Perspectives on Northeast India

TRADITION AND MODERNITY IN ARUNACHAL PRADESH

Perspectives on Northeast India

TRADITION AND MODERNITY IN ARUNACHAL PRADESH

Edited by

Sanjay Pulipaka
Rakhee Bhattacharya
Sarit K. Chaudhuri

Maulana Abul Kalam Azad Institute of Asian Studies, Kolkata

Anshah Publishing House

ISBN: 978-81-8364-089-3

First Published in India in 2013

Perspectives on Northeast India: Tradition and Modernity in Arunachal Pradesh

Published by:
ANSHAH PUBLISHING HOUSE
LG 18-19, Pankaj Central Market, Patparganj,
Delhi-110092, Tel: 91-11-2223 5152, 2223 6152
Br. Off. 4617/18, Ansari Road, Darya Ganj,
New Delhi-110002, Tel: 6594 6453, 9810522367

Contents

Introduction

Sanjay Pulipaka

"…I came in touch with the tribal people of the North-East Frontier of India, more especially of the Hill Districts of Assam. My liking for them grew and with it came respect. I had no sense of superiority over them. My ideas were not clear at all, but I felt that we should avoid two extreme courses: One to treat them as anthropological specimens for study and the other was to allow them to be engulfed by the masses of Indian humanity….I began to doubt how far the normal idea of progress was beneficial to these people and indeed, whether this was progress at all in any real sense of the word.[1]"

Prime Minister Jawaharlal Nehru
February 16, 1957

"In our ancient culture we, in India, are used to looking East every morning as we wake up to pray to the Sun God. We thank Almighty for the warmth and the brightness of the Sun. Arunachal is our East, our land of hope and promise. I assure you once again that a new Sun rises today in Arunachal Pradesh. There is a new ray of hope for a bright future of development, of education and of new employment opportunities.[2]"

Prime Minister Manmohan Singh's speech at a Public Rally in Itanagar
January 31, 2008

Tradition is often referred to as something 'old' and modern is used to refer to something 'new.' However, the terms 'old' and 'new' are very relative, as they are contingent on the interpretation of the user. However, in academic parlance, the words tradition and modernity have a more specific meaning. Traditional society was characterized by strong kinship ties and production was not driven by intensive technological processes. To borrow Daniel Bell's words, traditional society was "...'a game against nature' that centers on attempts to extract resources from the natural environment."[3] Religion/faith, in traditional society, played a big part not only in meeting the spiritual needs of individuals but also in explaining the social reality and various natural phenomena. On the other hand, the notion of modernity is located in the tectonic changes which England witnessed during 18th century. These changes were rapid technological growth, significant changes in the economy due to technological changes and a movement towards democratic/participatory forms of government. These shifts brought in fundamental changes in the society, as traditional kinship ties, rank-order and collective notions took a back seat and society tended to become individualistic. It was often assumed that the above technological and economic changes will result in more or less similar social organizations (first in Europe and later in other parts of the world) and it was also assumed that societies should become 'modern' to ensure faster economic development. This movement from traditional to modern society is often defined as the process of modernization. For the propounders of modernization, all societies evolve sequentially, viz., from traditional to modern.[4] Different scholars emphasized different variables, such as education, leaders as change agents, technology and urbanization for faster modernization, and often there was a debate as to which of the variables should be prioritized for better results.[5] So, for many developing countries, a menu of attitudinal/value changes or institutional changes required for faster development, were advanced. However, such an understanding has the following deficiencies:[6] first, implicit in the above arguments is the belief that the advent of modern institutions will also immediately prompt individuals to adopt 'modern attitudes.' It should be noted that institutions create culture and the advent of new institutions will not result in disappearance of the pre-existing culture; second, the nature of economic change is also context-specific and societies may take multiple trajectories in the realm of economic changes; third, it is also problematic to see kinship ties and collectivist notions as antithetical to the evolution of modern societies. Kinship ties, as in India, often become the fulcrum around which modern representative politics revolve. Technology facilitates communication of ideas and there is a discovery or imagining (re-imagining) a community. Such processes facilitate newer forms of solidarity which tends to get expressed in different realms; fourth, the modernization process is often conceived as consequence of changes ushered from within the society. However, societies also experience significant changes due to external influences. In many societies which experienced colonialism, or tribal societies which enjoyed relative autonomy, modernization processes were often state-driven. Such modernization processes engage/interact with the local social structures without completely obliterating them. Moreover, the absence of strong internal dynamics, relatively low-level of industrialization, state-led developmental processes may lead to mixed feelings towards the state-led modernization project, which may prompt a call for protection of local cultures and traditions.

Given the complexities of the modernization process, one must refrain from deploying simplistic sequential and causal analysis to understand changes in a given society. It is also important to desist from characterizing tradition and modernity as binary opposites. It is to reflect on the multiple trajectories of change due to the emergence of new institutions and processes, that a national conference was organized at Itanagar. The contributions in this volume make an attempt to reflect on the issues of modernity and tradition in Arunachal Pradesh.

Arunachal Pradesh

Arunachal Pradesh, often referred to as the land of the dawn-lit mountains, is the largest state (83,743 square kilometres) in Northeast India. Given the topography—snow capped peaks, alpine forests, valleys and plains—one can experience diverse climatic conditions in Arunachal. Situated in the Shivalik ranges of the Himalayas, Arunachal Pradesh has been blessed with big rivers such as Siang, Lohit, Kameng, Subansiri and Dibang and numerous other smaller rivers. Arunachal has a population of 13,82,611 (in 2011), which is one of the lowest in Northeast India after Mizoram (10,91, 014). Arunachal has the lowest population density in India. According to the 2011 Census, the population density of Arunachal Pradesh stands at 17 persons per square kilometre as against the national average of 382 persons per square kilometre. Arunachal Pradesh has a large number of tribal groups such as the Nyishi, Adi, Sulung, Apatani, Tagin, Memba, Mishing, Monpa, Sherdukpen, Mishmi, Khampti, Tangsa, Singpho, Nocte, and Wangcho, to name a few.[8] The diverse tribal groups have also contributed to rich cultural traditions and also art forms. Arunachal also has varied religious traditions such as Buddhism (Hinayana and Mahayana), Christianity, Donyipoloism and Hinduism, among others.

In the political realm, Arunachal Pradesh witnessed diverse administrative and political frameworks. At the time of independence, Arunachal was called North East Frontier Tracts, which was later rechristened as North East Frontier Agency (NEFA) in 1954. Through the NEFA Panchayati Raj Regulation (1967), a three-tier panchayat system was introduced in the state. In 1972, Arunachal became a Union Territory and on 20 February 1987, statehood was granted to it. The Arunachal state legislature currently has 60 members and Arunachal contributes two members to the Lok Sabha and one member to the Rajya Sabha. For years, the state apparatus was very weak and limited in Arunachal Pradesh. This can be seen from the fact that when Arunachal Pradesh became a Union Territory in 1972 and the capital was shifted from Shillong to Itanagar in 1974, it took more than six years for various departments to be shifted to Itanagar.[9] However, with the attainment of statehood there has been rapid growth of the state apparatus and allied institutions. It should be noted that there was no major political movement that demanded the creation of Arunachal Pradesh. Some scholars have also argued that the new political process and the representative institutions were aimed to "forge a distinct political identity, thereby to develop a new political culture… by integrating the different communities into larger national life.[10]" Like in other parts in India, the introduction of competitive electoral politics also gave a fillip to identity-based political movements; Arunachal has witnessed demands for greater autonomy from some groups. There are also apprehensions that local languages and local cultures may get subsumed due to rapid economic, political and social changes. Like in other parts of India, there are growing concerns in Arunachal Pradesh that corruption and nepotism are eating into the vitals of the political system.

Externally, Arunachal has been witnessing many challenges. The state shares international boundaries with Bhutan, China and Myanmar. The Chinese for long have been claiming the territories of the state and these claims have also contributed to hostilities between the two countries in 1962. It appears that China is very interested in taking control of strategic areas such as Tawang, as these give greater access to the Brahmaputra Valley and beyond. More recently, it has been reported that China is keen on Arunachal Pradesh as it has considerable resources of shale gas deposits.[11] It is important to note here that Chinese officials in the recent past have claimed the whole of Arunachal Pradesh as part of China. These Chinese statements invited protest demonstrations in Arunachal Pradesh. The absence of common perceptions about the boundaries is a source of anxiety in India and China and more so for the people of Arunachal Pradesh. The India-Myanmar border in Arunachal Pradesh is not contested. However, international trade across the borders has been constrained by the absence of adequate infrastructure and the presence of various insurgent groups in the close vicinity on both sides of the border. The increased trade across international boundaries in future, along with an upswing in economic activities, will also result in reconfiguring the identities and articulation of new spaces.

In the economic realm, Arunachal Pradesh witnessed significant changes since independence. During the early years of independence, the Indian leadership appeared to be apprehensive about initiating large-scale developmental activities. The apprehension about the consequences of faster economic development on local traditions and values may have contributed to the hesitation. The Indian government's policy towards the Arunachal region after independence has been substantially influenced by Jawaharlal Nehru. Nehru was keen on striking a balance between ensuring isolation and over-administering these areas, and suggested the following five fundamental principles: "First, people should develop along the lines of their own genius and we should avoid imposing anything on them. We should try to encourage in every way their own traditional arts and culture; second, tribal rights in land and forests should be respected; third, we should try to train and build up a team of their own people to do work of administration and development. Some technical personnel from outside will, no doubt, be needed, especially in the beginning. But we should avoid introducing too many outsiders into tribal territory; fourth, we should not over-administer these areas or overwhelm them with multiplicity of schemes. We should rather work through, and not in rivalry to, their own social and cultural institutions; five, we should judge results, not by statistics or the amount of money spent, but by the quality of human character that is evolved.[12]" The intentions of the policymakers during the early years of independence were to implement carefully calibrated development activities which do not fundamentally alter the socio-cultural landscape of the NEFA region. Further, because of the terrain, large parts of Arunachal were inaccessible, which also ensured that the 'processes of development' made a late entry into the state. For instance, citing the Techno-Economic Survey of Arunachal Pradesh, Tamo Mibang and M.C. Behera point out that "there were only two primary schools, 13 health units and only two jeepable roads in the territory covering 168 kms at the time independence."[13] However, the Chinese invasion and the continued threat perceptions from China, brought about fundamental transformation in the government policies towards Arunachal Pradesh. Nehru's policy of calibrated development gave way to proactive state-sponsored developmental programmes and also creation of a well spread administrative apparatus. The quotations at the beginning of this essay indicate the shift that Arunachal Pradesh witnessed in various development policies.

However, in the past few decades one can see considerable change in the attitude of the governments (union government and also state government) towards developmental activities. In the recent past, Arunachal Pradesh witnessed significant economic growth. During 2009-2010, it witnessed an economic growth rate of 22.43 per cent.[14] The expansion in the economic activities resulted in the creation of jobs in the government sector. Initially, outsiders were brought in to man the administrative apparatus and over time, local people with necessary qualifications were able to access the employment opportunities in the government sector. However, chieftain families, specifically those from dominant tribes, reportedly have been the major beneficiaries.[15] Moreover, Arunachal's growth rate looks impressive because it is starting from a low base line. Much of the growth came about due to substantial investment made by the state and central governments. The economic development in Arunachal Pradesh is due to the tremendous emphasis laid on creating physical infrastructure. Massive infrastructural projects such as power, communication networks, the trans-Arunachal Pradesh highway, and expanding rail networks have been proposed and some of them are being implemented. There are growing anxieties that the aggressive development activities will have negative consequences on the fragile ecosystem in the state. For instance, in order to harness the massive hydroelectricity potential of Arunachal Pradesh, massive dams are being planned across some of the major rivers. Reportedly, the existing dams have already started contributing to the floods downstream and more importantly the location of the proposed dams along seismic fault lines has contributed to the growing anxiety.[16] All this points to the necessity of factoring in local specificities and making local people effective partners in developing various infrastructural projects. While focus on creating physical infrastructure is indeed required, the emphasis on social infrastructure should also be unwavering. It should be noted that the literacy rate in Arunachal is 66.95 per cent (lowest in Northeast India), which indicates that there is a substantial population that is not in a position to access the fruits of economic development. This inability to benefit from economic development has resulted in tremendous economic disparity in the state. The disenchantment with the economic disparity may express itself along identity lines. The rapid economic progress does not necessarily mean that the debate about the impact of development on local traditions has disappeared. On the contrary, many voices have been raised calling for a re-engagement with the debate on the issues of modernity and tradition in Arunachal Pradesh, and the contributions in this volume seek to address precisely such issues. Senior policymakers, established academicians, members of civil society and young scholars have contributed to this volume and their chapters reflect on wide range of issues such as external policy, mapping the contours of modernization, transition in institutions, development strategies, employment challenges, educational policies and so on.

Issues of Modernity and Tradition

Krishnan Srinivasan's essay examines the external policy issues of Arunachal Pradesh and locates the state in broader interactions between India and its neighbours. Plotting the fault-lines such as India-China boundary dispute in Arunachal Pradesh, Krishnan Srinivasan suggests minor adjustments in unpopulated areas with possible conversion of the LAC into a boundary which facilitates trade and cultural exchanges for Tibetans to resolve the boundary dispute. Pointing out that the future of Northeast India is linked with neighbouring countries, Krishnan Srinivasan notes: "Confidence building with the neighbours is important, but that has to be complemented with first building confidence about the Indian state with the people of the Northeast."

Prof. Tamo Mibang in his article contends that tradition and modernity are two sides of the same coin and plots the numerous changes witnessed in the political, social, and administrative realms. After giving an overview of the social composition of Arunachal society, his article also reflects on the various social issues due to the advent of new attitudes and also refers to the poor state of medical infrastructure in the state. Pointing out that there is a visible shift away from insurgency among the youngsters, Prof Mibang laments the absence of industries to provide sustainable employment to youngsters. In the economic realm, he notes the increasing shift towards mega infrastructural projects and reflects on the necessity of giving space to indigenous economic developmental models. The article succinctly sums up changes in the administrative landscape of the state in the past few decades. Prof Mibang calls for good governance practices and points to the necessity of incorporating tribal institutions into modern democratic institutions. Annada C. Bhagabati's article interrogates the notions of tradition and modernity. Annada contends that the lived experience of people cannot be neatly boxed into such dichotomous conceptual straightjackets such as 'modernity' and 'tradition'. Annada argues that attempts at modernization of indigenous tribal and rural societies must make sustained efforts to understand the traditions, as they may be useful in conceptualizing inter-personal relations and in coping with change for progress. Sucheta Sen Chaudhuri in her article explores gender issues with reference to modernity in Arunachal Pradesh. Sucheta Sen Chaudhuri's article explores the notions of identity space with reference to modernity. In the process, she examines the constructs of 'private domain' and 'public domain' and their implications for gender equity in Arunachal Pradesh. The article details the important role being played by the Arunachal Pradesh Women's Welfare Society (APWWS) in eradicating gender discrimination and in facilitating empowerment of women. Based on field visits, Sucheta Sen Chaudhuri observes that in Arunachal Pradesh, while the rural women are participating in agriculture for livelihood, the urban women are participating in agriculture from the perspective of maintaining and celebrating their cultural heritage. Philip Mody and Teshi Sohang in their joint article, through a case-study of the Nyishi Tribe of the Doimukh Circle, seek to plot gender discrimination in terms of accessing education. Their field-study throws up interesting observations. While enrollment rates of boys at the primary school level are higher due to gender discrimination, the number of girls is higher than the number of boys studying at secondary schools. The authors believe this is due to greater consistency, sincerity and lower dropout rates among girls during adolescence. Similarly, the number of girls joining colleges and universities is lower than boys; the number of girls accessing non-formal education is higher. Based on the findings of their field research, Philip Mody and Teshi Sohang suggest a series of measures (such as increasing the number of non-formal educational centres) to ensure gender equity in terms of accessing education at all levels.

Tajen Dabi maps the negotiations with modernization at the level of society and politics in Arunachal Pradesh. He contends that in Arunachal Pradesh, "the broad contours of modernisation ….are suggestive of the fact that the ethnic assertions and religious movements seek to create a niche in the broader space of the Indian nation-state rather than an attempt to create an independent and differing ideology as posited against the latter." He observes that, unlike other northeastern states, the engagement with forces of modernization did not result in the emergence of insurgent groups in Arunachal Pradesh. This, he argues, is because of absence of necessary social and other attendant infrastructure to facilitate emergence of insurgent outfits in Arunachal Pradesh. Tajen Dabi opines that operationalisation of multiple dynamics—such as the formation of the state without a prolonged democratic movement, state-based employment generation, and inner line permit—ensured that the perception of alienation and consequent insurgency did not find fertile ground in Arunachal Pradesh. Tajen Dabi's article also gives an outline of significant changes that are happening in the realms of languages and religion. He suggests that in the recent past there have been attempts at redefining and/or 'preserving' the native faith. He advocates that such reinventing should also result in genuine reform. Sarit K Chaudhuri's article focuses on the healing traditions of Idu Mishmis. Referring to the renewed interest in shamans/shamanism, he examines the role of Igus (shamans) and their interrelationship with spirit (khinu) and supreme creator (inni) in the Idu Mishmi society. His article focuses on the processes that transform an individual into an Igu, the various classifications of sickness or diseases, rituals and other healing practices of Idu Mishmis. His article also reflects on the interaction of traditional healing processes with modern medical facilities and also the process of accommodation such interactions entail. Chaudhuri contends that the traditional healing processes will tend to endure in Arunachal Pradesh as long as the village life endures. Jayanti Alam reflecting on socio-ethical aspects of Buddhists in Tawang, West Kemang in India and Tibetans in China, states that Buddhist traditions can meet the spiritual demands of the 21st century. Her article elucidates various Buddhist religious concepts such as a suffering, Karma, seed consciousness, and dharma, and their impact on the way of thinking and everyday life of the Monpas, and Sherdukpens in Arunachal Pradesh. She states that Buddhism has impacted Tibetans, Monpas, and Sherdukpens "in every single aspect of their life, living, beliefs, thoughts." She opines that Buddhist religious scriptures, practices and norms have contributed to the evolution of less hierarchical and a more egalitarian society. Moji Riba opines that local languages and local traditions are withering away in the face of globalization and developmental processes. He argues that the 'language shift' is also a loss of repositories of knowledge articulated in the local languages. Hence, the focus should not just be on preservation but also promotion of local languages. So, how does one go about promoting local languages and local traditions? Moji Riba gives a comprehensive list of education-centred initiatives (such as promoting the mother-tongue by identifying teachers to teach in local languages and also formulating youth targeted programmes) and community-centred initiatives (strengthening traditional institutions and operationalizing community-driven participatory documentation models). Jagdish Lal Dawar in his article plots the changing contours of the state's policy with reference to various built environments and its engagement with local cultures and local norms. In independent India, Dawar contends that bureaucracy became the custodian of local knowledge, tribal culture and traditions, which provide an opportunity for exercising 'cultural hegemony' through various appropriation strategies and his article seeks to demonstrate such appropriation strategies in built environments. After plotting various approaches that defined architectural designs in the construction of public buildings, Dawar argues that policy- makers by infusing values of 'modernity', tried to hegemonize local traditions. Dawar argues that the Indian state, after the 1962 war with China, gave up on appropriation strategies and started deploying more of mainstream 'cultural values' and 'norms.' Mrinal Kanti Chakma also dwells on similar issues. He examines the dynamics of the state-led development strategy and its impact on social changes that are taking place in Arunachal Pradesh. Mrinal contends that post-1962, the 'development' and 'modernization plan' of the Government of India treated various agencies of the state as 'introducers' and the traditional communities in Arunachal Pradesh as 'receivers.' Mrinal elucidates his point by taking a few sectors as case study. In the realm of education he argues that the government's linguistic policies are endangering the local languages which is also contributing to the erosion of local knowledge system associated with the local languages. Mrinal states that the shift from *Jhum* cultivation to settled farming, along with increasing agricultural production also had 'spiritual consequences' and impacted the "cognitive functioning of the faith system of the human mind which is beyond the scope of assessment by technocratic tools of modern science." Mrinal also identifies various challenges confronting Arunachal Pradesh such as inclusion and exclusion strategies associated with identity politics, environmental impact of various development initiatives and growing inequity.

Deepak K. Mishra in his article seeks to explain the economic transformation of Arunachal Pradesh through the transitions in institutions. The article looks at the evolution of local institutional mechanisms which facilitated "tribal elites to accumulate and invest the surplus generated within and outside agriculture." Mishra suggests the necessity "to move beyond the analytical prism of the state-versus-community or the state-versus-market framework and to take note of the existing and emerging differentiations within and across the communities." N.C. Roy attempts to map the factors that have impacted the growth of technology and industrialization in Arunachal Pradesh, which are often not assigned a central position in the understanding of the socio-economic dynamics. Manufacturing industries in the state are substantially home-based with a very low contribution (2.28 per cent in 2007-2008) to the State Gross Domestic Product (SGDP). What is the explanation for this low contribution of the manufacturing sector to the SGDP? According to Roy, the reasons for this are: First, the industrialization process in the state did not factor-in two sub-processes, viz., translational (scatteredness to concentrations) and transformational (the members of different primary groups are transformed into a secondary group whose members operate the factory). Second, "the project of industrialization did not take into consideration the tastes and preferences of the local people, their strengths and their weaknesses." Third, "the approach was from industry-to-people, not from people-to-industry." The weakness of the manufacturing sector also has impacted on employment opportunities in Arunachal Pradesh. Vandana Upadhyay in her article uses the data from the 50th, 55th and 61st round of the National Sample Survey (NSS), to explore the employment scenario in Arunachal Pradesh. Upadhyay gives a comprehensive analysis of the patterns of employment, distribution of workers across industries and other relevant categories. Pointing to the marginal presence of the manufacturing sector, she refers to the provision of expanding government sector employment. However, she quickly adds that expansion of government sector employment with a job-creation motive, rather development motive, is not sustainable in the long run. She suggests that there is a need to kick-start employment creation in the non-agricultural sector in Arunachal Pradesh by expanding non-farm occupations, which require credit and marketing support. For Upadhyay, broad-based employment strategies with a focus on ensuring access to quality education is critical to ensure inclusive development, viz., equity, equality of opportunity and protection in market and employment transitions. Given Arunachal Pradesh's natural beauty, tourism can play a major role in generating employment, increasing revenues for the state and hastening the development process. Maila Lama and Amitava Mitra in their joint article, identify numerous possibilities (heritage, pilgrimage, cultural, nature and adventure tourism) and also challenges (infrastructural, institutional and marketing) for enhancing the tourist potential of Arunachal Pradesh. They also give a few policy suggestions such as the necessity of drafting a tourism masterplan, ensuring public-private partnership for better management of tourist facilities and the need for ensuring local participation in various tourist promotion activities.

Apart from strategic location, Arunachal Pradesh is also critically important for peace and prosperity of Northeast India. It constitutes a watershed for large rivers that sustain the agro-economy of the region. Hence, the nature and quality of developmental activities will have positive or negative spin-offs for the whole of Northeast India. The option of trade across borders looks bleak at the moment. But, in the long-run, Arunachal has the potential to be one of the important centres for international trade in Northeast India. To meet the future challenges developmental activities have to be sustainable. Sustainability should not be judged merely in economic and technical terms; sustainability should also be seen in terms of the impact the policies and developmental activities have on local cultures and traditions.

In the past few decades Arunachal witnessed many shifts in social, political and economic realms. There has been movement from shifting-cultivation to settled farming. Further, there have been consistent efforts to usher-in development, industrialization and strengthen market mechanisms. There has been a quantum jump in the number of educational institutions such as schools and there has been increased access to university education. Today, the state apparatus with its multiple organization/agencies and processes is a major player in Arunachal Pradesh. Many representative institutions and processes have taken strong root in the state. This is not to suggest that traditional modes of interactions, relations and institutions have completed disappeared. On the contrary, the 'old' and the 'new' have been negotiating, contesting and altering each other. Given the above interactions it is important not to see tradition and modernity as binary opposites. As Rajni Kothari stated, it is important to note that "not until the institutional changes introduced in a particular society become part of the working relationships of that society, can they hope to gain stability and legitimacy."[17] Reflecting on issues of tradition and modernity, he added, "for any political system to get stabilized it is necessary that its procedures and symbols are both internalized and traditionalized; they should not be accepted just for their utility but should be valued as such, as intrinsically meritorious and valuable, endowed with inherent goodness. In other words, the new procedures and values must themselves be turned into 'tradition', something that must be nurtured with care, developed further and made strong."[18] This volume is a modest attempt to understand Arunachal Pradesh's engagement with such issues of modernity and tradition.

Notes

1. See Foreword in Verrier Elwin, *A Philosophy for NEFA*, (Delhi: Isha Publishers, 2009).
2. 'Prime Minster Manmohan Singh's speech at Itanagar Public Rally,' *Prime Minister's Office*, available at http://pmindia.nic.in/speech/content.asp?id=647
3. Malcolm Walters, *Daniel Bell*, (London: Routledge 1996), p. 109.

4. For instance see Gilbert Winham, "Political Development and Lerner's Theory: Further Test of a Causal Model," *The American Political Science Review*, Vol. 64, No. 3 (Sep., 1970), pp. 810-818.
5. See Myron Weiner, *Modernisation: The Dynamics of Growth*, (New York: Basic Books, 1966).
6. For more details see David Harrison, *The Sociology of Modernization and Development*, (New York: Routledge, 1990). Also see Adam Przeworski and Fernando LimongiSource, "Modernization: Theories and Facts," *World Politics*, Vol. 49, No. 2 (Jan., 1997), pp. 155-183; Ronald Inglehart & Christian Welzel, *Modernization, Cultural Change, and Democracy: The Human Development Sequence*, (Cambridge: Cambridge University Press, 2005)
7. The Brahmaputra river is formed after River Siang joins River Lohit.
8. See Government of Arunachal Pradesh, *Arunachal Pradesh Human Development Report 2005*, (Itanagar: Government of Arunachal Pradesh, 2006), p. 5
9. R.P. Bhattacharjee, *Economic Development of Arunachal Pradesh*, (New Delhi: Himalayan Publishers, 2000), p. 162.
10. Tanya Dabi as cited in Sanjib Baruah, *Durable Disorder: Understanding the Politics of Northeast India*, (New Delhi: Oxford University Press, 2005), p. 48.
11. Swaminathan S.A. Aiyar, "Will China eye Arunachal Pradesh's shale oil?," *The Times of India*, 25 September 2011, available at http://economictimes.indiatimes.com/opinion/columnists/swaminathan-s-a-aiyar/will-china-eye-arunachal-pradeshs-shale-oil/articleshow/10111977.cms (Downloaded on 26 September 2011)
12. Verrier Elwin, *A Philosophy of NEFA (Arunachal Pradesh)*, Director of Research, Government of Arunachal Pradesh, Itanagar, available at http://www.arunachalpwd.org/pdf/Philosophy%20for%20NEFA.pdf
13. Tamo Mibang and M.C. Behera, *Dynamics of Tribal Villages in Arunachal Pradesh: Emerging Realities*, (New Delhi: Mittal Publishers, 2004).
14. 'Arunachal Pradesh registers 22.4 per cent GDP in 09-10,' *The Hindu*, 23 February 2011, available at http://www.thehindubusinessline.com/industry-and-economy/economy/article1483263.ece
15. Ela Mukhopadhyay, "Arunachal: The Changing Profile of a Closed Culture," *Social Scientist*, Vol. 20, no. 3/4 (March-April 1992). pp. 71.
16. Hiren Gohain, "Big Dams, Big Floods: On Predatory Development," *Economic and Political Weekly*, Vol. 43 No. 30 July 26 - August 01, 2008, p. 20
17. Rajni Kothari, *Caste in Indian Politics*, (Hyderabad: Orient Longman, 1970), p. 3.
18. Ibid., p. 23.

1

External Policy Issues of Arunachal Pradesh

Krishnan Srinivasan

This short essay outlines and confines itself to the concerned external policy issues of the state of Arunachal Pradesh in Northeast India. Arunachal Pradesh shares external borders with Bhutan, China and Myanmar, and with all three nations, there are some questions that need to be addressed.

Bhutan

Bhutan is the most straightforward of the three neighbours because since Indian independence, India has enjoyed and benefited from excellent relations with the Kingdom. As far as it is known, the only matter for concern here is the unsettled location of the tri-junction of the Bhutan-India-China border which remains unsettled because the Indo-Chinese border in this sector is still disputed.

Myanmar

The tri-junction with Myanmar would of course face the same difficulty; China has delineated the boundary with adjoining Burma (Myanmar). There was no reason why the same principles used to delineate the boundary between China and Myanmar could not be used for the Arunachal Pradesh-China border, but that is now water under the bridge.

In the case of this neighbour, there are some other issues as well. There is some anecdotal view that China is assisting some Northeast insurgent groups via NGOs in (Yunnan). True or not, the Chinese influence in Myanmar will always cause unease in India, especially in Arunachal Pradesh. Myanmar has allowed most of the Northeast insurgents to operate out of its territory, where they enjoy a safe haven for training and weapons procurement. The NSCN insurgents active in Tirap and Changlang have Indian and Burmese Nagas in their ranks. Burmese troops have crossed into our borders time and again since 1991. From 1993 we have had constructive engagement with Myanmar as against the previous policy to support the pro-democracy movement and the Chin, Arakanese and Kachin groups. Among the Indian motives were the new priority to ASEAN, with Myanmar as the nearest member and so of consequence to India and the Northeast, and trans-border linkages to restrain smuggling, insurgents, and of course, the influence of China. But joint action against insurgents has not taken off because the Burmese action against Indian insurgents has been only cosmetic. With much smaller armies than Myanmar, Bhutan and Bangladesh have acted against Northeast insurgents but not Myanmar. Connectivity—such as the 160 km Tamu-Kalemyo Road—has improved but roads can also be used by insurgent groups, illegal traders, and the Chinese. The Stillwell Road connects Ledo in Arunachal with Kunming in Yunnan through Mytkyina in Myanmar. Roads could be a source of insecurity but the Chinese and some academics and politicians in the Northeast are keen on re-opening this road. The Kachins have a good hold on the Stillwell Road area in Burma and could ensure a supply of essential goods and armaments for the NSCN. ULFA has routes through Arunachal Pradesh for weapons from China. Some parts of Arunachal such as Lohit and East Kameng have a history of insurgent activity, which increases the vulnerability to the Chinese. Trade would increase but the fear is of Chinese goods flooding the market—though the Chinese already have the ability to run a parallel market in the Northeast. There is also concern as to how much the local population would actually benefit from employment opportunities from the re-opening of the Road.

China

China is yet to provide any maps indicating its position on the disputed border. China persists in centring attention on Tawang on grounds that it has a special place for Tibet and as the birthplace of the 6th Dalai Lama. The Chinese envoy to India said in 2006 '*In our position, the whole of the state of Arunachal Pradesh is Chinese territory. And Tawang is only one of the places in it. We are claiming all of that. That is our position*'.

Construction of the railway, the deployment of missiles and the construction of roads and dams in Tibet add to the security concerns that plague Arunachal Pradesh. The fact that India and China are engaged in prolonged discussions do not seem to be indicative of any warlike situation that will retard development in both countries by many years if not decades, and frustrate China's intention to be a superpower to rival the US as a long-term objective.

My personal involvement with the Arunachal Pradesh border was in 1994. In 1983, an Intelligence Bureau team went to the pasturage of Sumdorong Chu which is north-east of the confluence of the Namka Chu and the Nyamjiang Chu. The area in question was a grazing ground at Wangdung. The Government of India tried to maintain its legitimacy over Wangdung by sending citizens to use Wangdung for grazing during the summers just as the Chinese do in other areas. The defence forces stayed through the summer and returned in winter. This procedure was followed for two years. The Chinese prevented this by pre-emptive occupation of Samdorong Chu by a small army post and in 1986, Indian forces found that the Chinese had preceded them and set up semi-permanent structures there. The fallout of Sumdorong Chu and the resultant military build-up was that India and China decided to restart their dialogue on a new and more urgent basis. In 1993, the two countries signed an agreement to ensure peace along the Line of Actual Control. The situation however remained one of "close proximity" where the respective posts were only 50-100 yards apart.

At talks in Beijing in 1994 I proposed to the Chinese that the stand-off could be resolved by the Chinese withdrawing a certain number of metres which would then be followed, after verification, by our Army doing the same. I suggested the same formula for Thag-la/Hathung-la. The Chinese were taken by considerable surprise, and as usual were not able to respond, because it takes time for the implications of any new proposal to sink in for them, and to be considered at higher-up levels in the party hierarchy. However, a year later, at the meeting on April 1995, I was happy to see the two sides agreeing to a simultaneous withdrawal of their troops from the four border posts—two Indian and two Chinese—in the Sumdorong Chu valley. As of 2000, the valley was not occupied by either army, and their respective posts in the area were close to a kilometre apart. I am afraid I am not informed about the latest situation.

In 2003, a similar problem arose when the media and parliament forced a reluctant External Affairs Minister Yashwant Sinha to admit that there was a transgression of the LAC by a Chinese patrol in the Asaphila area of Upper Subansiri district. This and earlier such incursions could have been avoided if the two countries had a common perception of the LAC, he said. Of course, there are no common perceptions of either the international border or the LAC.

On the broader question, how can the border be settled? Perhaps in time, with minor adjustments in unpopulated areas; possibly by converting the LAC into a boundary with a special zone for trade and tourism can attract Tibetans to visit Tawang, and access trade and religious sites.

Rivers

Other matters that have a bearing on Arunachal's external relations are river waters, immigrants and tourism.

In 2000 Arunachal Pradesh faced its worst floods due to a dam breach in Tibet and major dams are being constructed at the Great Bend of Brahmaputra to divert waters to the drought-stricken north. Fifty-nine storages are planned on rivers flowing out of Tibet to save glacier run-off and at least 6 major river power projects on the upper Brahmaputra. China's activities upstream cause great anxiety, apart from our own plans because Arunachal Pradesh accounts for a large percentage of India's untapped hydroelectric power production potential. The Government of India's plans include some 42 hydroelectric schemes that will produce electricity in excess of 27,000 MW. Construction of the Upper Siang Hydroelectric Project, which is expected to generate between 10,000 to 12,000 MW, began in April 2009. Then there are Subansiri with 2000 MW, Kameng with 600 MW and Dibang with 3000 MW, and all have ecological, environmental, biodiversity and displacement issues to settle before they can take off.

Recent blockades by Assamese student groups to prevent dam-building equipment from reaching Arunachal provoked some people to describe them as 'anti-national' but as a lower riparian located in a very sensitive seismic zone, Assam has reasons to be concerned with so many big dams upstream.

Immigration

One needs to refer in passing to the Chakmas and Hajiongs from

East Pakistan, numbering around a lakh that affect Arunachal's delicate tribal balance. Can they ever go back, even supposing they would want to? How can we, who settled them in erstwhile NEFA as part of our commitment to settle East Pakistani refugees, push them out? But people here in Arunachal Pradesh feel uneasy at the prospect of the Chakmas and Hajongs getting Indian citizenship because they will impact on the political situation.

Tourism

A great economic opportunity is tourism. Boasting a scenic natural beauty that equals and in some respects surpasses that of other Himalayan regions such as Sikkim, Bhutan, and Nepal, Arunachal Pradesh's "Restricted/Protected Area Permit" scheme and very poor connectivity, both ensure that no more than a trickle of foreign tourists are able to visit the state each year, and little if any benefit from tourism is able to reach the general population. But with the trouble in Kashmir, it may be good for India to relax entry of foreigners into Arunachal Pradesh and develop infrastructure for tourism in the state—such as golf courses, angling, river rafting and other forms of adventure and eco-tourism. But a balance has to be struck beween the good effect of tourism and harm to local ecology and unique way of life.

Conclusion

The future of the Northeast is to a considerable extent governed by the neighbouring countries. The challenge is, how to relate that future with the interest that India wants to show with cross-border contacts to the eastern neighbours and the need to reiterate the identity of the Northeast within that of India. Confidence-building with the neighbours is important, but that has to be complemented with first building confidence about the Indian state with the people of the Northeast.

2

Arunachal Pradesh

Issues of Modernity and Tradition

Tamo Mibang[1]

The issues of modernity and tradition or tradition and modernity are not contradictory. They are merely two sides of the same coin; which can interact beneficially. Tradition is still often considered a thing of the past without contemporary legitimacy and modernity and is often mistakenly considered as modernism. Tradition is defined in a context of practice of virtue in the perspective of good life based on the potentials of our own time and selected wisdom of the past such as wise sayings, folk tales, song, dance, festivals and rituals. Time, history, progress, spirituality, love, culture and the spirit of evolution remind us that the word tradition is unlikely to be replaced by another word to represent its universality. It is not related to village folk alone as today's town dwellers think but tradition implies presence of the past in the present. Therefore, modernity and tradition are not competitive but complementary. Mankind has experienced and observed for years that yesterday's modernity is today's tradition and today's modernity is tomorrow's tradition. Yesterday's wooden plate is today's artifact and today's aluminum or steel plate is tomorrow's artifact and so on. Modernity in essence is nothing but tradition re-defined and restructured on the strength of what we assimilate from our works and experience with the new trends and techniques.

To enlighten ourselves, let us have a glimpse of the social scenario of our great nation India. Today, in India, most of the politicians are

1. This paper was delivered as the Keynote Address at the National Seminar on "Arunachal Pradesh: Issues of Modernity and Tradition," held at the Rajiv Gandhi University, Rono Hills, Itanagar, Arunachal Pradesh on 07-08 September 2010.

talking of shining India or India shining. And a few intellectuals are talking of India as an emerging superpower. We hope for the best. It may be a good prediction; yet we have not made enough efforts to educate the rural masses who comprise 70 per cent of our total population. We cannot say how long it would take to educate the rural populace as we are becoming more urban and utterly failing in our planning for rural upliftment. India's strength and future lies in rural India; there lives the soul of India. Rural India feeds the million mouths of urban India.

A series of murder cases of young men or women for marrying outside the caste or against the family's wishes have come to light in recent times in India's metros and villages. How many of us have openly come out to protest against such crimes? And how many voluntary organizations have boldly taken up such cases to court? Is it modernity or tradition in continuity?

It is said that in India, the dowry system has a historical tradition. How many cases of bride burning have been brought to light? Why are young and even highly educated women burnt for dowry? Is it a tradition to be preserved or promoted in tune with so-called modernity? Society must look inwards keeping in view the current discourse of modernity and tradition in a world increasingly dominated by technology and rapidly changing values.

Arnold Toynbee writes that there were twenty-one cultures in human history; they have all come and gone, repeating a recurrent cycle of birth, growth, breakdown and decay. He attributes the breakdown of civilizations not to any cosmic law, but to the people; they exhaust themselves as their response to successive challenges becomes sterile. His formula of 'challenge and response' is based on the distinction between those who can cope with a changing environment, and those who cannot. It shows that a successful life is a continuous succession of problems met and solved. Likewise, 'a society can grow if it can constructively respond to the new challenges. The initial challenge comes from the environment. Later on, the challenges are social rather than physical and geographical; they are internal rather than external' (Toynbee: 1965). Toynbee has shown how the creative minorities can respond to the challenges.

Whether one accepts Toynbee's thesis as correct or not, this observation has great relevance to the contemporary Indian situation. Though in the euphoria of independence, a strong central government with ideals of equal opportunity, social justice, secularism and so on, was accepted, the tribal feelings with respect to caste, creed, language have come in the way of developing national sentiments and of looking upon all Indians as members of a nation. As Toynbee calls it, troublesome is a formidable habit and it is nothing more than a habit of thought and sentiment, it is something which man created for himself ages back and it is possible for man to free himself from it. Therefore, first, we want a happy India and then a superpower India. Unless we are happy, we cannot prosper to emerge as a superpower.

With this backdrop on the issues of modernity and tradition, let us now have a bird's eye-view of the historical landscape of Arunachal Pradesh. The history of the state can be traced from the time when Ahom Kings began to rule Assam in the 13th century, mainly from the history of Ahom tribal relations, the payment of posa by King Pratap Singha to tribals by way of appeasing them from frequent raids on the Assamese ryots along the foothill areas. The British took over Assam in 1838 and defined their administrative jurisdictions by drawing an Inner Line in 1873 in relation to the frontier tribes and kept them out of the purview of their administrative jurisdiction. But then they followed the policy of gradual penetration and in 1946 the North-East Frontier Tract was re-organized into four frontier tracts—Sadiya, Lakhimpur, Tirap and Sela-Sub Agency. After the achievement of independence, by virtue of India's independence Act 1947, the Government of Assam assumed the administrative jurisdictions of North-East Frontier Tract (NEFT) and administered the region from 15 August 1947 to 26 January 1950.

The Government of India appointed a sub-committee headed by Gopinath Bordoloi to recommend the future pattern of administration of the North-East Frontier Tract. The Bordoloi Committee recommended that the Government of Assam should take over that area by the strength of a notification. However, in consideration of various geographical reasons and defence, the Government decided to administer the region as an "Excluded Area" through the Governor of Assam. In 1950, the plain portions of the tract, Balipara Frontier Tract, Tirap Frontier Tract, Abor Hill district and Mishmi Hill district were transferred to the Government of Assam. In 1951, the units of the tracts were reconstituted again and the Tuensang Frontier Division was created which later merged with Nagaland. The North-East Frontier (Admn) Regulation of 1954, re-designated the name as NEFA, and the administration was brought under the Ministry of External Affairs (MEA) and in 1965 it was brought under the Ministry of Home Affairs (MHA). It attained Union Territory (UT) status in 1972 and statehood on February 20, 1987. Its evolution and functions is a tribute to a farsighted vision and the tribal policy of Pt. Jawaharlal Nehru and Verrier Elwin. The various phases of evolution highlight the march of the people towards modernity in terms of socio-economic and political development.

In terms of geographical area, Arunachal Pradesh, is the largest state in the Northeast, covering an area of approximately 83,743 sq. kms. It shares an international boundary with China (1060 km) in the north, Bhutan (160 km) in the West and Myanmar (440 kms) in the East. The McMahon Line defines the international boundary between India and China. The state is now divided into sixteen districts. Traces of cultural influence of Hindu civilization are noticed from the ruins of Bhismaknagar in the Dibang Valley, Parsuram Khund in Lohit, Malinithan in Likabali of West Siang district and so on. Arunachal Pradesh is highlighted in this perspective because administrative growth is a historical transition from a tradition-bound society to modernity.

The state is inhabited by 26 major tribes and is further divided with a number of groups who profess different religions. The total population of the state is 10,97,968 and is scattered over 17 towns and 3863 villages (Census 2001). Most of the tribal groups are ethnically similar having derived from an original common stock i.e., Mongoloid, but geographical isolation has brought among them certain distinct characteristics in language, custom and dress. They are divided into three cultural groups on the basis of their socio-religious affinities, viz., Buddhists, the central groups—Adis, Apatanis, Nyishis, Tagins and Galos—who worship Donyi-Polo; and the third group comprises Noctes and Wanchos of Tirap and Changlang districts, who practice an elementary form of Vaishnavism.

The tribal people of Arunachal Pradesh were not familiar with the written word until recently except the Monpas and the Khamtis of Kameng and Lohit districts. As a result knowledge was passed on from generation to generation verbally and learning by doing. The older people used to teach them song, music, dance and folktales which were rooted firm in tradition. The languages of the tribal people of Arunachal Pradesh reveal diversity rather than the unity of origin. However, the Tibeto-Burman family is most important amongst the group of Indo-Chinese-languages spoken by the people. Adi, Apatani, Nyishi, Tagin, Galo, and Mishmis constitute the larger group of speakers having cultural affinities with each other. They belong to the North-Assam group of the Tibeto-Burman family.

Monpa, Sherdukpen, Membas, Khambas and Meyors speak languages of the Tibeto-Himalayan group of the Tibeto-Burman family. The Khamptis belong to the same religious group and speak a language of the Tai group of the Sino-Siamese family. The Singphos speak a language of the Kachin group of the Tibeto-Burman family and the Noctes, Wanchos and Tangsas speak languages of the Naga group of the Tibeto-Burman family. Thus, there are two language families and four groups of languages prevalent in the state. Most of the groups have been writing with the Roman script. The Monpas write in the Tibetan script and the Khamtis in the Tai Khampti script. Their literature is mostly religious and ritualistic. The other groups like the Adis, the Nyishis, the Mishmis, the Apatanis, the Galos and so on, have been writing with the Roman script but without much headway towards growth of their language and literature. The medium of instruction in the schools right from the elementary level is English and Hindi. The result is that avenues for the growth of the local language have been few; therefore, in comparison, it seems that there is a retardation in the growth of the local language. It is found that Hindi is gaining popularity among the tribal people of the state. But nobody can say that it has been imposed from outside. People have accepted it spontaneously. The effort of the state government has been to at least try and introduce the mother tongue at the elementary level. I have given importance to language because without language culture cannot survive. In the name of modernity, tribal languages of the state are going to be marginalized within the next few years as most of the youth in urban areas are switching over to other languages.

Tribal foods have medicinal values as they mostly produce their food without use of artificial manure. Their staple foods are rice, meat, and green leafy vegetables that are rich in vitamins and minerals. This to some extent cures hypertension, blood pressure, dehydration and many common ailments. Apong is another important food item. It is a local beverage prepared with a few herbs by female folk and is consumed by family members irrespective of age in moderation in the evening before a meal. It gives stamina and is good for health. It is prepared in plenty during local festivals. It is said that without apong there can be hardly a good celebration. But now, times are changing. Foreign liquor in the markets is becoming more popular and it has percolated down to the villages with school and college-going youth habituated to this drink these days. Arunachal was declared as a dry belt to restrict the sale of foreign liquor. However, these days there are liquor shops in every town. This has created a social problem in fast changing tribal society. I wonder how we are going to address this issue in days to come.

Though there was no modern health infrastructure till 1947 in the state, people were healthy with exposure to nature and natural food habits. Many of the modern diseases were unknown to them. Life expectancy was good though child mortality was common due to an unhygienic environment within the village setup. It is now common knowledge that life expectancy in Arunachal Pradesh is not very encouraging except in two districts viz., East Siang district and Papum Pare (60.08 years and 61.80 years respectively according to Arunachal Pradesh Human Development Report), which may be because of comparatively good health infrastructure for being the capital of the state. Without health and food one cannot think of culture, tradition, change and continuity.

The question of sanitation in traditional villages draws our attention. In local tribal houses made of bamboos, wooden and *toko* leaves in interior villages, the lavatory is attached where pigs are kept to act as scavengers. Verrier Elwin in his book, *Philosophy for NEFA* (1958) had pointed towards the need for the separation of the lavatory from the main dwellings. Here, pigs can be easily shifted from the ground floor to a little distant area where they are free to roam. In the process, more healthy livestock can be expected. In the foothill areas of the Adi land the people have now separated such traditional lavatories from their houses which is a significant departure from the tradition. A better hygiene and sanitation is required not only in rural but also in urban areas to help reduce the incidence of many infectious diseases which often proved fatal. In Arunachal Pradesh, till now, there is not even a single medical college and therefore the people depend on other neigbouring states particularly Assam. In the existing hospitals like Pasighat, Naharlagun and R.K. Mission, Itanagar there is a shortage of trained personnel and specialists. Above all, within the limited resources available, there is again unequal distribution of manpower; most of the medical personnel even with rural background do not want to go back to rural areas because of remoteness of the area as well as poor communications, lack of power supply, poor working and living conditions, and meagre opportunities for their professional growth.

The tribal people are blessed with a rich cultural heritage in terms of language, literature, faith, practices, festivals, songs and dance. But of late, there has been a strong current of religious conversion among the people. The spread of Christianity adversely affects the cultural life of the Adis, Apatanis, Nyishis, Galos, Thangsas and Noctes. Christian converts help each other, at the hour of need, whenever called for, such as healing prayer, funeral ceremony, etc. Their customs and traditions have captivated the local populace, particularly the aged,. They decline to participate in the local festivals, traditional dance and music, creating social disunity and disharmony. In such, situation, to counter the process of conversion, there has been a resistance movement under the banner of Donyi-polo Yelam kebang among the Adis, Rangfrah of the Thangsas and Indigeneous Faith and Practices Society of Arunachal and among many other tribal groups in the state. Some like-minded Hindu organizations like Arunachal Vikash Parishad, Vivekananda Arunjyoti, etc., extend moral support to this movement for the preservation and promotion of tribal culture. Today the tribal society is found to be divided on two lines viz., Christians and the indigenous groups. But for how long? We are dependent on each other. I firmly believe that it is only education that can salvage the current situation and in the course of time, many will realize the importance of one's own roots and culture, and return to the fold.

In the problem-ridden Northeast, Arunachal Pradesh still remains peaceful; this may be because of constitutional safeguards; more specifically, due to operation of Inner line regulations. However, two districts viz., Tirap and Changlang, have been affected by extremists from across the border with Nagaland, which causes concern. But most of the educated youth now realize by and large that joining insurgency and creating violence among the people would lead them nowhere. A change of mindset for peace and stability is visible. In reality, there are no industries in the state to employ the unemployed local youth as government jobs are already saturated. However, there is a great future, ample opportunities to grow economically when we see the natural resources of the state. But it depends upon the vision of the planners how they plan for the future of the state. Economic development is the cornerstone for peace and stability. People want constructive plans for sustainable development.

The beautiful forests and rivers are invaluable assets of our past, which need to be preserved and exploited judiciously in tune with the aspirations of the people. The reckless exploitation of natural resources will cause irreparable damage to the people leading to ecological and environment problems. In other words, there would be a serious fallout of present-day development activities. We must remember that in today's world development is measured in terms of basic amenities—health, child care, and education which is inclusive and sustainable. In the name of development as perceived by the state government, the modus-operandi at present, to exploit the water resources of rivers like Kameng, Subansiri, Siang, Siyom, Lohit etc. in the state, may not be the right direction, ignoring the imminent environmental problems. Is it that "Mega Dam" projects over our rivers will transform the socio-economic life of the innocent tribals within a fortnight? Is it the only way out to boost the economy of the state? What about inter-village connectivity? What about education and health care? What about modern agriculture and horticulture? What about promotion of eco-tourism? In the Indian context, rivers are considered holy as they play a pivotal role in the socio-religious milieu of India. Water and earth are considered sacred, life-giving and nurturing resources. They are worshipped in many ways. In tribal areas, the land, forest and water are considered to be the heart, mind and soul of the people. In this context, it is my rare privilege to spell out the idea of Pandit Jawaharlal Nehru, who said, let tribal people develop along the lines of their own genius; tribal rights in land and forest should be respected and tribal art and craft should be encouraged. Why should not the people be allowed to choose their own path of development?

Change is the law of nature. Nobody can stop it but the trend of change must be evolutionary to keep pace with time and space. Revolutionary change is a high and long jump, which may create a big vacuum and in the long run it would not be so easy to fill such a vacuum. The history of human civilization began from naked barbarianism to city civilization which implies gradual development. So the policies we initiate must be in tune with the aspirations of the people for their development. Government must aim at inclusive growth accompanied by accountability and transparency in the implementation of schemes and projects that are for the long-term benefit and welfare of the people.

We can look at Nehru's tryst with modernity. Being educated at Cambridge, English in style, taste and outlook yet Indian in blood and colour, was culturally and physically alien to 20th century Europe. Indians could hardly challenge his lofty vision. He could address

Indian masses and their problems. Indian masses welcomed the planning and establishment of heavy industry and elite universities which created opportunities in the family and grand projects, but basic education, health for rural areas were neglected and in the process Indians languished in abysmal poverty. Here is the question, the tryst with modernity on the Western model to some extent seems to be self-defeating. In India, till today, 350 million people are illiterate and have the second highest mortality rate; while 40 per cent of its pre-school children are reported to be underweight.

The state of Arunachal Pradesh is treated as a special category state by the Centre for its socio-economic and cultural diversity; which used to pump funds liberally, but the pace of development is not on par with the expectations of the people. The feeling among the people is that funds are not utilized in a judicious manner; rather we throw more money into politics than the developmental schemes and our legislators have failed to live up to the aspirations of their people. There has been a strong feeling among the people that funds, whatever allocated, are neither properly appropriated nor are the representatives accountable. The question of the hour is good governance and accountability. If the people in power have integrity, the second wing of governance will automatically follow suit. At the village level, Panchayati Raj has been in operation for more than four decades, but the situation in rural Arunachal is still miserable in terms of road connectivity, power supply and modern medical facilities. In real sense of the term, in Arunachal Pradesh, Panchayati Raj is not working as per the aspirations of the people due to certain practical reasons. The state has no revenue generation of its own; whatever it gets, is from the state government. Therefore, we are still to try our tryst for an effective system of Panchayati Raj for rural development. At the same time, the age-old village councils of various tribal groups, for instance, Kebang of the Adis of Siang Valley, are also functioning side by side as a judicio-administrative body in the villages and are quite competent to safeguard and preserve the traditions, customs of the people, cultural identity, manage community resources and resolve disputes. They are found to be more effective and are led by elderly persons unlike Panchayati Raj, which has been taken over by semi-educated youth through party politics. Therefore, considering the dynamics of the village councils, there has to be a new arrangement to incorporate the tribal institutions into modern forms or modern democracy must treat traditional structures with respect.

References

1. Census of India, Arunachal Pradesh, 2001.
2. V. Elwin, *A Philosophy for NEFA,* Shillong, 1957.
3. *Human Development Report*, Arunachal Pradesh, 2005.
4. P.N. Luthra, *Constitutional and Administrative Growth of the Northeast Frontier Agency*, Shillong, 1971.
5. A. Toynbee, *A Study of History,* Vol. 1, University Press, London, 1965.

3

Between Tradition and Modernity

The Horizon of Anthropology

Annada C. Bhagabati

The two terms *tradition* and *modernity* have been used often enough in Anthropology. There has been no respite in the discipline from exploring the meanings and implications of the terms. This is because the terms just about represent the two extreme points between which most anthropological studies are ranged.

As a scientific discipline, Anthropology began in the nineteenth century with an overwhelming emphasis on the study of traditions and customs in simple societies. Since those early years, Anthropology has fairly consistently been looking at tribal or folk communities primarily in terms of their stable social structures and age-old cultural resources. But in the recent decades this kind of a focus on traditional patterns of life has become increasingly untenable in view of spectacular, frequently externally-induced, changes occurring in these societies. A book with a title like *Traditional India: Structure and Change* (edited by Milton Singer) neatly reflects the ground-level realities; or, for example, *Old Societies and New States* (edited by Clifford Geertz). Traditional ways are being substituted, supplemented or modified by the impact of newer elements, ideas, modes of acting and patterns of relationships. Anthropologists, as a matter of course, had to take cognizance of the emergent, non-traditional situations in various societies they studied. It is in this fashion that tradition and modernity between them have come to represent, so to say, the two ends of a spectrum, within which many anthropological studies are conceived and carried out.

Tradition and modernity are often conceptualized as opposing entities unable to combine, co-exist or blend. This is anything but the truth. Let me take recourse to an example: Some years ago while waiting at one of the terminals of New York's Kennedy Airport for the plane to Delhi, I noticed a group of fellow Indian travellers engaged in an act commonplace and innocuous in itself but with interesting cultural implications. In one corner of the lounge the group—all members of the same family as it turned out later—had settled down to a typically Indian snack consisting of *jalebi, laddu* and other *desi* tidbits. In the land of hotdog, hamburger and other fast food, this devotion to traditional delicacies in the busy and crowded surroundings of the airport lounge was what I thought to be interesting and therefore, worthy of notice. Eventually, in the course of the long and tedious flight, I got to know some members of the group: they belonged to a very prosperous Gujarati family having business interests in the US. for over twenty years, including ownership of a chain of motels. There is nothing traditional about the cut-throat competitive state-side business world. In order to succeed overseas, they certainly had to be very modern in their means and methods of commerce. Yet in matters of personal satisfaction, especially in the realm of food preference, twenty years of residence abroad had little meaning and tradition held its sway.

It will be appropriate at this point to look at the dictionary meaning of the terms, tradition and modernity, and then to proceed to examine if they represent opposing social realities. The *Concise Oxford Dictionary* defines 'tradition' as opinion or belief or custom handed down from ancestors to posterity. The word 'modern' and its cognate 'modernity', besides implying things of the present or recent time, also stands for things that are contemporay and not antiquated.

Having had this clarification from the dictionary, how do we classify our fellow travellers from New York? Are we to call them traditional because of their food preferences or label them modern because of their success in Western commerce in a Western land? I think they are bits of both really; traditional in one sphere of life and modern in another. Tradition and modernity are thus not always at loggerheads. But of this, more later.

Stepping outside the sphere of dictionary meanings, what really do we imply when we use the term 'modern' or 'modernity' as a social concept? All over the world and especially in a developing country like ours, there exists much concern about the persistence of the old order and tremendous enthusiasm for the notion of modernizing. Nearly all of us are keen that we as a people should become modern as quickly and as surely as possible. In other words, we presume that the term 'modernity' designates something good and therefore desirable. We also presume that in the path towards this desirable goal, traditions, that are antiquated beliefs and customs, raise their woolly head as barriers and these we must weed out. To be modern we must cast aside traditions.

But the question arises: are all things modern necessarily good and desirable? Let us take an extreme, even if widely used, example: few things are more modern than nuclear weapons. Should it therefore be a desirable goal for national society to acquire and stockpile this very modern weapon system? In contrast to nuclear weapons, the concept of *ahimsa*, non-violence, revivified by Mahatma Gandhi is very traditional. Should we, therefore, discard this old-fashioned idea because it runs counter to attributes of modernity such as nuclear warheads?

Let us look at some other examples of modernity and then ask ourselves if these too should form part of our goals. Urban-industrial growth is considered to be the best indicator of modernity for India. But an almost universal consequence of this growth has been the emergence of vast slums. Slums too are facets of modernity. Slums even if modern, cannot surely be regarded as desirable. An even better example of something that is very modern, and yet none will say is desirable in the least, is population increase of almost explosive proportions.

In fact, Professor W.C. Smith, a historian of Islam, goes so far as to say that in many ways modernity is a threat instead of being a boon. He cites the example of how traditional India was securely protected by geographic barriers from foreign conquest. Those who did come as invaders in ancient times had to settle down here and therefore become Indian in the long run. It was the beginning of the modern process that enabled this country to be conquered from the sea, and then to be ruled from outside by foreigners who remained foreigners. Likewise, external aggression has become possible on a new scale as a consequence of modern developments, he points out.

As a rule, anthropologists would be the last to defend the idea that everything new, without exception, is admirable; that every change, every innovation is a change or innovation for the better. They have knowledge of far too many societies where modern influences have caused havoc, and worthy traditions, including traditional skills and competence, have disappeared in the wake of the so-called modernization process. This last point was tellingly brought home by an elderly Nocte whom I met decades ago at the Naharkatya Inspection Bungalow on my way to Khonsa and Longding of Tirap District in Arunachal Pradesh for field work. He was very critical of the youth of his tribe who were getting educated in the high school at Khonsa: "Of what use is this education, if it makes them forget how to hold and wield a *dao* and makes them shy of repairing their own house?", he asked. He was alluding to the thatched hostel of the school which had been damaged in the storm the preceding summer but had been left without repairs for months by the authorities. In the village setting a fallen house would have come up the very next day, he told us.

There cannot thus be blanket support for modernity. By the same token, one cannot support the views of the traditionalists for whom what is good, lies in the past, in some golden age of long ago, and who find fault with most aspects of contemporary life. To such persons, 'modern' may be a term of abuse; it stands for something bad. We do come across such persons to whom modernity and decadence are synonymous. Some among them we call 'conservatives' for they stick to the old ways and outlooks as far as is possible in a changing world. A few among them we call 'revivalists' because they go a step beyond the conservatives. They would like to restore the lost ways, the lost grandeur, and reintroduce what had once been and to re-implement their traditionalist ideals.

I hope by now we have some idea of the social implications of the terms tradition and modernity. In a country like ours, the notion of modernity is closely tied up with the notion of progressive change and positive achievements that have taken place in the West in the spheres of science and technology, education and communication, growth of rational thoughts and secularism, and so on. Hence modernization is thought by many to be the same thing as Westernization. Since the bulk of ideas, ways and material traits that make up the outward garb of contemporary modernity originated in the West, the proposition is partly true. But modernization is no mere Westernization. Anthropologists know it very well that there can never be a complete transfer or transplantation of culture from one area to another. A rather distant example that comes to my mind is that of the Maori of New Zealand. Since the year 1814, when the Anglican missionary Samuel Marsden landed and established the first church in the far north of that island country, till the 1960s when I came to know some of them, the Maoris had been under the most thorough and deliberate pressures for changing their lifestyle, economic patterns and social relations into the predominant *pakeha* (white man) or the white Western model. Yet this simply did not happen. The Maoris did become modern in the sense that they took to modern education, employment and the intermediate technology and commerce of modern farming. But they did not become Western in the sense of being converted into 'brown *pakehas*'. The combination and blending of old ways with new influences emanating from the West could not be called 'acculturation' pure and simple since the change was not along a single gradient. Instead, as Professor Ralph Piddington pointed out, this was *emergent development.*

Japan offers us an even better and widely known example to make the point: As we know, it is one of the most industrialized and modernized nation-states of the world. Since the Meiji Restoration of the 1860s, and more particularly since the Second World War, Japan never really has looked backwards in the path towards modernity. Basing its industrial-economic development on Western scientific and technological achievements, Japan has outpaced most Western nations. The Japanese are highly modern but perhaps we cannot call them a highly Westernized people. For, it is said that typically Japanese mores and values persist and pervade even in the working of giant industrial concerns. The technology and the market forces that inspire production and commercial enterprises are totally Western; yet the cultural frame in which they operate is essentially Japanese.

Much of this is true for our country as well. I need not go into citing examples for we all can make up our own from the lessons of history, our surroundings and day-to-day experience. Modernization here is not Westernization pure and simple; but a combination and blending of two separate ways and the emergence of a new one.

Do traditions pose as barriers to modernity? Do these represent opposing and irreconcilable forces so that one has to be destroyed to have the benefits of the other? While it is easy to pose such questions, no simple and straight-forward answer can be given. However, most anthropologists, who are always a little cautions and a little partial when talking about old and established ways of life, would say that since traditions take a long time shaping and since they constitute the foundation of any society, they must be understood properly before being tampered with to pave the way for modernity. Besides, there may not be any real conflict between tradition and modernity. The two have been known to co-exist, integrate and blend with one another to create new social orders. On the other hand, there are examples of peoples whose traditions have been thoroughly violated by the forces of history. Yet it is not modernity that grew in such a tradition-free environment. What grew in extreme cases was despondency leading to a lack of will to survive on the part of these people. Many of us know of the rise of the *cargo cult* in the Melanesian Islands in the wake of the Pacific War of the 1940s inducing islanders to give up work and normal living and escape into the realm of mass fantasy. Nowhere is the poignancy of the passing away of traditions better epitomized than the statement of Ramon, a Digger Indian of California, to the anthropologist, Ruth Benedict, immortalized in her well-known book, *Patterns of Culture.* He said, "In the beginning God gave to every people a cup, a cup of clay, and from this cup they drank their life. They all dipped in the water, but their cups were different. Our cup is broken now. It has passed away".

I have continued this far tossing about the two terms, tradition and modernity, in what might seem an aimless fashion. But I have a certain limited purpose in doing this: In our attempts at modernization of indigenous tribal and rural societies, the first task, as part and parcel of the planning process for development, is to try to understand the traditions—the old ways of doing things, of acting and of conceptualizing inter-personal relations and the social universe in general. There may be much in the traditional culture that is meaningful and relevant even for coping with change for progress.

4

Issues of Modernity, Identity, and Women of Arunachal Pradesh

Sucheta Sen Chaudhuri

This chapter explores modernity as the identity space for women. Modernity as perceived an influence of Western education shaped up thoughts and actions of the people of state and non-state societies of the world. Modernity in principal created a space for women and embracing Western education, women of the non-Western societies reoriented the traditional views and living patterns. The parameters of modernity maintain different configurations, which differ from society to society. Moreover, nothing is considered constant in the issues of modernity except education. However, modernity is cultural, economic and political too. Even in the practices of modernity religious issues are interpreted in a new way. It refers to new habits and activities shaped by ideologies. In arguments, modernity refers to rationality of thoughts. While modernity as a parameter is historically determined by some scholars as the backdrop of traditionalism, primitivism, and post-modernism, others consider it as referring to the identity space determined from the perspective of structuralism.

Context

I reached Arunachal Pradesh at a point when tribal communities of this part of India received statehood, and the UN declaration on the CEDAW, tribal women organizations, as well as the Government[1] ratified it as a document and acknowledged its principles. After reaching here, I had the opportunity to meet women activists of the state and NGO workers at local, regional, and national levels, who had diverse experiences of addressing women's issues at the organizational level. Problems of gender inequalities were coming up as an agenda for tribal women after statehood. In a research paper, Basar (2006: 208)[2] mentions how education enlightened and created consciousness. She writes: "This consciousness along with other factors made us aware of discrimination against women in the society, due to which women organized themselves to protest against the inequalities and other traditional maladies prevailing in the society...". She continues that an ideological conflict happened after the exposure of women to different jobs, and businesses of their husbands. The women realized that they were discriminated in society, marginalized in development, and were least secure as they were outside the protective cover of their respective community. Here Basar quotes Jarjun Ete, who is one of the Indian women activists and a pioneer in Arunacahal Pradesh, who says, "The women came together to look at their lives in a society in transition and to dream of a strong society with traditional strength and wisdom" (Basar Ibid). Both Ete and Basar referred to "modernity" as a pressure point for women and children within communities, vulnerable to attacks from within and outside their community. Even the use of words "within and without community" by these authors refers to a structural change in society, whether perceived in mind or as a reality. Again in the same article, the use of the words, '...struggle for more egalitarian society" signifies a momentum generated by women specifically after they established a women's organization (1979), which is now popularly known as Arunachal Pradesh Women's Welfare Society (APWWS)[3]. Speaking at the Rajiv Gandhi University on 05 September 2009, Jarjum Ete stated: "in May 1985, dealing with various womenfolk, rural and urban, educated and illiterate—our collective comprehended that those problems would not have been there if the womenfolk were treated as equals, as humane as their male counterparts, in the society or within the families in the schemes of community life"[4]. Basar (Ibid: 209) mentioned that the APWWS has sixteen branches and affiliated bodies all over Arunachal Pradesh. Apart from fighting for issues concerning problems faced by women and children, the organization also extends moral support, counsels and negotiates cases of moral discord, and organizes seminars and workshops to sensitize women on gender realities.

Analysis of tribal women intellectuals, provided evidence of gender discriminations, a phenomena not observed in dominant mainstream Indian hierarchical caste societies alone. Experiences of tribal women after statehood, on gender equality, interpreted some customary norms and practices as 'dominant', 'hegemonic', and 'discriminatory' for women. Boserup (1976)[5] and Simone de Beauvoir (1949)[6] evolved perspectives to study the matter, locating and searching for gender relations in all activities with a view to document the position and development of women at various levels—within traditional, social and economic institutions and organizations.

This is an attempt to understand the contemporary modernity of Arunachal Pradesh through contributions of women and their interpretations of their own society. Traditional ideas of gender construction limited the role and contributions of women of this state to food production, weaving technology, and household work that are regarded as less strenuous and thus classified as women's jobs. Work participation of women of the region is generally considered as an indicator of economic self-dependence, categorizing tribal women as bread earners for self and children in everyday life in the rural situation. In India, 'economic self-dependence for women, which is measured through work participation and earning, is perceived as the basis of gender equality'[7] and invariably women of Arunachal Pradesh enjoy better status than their counterparts in the rest of India. However, socio-economic and demographic findings (mentioned in the Human Development Report, 2005)[8] do not indicate a better social status of women. Therefore, this study intends to understand the concept of space for women in modern times, in terms of roles and rights they enjoy in their own societies, at the backdrop of women's contributions to subsistence economies. Specifically, references of Boserup (Ibid) remind us of a similar situation in Africa where agriculture heavily relies upon women and developmental activities disassociated women gradually from the production system. Moreover, patriarchy influences all ideas, opinions and dialogues even to understand women's subordination in all communities. Whether this is the situation among tribal women as well, not clear. Therefore, this chapter further explores modernity as an identity issue[9] for tribal women and specifically aims to understand relations of modern technology, education (44 per cent for women in 2001 census), with a culturally perceived private domain. Subsequently, this variable will be the centre of enquiry.

In agricultural activities, women contribute substantially in production systems. According to the culturally perceived scales of division of labour, cleaning of cultivable land, digging and sowing seeds, weeding, harvesting, carrying, threshing, and storing seeds in the granary, all are women's jobs. In the Apatani plateau, old women remain busy in repairing the bund during the winter season. In Adi villages, women remain busy in vegetable and horticultural production of ginger and orange, after paddy production is over. These attachments refer to full work participation of women in food production throughout the year. Does their contribution in the family ensure equal rights and space for women in the private as well as the public domain? Does indigenous knowledge carried by women from one generation to another ensure rights to women for participation in the decision-making process for future development? Do state-level development facilities create better opportunities for women?

Modernity and the Private Domain

Private domains as a construct both in cultural traditions as well as in academics perceive 'household' as the unit to understand the domestic production system. That space, traditionally, and in academics is distinguished as space for women. In that domain, the role of women in food production is not only compulsory but also inevitable. Culturally, the knowledge of food production is learnt and practiced by women, generation after generation and is considered as a woman's job in the tribal societies. In modernity, when the individual's choices guide life in urban societies, the tribal women in the urban family have redefined their workspace in the family production system. Ethnifications of tribal identities engage women in the work of redefining 'culture and tradition' as 'heritage'. Modern education created new working space for women. Modernity also created the urban living space. Their rural counterpart embraces modernity differently. Whatever it is, the urge for food security remained the responsibility of women in the real and symbolic senses. Now, white-collar jobs of many women both in urban and rural situations categorized the work of agricultural production as secondary activities. Families with landed property practice wet-rice cultivation with the help of hired labourers. Women practice shifting cultivation, and cultivate kins'/clans' land. The status of women farmers differs, and follows traditional institutional pactices.

Urban Women Farmers and Their Identity Space

Mrs. Gumri Ringu, a founder-member of the State Women's Commission said in the summer of 2010 that she would not be available for some days for any work during the seedling transplantation in her cultivable field. She would be at the farmhouse. In another interaction, she was remembering her trip to Nagaland when she visited entrepreneurs engaged in Bamboo production and technology. Recently, the Government of India and the North Eastern Council's initiative to the Bamboo Mission attracted progressive farmers and Gumri was one of them.

Mrs. Dakter Basar, a schoolteacher and wife of the Director, State Health Services, passionately remembered her experiences of participation in cultivation on her in-laws' cultivable land. This interaction took place before she contested the state assembly election for the first time in 2009. In fact, for her and for many other women settled in urban areas of the state due to family commitments or for own careers participation in cultivation as well as in get togethers in the rural household, follows institutionalized tradition of reciprocity. This is part of celebration and heritage. In these cases the investment cost of agriculture sometimes does not reach levels of high surplus or sometimes even the expenditure related to a common feast and merry-making may be the same as the investment cost. But Mrs. Basar derives immense pleasure in community participation. For her the cultivation is not a primary occupation, not even for any member of her family, who are otherwise highly educated and well placed. Participating in the tasks of cultivation maintains a good tradition, utilizing cultivable land to help members of one's own society that has remained rural. I felt that the acts of Ms. Gumri Ringu, Ms. Dakter Basar and many women like them were conscious and progressive acts that blended tradition with modernity. Here, participating in cultivation is like participating in the traditional activities. These educated tribal women are used to urban living. Therefore, modernism is the order of the day for them. Friedman (1998: 285-300) identified modernity as identity space which is "cultural", and "natural". For him "traditionalism" stands for "culture" and "primitivism" stands for "nature". He said all the categories, like "modernism", "post-modernism", "traditionalism" and "primitivism" may be historical categories to some scholars but for him those are structurally designated identity spaces in the post-colonial contemporary world.

All the identity spaces in the post-colonial, globalized world symbolize trans-nationalization...and ethnification as expressions of declining global hegemony. Therefore, the urban tribal women going to the forest for the collection of seasonal leafy vegetables, mushrooms, roots, fruits is cultural and traditional heritage. Here I cannot resist sharing the closeness of modern tribal women with forests. In one conversation, Mrs. Tariang[10], Mrs. Hungyo[11], and Mrs. Pakma[12] were discussing about mushroom gathering being one of the favourite pastimes. They referred to going to collect mushrooms to the forest whenever they went to the village or had time. Urbanism for tribal women, was not yet completely detached from the cultural use of nature, though none of them were sure that the habit would be transmitted to the next generation.

The circumstances of the rural women in all cases are not the same. There are tribal families living at subsistence levels; there are tribal families at village level who are surplus growers, too. For many rural women, agriculture is the primary occupation. Their work schedule is the best way to understand that. During the whole season of cultivation, these women spend major working hours in domestic production. An attempt by the Womens' Studies Research Centre of Rajiv Gandhi University (RGU) observing activities of women cultivators, is presented in two Tables below. These data were collected through a documentation project entitled, "Women Work and Land Right" by the members of the Centre in the month of March and July 2010. The workshops aimed to understand the issues and concerns of women cultivators. The women participants were from the areas of Sagali and Leporiang of the Lower Subansiri district, and Takpu Bagra, Gori I Gori II, and Soi villages of the West Siang district of Arunachal Pradesh.

Table 4.1 shows the nature of participation of women in family production systems. This is a sample of women participants who attended the workshop.

According to responses, 87.5 per cent of the women started agricultural work in the family production system before the age of puberty. Each of these members contribute at the subsistence level. The shifting cultivation is a mixed production system. They grow paddy, maize, arum, different types of gourds, cucumber, chili, leafy vegetables, brinjal, pulses, and beans. The concept of kitchen garden is practiced with paddy production through shifting cultivation. In the Table 4.1, the separate category of vegetable growers refers to

Table 4.1: Women Cultivators

Age at the beginning of work		*Family production*	*Types of cultivation*			*Village*
Pre-Menstrual	*Post-Menstrual*	*Working in kins' land*	*Vegetable, fruit cultivation*	*Shifting hills*	*Wet rice*	
25	4	29	13	28	15	Takpu Bagra
25	13	33	08	24	25	Gori I
11	6	17	05	13	11	Gori II
21	03	24	03	21	19	Soi
30	0	30	19	29	28	Sagalee

Source: Women Studies and Research Centre, Rajiv Gandhi University, 2010.

the commercial ventures undertaken. Women sell products of Jhum cultivation in local markets and most of the income is utilized as expenses for children's education, purchasing food and vegetables that they do not grow in their own fields and to meet family requirements. They spend money on cloths also. The family production system is extending its reach and venturing into vegetable production at the commercial level, as well as fruit production. In the extended horizon, tribal women became experts in both hills and plains cultivation. A few women referred to their experience of commercial horticulture. All this work participation among women needs separate sets of expertise and experience. The division of labour identified most of the tasks of cultivation as the responsibility of women. In the hills these include cutting, clearing forests, and burning wood and leaves as well as tasks like seed sowing, weeding, fencing, harvesting, drying, cleaning, and storing. Earlier cutting/felling of trees and fencing were men's jobs, now women do men's jobs as well. Similarly, operating the mechanized plough (Japanese brand 'kubuta') is the job of both men and women in wet rice fields. The rural women are now doing men's jobs. Is the horizon for women expanding due to technological developments? (Table 4.2)

Among the 34 respondents at Sagalee, at least 20 women claimed that they inherited landed property or purchased landed property with or without Land Possession Certificates in their names. In Bagra circle, among 100 respondents, only one woman claimed that she had the land possession document in her name. These women of Sagalee and Bagra may be very insignificant in percentage but are an important pioneer group among women farmers, who are enjoying rights over

Table 4.2: Women Land Owners

No. of Respondents & Circles	*Inherited landed Property*		*Purchased landed Property*	
	With document	*Without document*	*With LPC*	*Without LPC*
34 (In Sagalee and Leporiang circle)	3	3	8	6
100 (in Bagra circles)	1	0	0	0

Source: Women Studies & Research Centre, Rajiv Gandhi University, 2010.

their land or influence of modernity, where parents/husbands wanted to ensure security for women family members. However, this data really exposed us to a complex phenomenon when the marital status of the sample of Sagalee was compared with the right to inheritance. Among 34 respondents of Sagalee 13 women live in polygamous marital relations.

Tribal Women in Public Domain

Both concepts of "Traditionalism" and "modernity" share similar views on "private" and "public" domains as "women's space" and "men's space". In traditional tribal wisdom, physical space of women is never confined within the household for activities in different shifting cultivable plots, forest for gathering food, or collecting firewood. In the public domain, women do not have access to the political organizational meetings if they are not a party—either accused, victims or aggrieved; as such political spaces are open only for men.

Therefore, the establishment of APWWS is significant in many ways. In the Constitution, Article I claims, the women's organization is formed for all the women of Arunachal Pradesh, in order to bring integration and foster understanding among the younger generation to exploit the exuberance of youth for the greater interest of women in Arunachal Pradesh and to preserve, promote and protect culture and tradition. It further claims to fight for the human rights for women of Arunachal Pradesh and to eradicate all forms of social evil and bad practices from society and thereby, to bring a new dawn for the women of Arunachal Pradesh (Basar, Ibid). In reality, from the beginning, this organization had to concentrate on eradicating all forms of social evil related to child marriage, polygamy, forced marriage, bride price, abduction, divorce and desertion of women. This organization articulated the voice of the people and specifically of women of Arunachal Pradesh. Since 1989, this organization was making people in general and women specifically aware of reform in the practice of tribal customary law, especially in the law of marriage, divorce, and inheritance of property rights. To establish subsistence rights for women, the society was advocating for rights to property for women through regional level meetings workshops, and seminars. At present, according to customary law, women and widows enjoy right over cultivable land of husbands. The male child inherits the father's property and daughters do not. The rules of divorce for a woman and that for a man show inequalities. Basar mentions that even a widow 'is' property after the death of her husband, and her husband's clan or lineage inherits her (2006: 210).

In Table 4.3 the activities of APWWS refer to the issues of gender discrimination identified in tradition and the initiatives of women to eradicate the institutionalized forms of such discrimination.

Cultural Identity and Tribal Women

"Culture", which according to its modern definition is equivalent to "identity", incorporates political dimensions. "Political" refers to "tribal identity". Both educated men and women in Arunachal Pradesh are politically tribal today as Arunachalee. The identity is again plural. Therefore, the Arunachalee identity of the community is equally important besides the Scheduled Tribe identity and the identity of the clan/lineage within the community. This identity has created a larger circle of women who share similar experiences. Colonial administrators referred to the "tribal" as 'primitive' and in the post-colonial situation, in the modern parlance, the tribe comprises marginalized/indigenous people, who are socio-politically very close to nature.

Tribal Women and Political Empowerment

An excerpt from a lecture of Jarjum Ete, Founder Chairperson of the State Women's Commission of Arunachal Pradesh, given on the occasion of the inauguration of the Women's Studies and Research Centre at Rajiv Gandhi University, on 5 September 2009, clearly spells out her views on women's empowerment:

Table 4.3: Role of APWWS for the Eradication of Gender Discrimination

Year	*Issues and Demands*	*Programme*	*Remarks*
1989	Reform of Customary Law	Demanded women representative in traditional council	
1989 February	Demanded compulsory and uniform marriage registration act in Arunachal Pradesh	In First state gathering of women	
1989 February	Reform and review value system to enhance security of women	In First state gathering of women	
1989 February	Elected representatives of assembly work to eradicate inhuman practices like forced marriage, child marriage, and multiple marriages	First state gathering of women	
1989 February	Demanded social initiative for intertribal marriages	In First state gathering of women	
1992 March	Demanded State Women's Commission	Submitted memorandum to the then Governor; Networking with national & international women's organizations; national Commission for Women; and National Alliance of Women	Consistent campaign, meeting, rallies, memoranda, representation through media continued. In 2005, SCW formed under the chairmanship of Ms. Jarjum Ete
1993	To abolish practice of child marriage	A private members resolution was moved	The resolution was stone walled and ultimately withdrawn
1994 March	Demanding State Commission for Women	A private member resolution for the constitution of SCW	

(*Contd.*)

Year	Issues and Demands	Programme	Remarks
1994 October	Demanded Equal Right and necessary modification in the customary practices to ensure gender equality	First all tribal women state conference on 10th October 1994	For the protection of customary rights, laws, social and cultural practices the bill was accepted in the assembly without debate.
1995 June	Demanded review, debate, etc. at the level of civil society, rural leaders, lawyers, social workers , politicians, human right activist before codification	Hold a meeting and sent the document to Guwahati Law Research Institute, Gauhati High Court	
1995	Demanded Women's Studies and Research Centre in RGU		The center is established on 5th September 2010
1996 October	Demanded State Human Rights Commission	Submitted Memorandum to Prime Minister Deve Gouda	
1996 October	Demanded implementation of 73rd amendment act for women	Submitted Memorandum to Prime Minister Deve Gouda	
1996 October	Repeal of the Armed Force Special Powers Act	Submitted Memorandum to Prime Minister Deve Gouda	

"As women of the particular tribe—some lenient and most others not being so—from their infancy to their graves, the women of Arunachal Pradesh, like most of their counterparts in the world, have to negotiate their lives within the parameter of the society. Yes, some of us had to break grounds and be known as rebels by the conventionalists—both men and women. However, someone had to do it. We did it. In addition, we take pride in that. The establishment of the State Commission for Women, the coming of more than 38 per cent of women PRI leaders in the three-tier panchayat of the state, and the legislation known as the A.P. Bill for Protection of Customary Law and Social Practices 1994, pending review, are the landmark achievements of the pioneering tribal women's network, APWWS."

Regarding her experiences with the State Commission for Women of Arunachal Pradesh (APSCW), which she headed as founder-chairperson, she added:

> "We dealt with cases of child marriages besides the ones of polygamy, maintenance, child custody, divorces, etc. We lobbied hard for a private members' resolution for a ban on such practices in the last assembly session of 1993. It had to be withdrawn. Then, on 8 March 1994, another private members' resolution was tabled for establishment of the State Commission for Women. It also had to be withdrawn. Women were used to scuttle this move in the state legislature. That was one of the most unfortunate Women's Day for us in Arunachal. And for having highlighted the manipulation and intrigues used by the state, yours faithfully was got thrown out by the publishing house of a regional daily, for which she used to report."

Her writing continues, and she maintains, "Many years later in 2000, the state under a new leadership, a friendlier one, constituted an all-woman committee to draft the State Commission for Women Bill for Arunachal Pradesh, in which the former president (of the State Women's Commission) and president of the APWWS were appointed as members, the latter being Member-Secretary. Finally, the bill was passed in the early 2000s but the first commission began its work only in first week of January 2005." (Ibid)

The establishment of State Commission for Women is a big victory for women of that state. The whole concept of patriarchy that relates all values and systems to gender inequality was a very new concept in tribal societies. "The first team focused on raising awareness about the body *per se*, the need for women's empowerment, the various laws and policies for the protection of women's rights and privileges in democratic India, even in traditional, tribal, patriarchal Arunachal. The fact that the state had established the body to look into the needs and aspirations of Arunachalee women made the village council elders stare back at us in amazement and disbelief. But, finally, in three years, we see a palpable change, in their attitude. One, even acknowledged that no political leader nor any administrative officer, not even the magistrates had ever told them about the rights of women!!" (Ibid.)

The Arunachal Pradesh State Commission for Women rekindled the aspirations of women's organization. Jarjum Ete wrote, "From...January 2005 to March 2008, we tried and involved the representatives of the women's organizations like APWWS, NAWO, the SHGs and various local women's groups, and other NGOs like the Human Rights Laws Network, Arunachal Citizen Rights, and even interested individuals around various subjects—economic empowerment, social mobilization, legal awareness, gender sensitization, etc. We tried interfacing with policymakers and civil society representatives. We roped in media-persons also to highlight the issues." (Ete 2009)[13]

Summing Up

For women of Arunachal Pradesh, modernity is the instrument of engendering and reformation of social processes. Structurally, the approach is embracing both traditionalism and modernity and perceives cultural identity as political identity. The cultural identity within the concept of modernity celebrates the closeness with cultural ecology and at the same time, locates gender discrimination that persists within tradition. The tribal women of Arunachal Pradesh, despite the separate community affiliations within the state are united in fighting the evils created by the inequality in gender relations.

The educated urban women practice cultivation as part of their cultural heritage. For them, the season of cultivation is a season of getting together. For rural women, a section lives at subsistence level while another is producing surplus. Women learnt and practiced new technology to plough land and techniques of fruit production. The women of the village are performing all jobs, beyond the traditional concept of 'division of labour'.

There may be a gap in modernity as perceived and as practiced, but the gap would be from the standpoint of gender inequality. Women are sharing more of the burden in the rural areas for livelihood, and urban women are reinterpreting agricultural activities as their heritage.

Notes

1. Basar, Jumyir. 2008. "Women Movement in Arunachal Pradesh: A Case Study of APWWS ", in A.K. Danda, S.B. Chacrabarti, A. Basu Ed.

Social Unrest, Jhargram, Pub. by Indian National Confederation and Academy of Anthropologists, pp. 197-206.

2. *Ibid.*
3. *Ibid.*
4. In her key note address during inauguration of Women's Studies and Research Centre, Rajiv Gandhi University, Itanagar, dated 5th September, 2009
5. Boserup Esther, 1976.
6. Simone de Beauvoir, *The Second Sex, Penguin 1972*
7. UNDP State Development Report, 2005, published by Government of Arunachal Pradesh, India
8. *Ibid.*
9. See Jonathan Friedman, "Transnationalization, Socio-political Disorder, and Ethnification as Expressions of Declining Global Hegemony", in Joan Vincent Ed. *The Anthropology of Politics,* 2002, Blackwell, 285-299.
10. Mrs Tariang was one of my colleagues from Anthropological Survey of India from 1992-1999, at Shillong. She was a Khasi from Meghalaya
11. Mrs. Hungyo, was one of my Tangkhul Naga Colleagues from Manipur, in Anthropological Survey of India, Shillong
12. Mrs. Pakma, was one of my colleagues from Meghalaya, in Anthropological Survey of India, Shillong
13. Jarjum Ete 'Narrative Experience of the Founding Chairperson of State Woman Commission of Arunachal Pradesh', Keynote address delivered at the inauguration programme of Woman Study Center, Rajiv Gandhi Universiy, 5th September, 2009, Rajiv Gandhi University Conference Hall, Itanagar.

References

Basar, Jumyir. 2008. "Women Movement in Arunachal Pradesh: A Case Study of APWWS ", in A.K. Danda, S.B. Chacrabarti, A. Basu (Ed). *Social Unrest,* Jhargram, Indian National Confederation and Academy of Anthropologists, pp. 197-206.

Boserup, Esther, 1970. *Women Role in Economic Development,* New York, St. Martin's Press.

Friedman, Jonathan. 1999. "Transnationalization, Socio-Political Disorder, and Ethnification as Expressions of Declining Global Hegemony" in Joan Vincent (Ed.) *The Anthropology of Politics,* Blackwell, 255-289.

Simone de Beauvoir, The Second Sex, Penguin 1972.

UNDP State Development Report. 2005. Government of Arunachal Pradesh.

5

A Study on Gender Discrimination in Education among Nyishi Tribe of Doimukh Circle of Arunachal Pradesh

Philip Mody and Teshi Sohang

It has been rightly remarked that societies where women are not afforded equal rights, the men can never achieve development in a sustainable manner. In tribal societies, by virtue of recognizing and addressing discrimination in the field of education against girls and women, the success in the fight against all forms of discrimination like colour, class, race, ethnicity and age will be more sustained and the results lasting. In fact, entire societies develop when girls and women are reasonably educated and productive. Gender equity in terms of education is felt as a primary human right that makes sure that all children are afforded quality education, one that prepares them for a participative and productive life. The Papum Pare District is the capital district of Arunachal Pradesh. It is located in the latitude 26 55'N and 28 40' and longitude 92 40' and 94 21' and is surrounded by the Kurung Kumey district in the north, Lower Subansiri district in the East, East Kameng district in the west and Assam in the south. The district is divided into two administrative subdivisions—the Sagalee Sub-Division and the Itanagar Capital Complex Sub-division with nine administrative circles namely Sagalee, Mengio, Toru, Laiporiang, Kimin, Balijan, Doimukh, Itanagar and Naharlagun. It is the abode of the Nyishis who are known in history for their courage and belong to the Indo-Mongoloid group of people speaking the Tibeto-Burman language. So far as education in the district is concerned, it has 72,021 educated persons with 42,602 literate men and 29,419 literate women respectively[1]. It is observed that, 13,183 male are more educated over and above the literate women, reflecting dominance of the men over the women and thereby, signaling predominance of the gender discriminatory tendency among the Nyishi community in education. Therefore, the Nyishi community needs to have a level playing field by ensuring that all the children irrespective of sex, have equal opportunities for education so that girls and women become active catalysts of social change and social reformation. Thus, promoting gender equality through education among the Nyishi community of the Doimukh circle in particular and the Papum Pare district in general, is seen as an effort towards greater socio-economic prosperity.

Objectives

The main objectives of the present study are:

1. To ascertain the presence of gender discrimination in education among the Nyishi tribe of Doimukh circle in Papum Pare district.
2. To study the present position of education among the Nyishi tribe in terms of boys and girls pursuing education at different stages of the formal educational and non-formal education system.
3. To analyze the amounts spent on girls' education by Nyishi parents in comparison to boys.
4. Tc offer constructive suggestions to bolster girls' education among the Nyishis.

The Expanse of the Study

The present study has been conducted in four villages of the Doimukh Circle in Papum Pare district, namely, Gumto, Emchi, Doimukh and Rono, during August, 2009. The villages have been selected deliberately on the grounds of being major Nyishi-dominated villages in the entire circle. Data over the last five years, i.e., from 2005 to 2009, has been taken into consideration.

Methodology

During the present study, an effort has been made to make the study empirical, based on a field study. However, the present study is entirely based on both primary and secondary data. For the collection of primary data, a field study was conducted in four villages and twenty heads of families from each village have been interviewed personally with the help of well-designed questionnaires. Altogether, eighty respondents have been selected at random and interviewed to ascertain the present position of education among the Nyishis in the study area with special focus on women's and girls' education.

As for secondary data, various articles, government reports and official websites have been referred to for better understanding of the problem. However, the Internet has been one of the most used sources of secondary data for the present study.

Analysis and Interpretation of Data

The information/data obtained during the course of survey has been analyzed and interpreted under the following heads:

A. Nyishi Girls and Boys at Different Stages of Formal Educational System in the Study Area

It can be observed from Table 5.1 and Diagram A that both, the total number of girls and boys, at different stages of the educational system are on the increase each year from 2005 to 2009, demonstrating positive behaviour. Looking into the present trends in terms of numbers of both girls and boys at different stages of the formal educational system, the improvements in the literacy position in the study area can be clearly seen. It is evident from Table 5.1 that, the

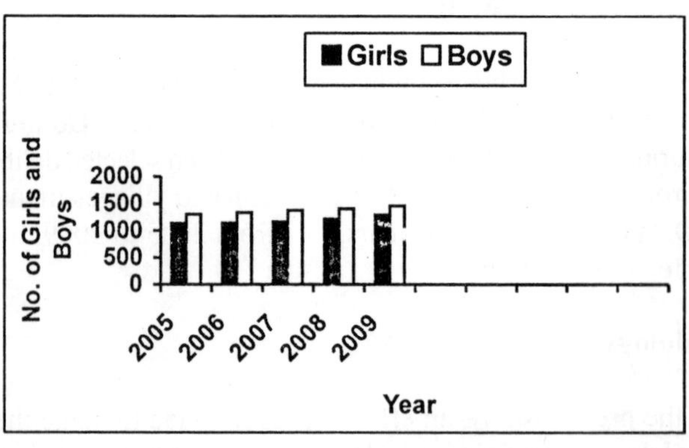

Diagram: A

Table 5.1: Total Numbers of Nyishi Girls and Boys at different stages of formal educational system (including non-governmental educational institutes) in the Study Area

	Girls/Women (in numbers)						*Boys (in numbers)*					
Year	05	06	07	08	09	Total	05	06	07	08	09	Total
Pre-schooling	67	64	73	79	88	371	82	86	102	112	117	499
Primary school	627	631	633	646	649	3186	727	741	744	752	789	3753
Middle school	190	196	198	207	231	1022	236	245	256	251	254	1242
Secondary school	181	187	191	199	213	971	145	145	152	156	163	761
Higher Secondary	45	48	46	58	69	266	72	76	78	81	84	391
College	22	19	21	26	38	126	35	38	41	45	46	205
University	04	02	02	04	06	18	06	09	09	08	11	43
Total	1136	1147	1164	1219	1294	5960	1303	1340	1382	1405	1464	6894

Source: Field Survey.

total strength of boys surpasses that of girls at pre-school, primary school, middle school, higher secondary school, college, and university levels. However, girls are found to have dominated boys right from 2005 to 2009 at secondary school levels as total numbers of girls stood at 971 against 761 boys. Moreover, analysis of present data reveals that enrollment of boys as well as girls (789 boys and 649 girls), was highest in 2009.

It is important to note that, the annual growth rate in terms of the number of girls in middle to college level education is sharper than boys, indicating the beginning of girls' reign over boys in the educational sector probably after 6-10 years, in the Doimukh circle in Papum Pare district. Altogether, 5960 girls and 6894 boys are found to have been educated under the formal education system running from pre-school to university during the study period.

B. Nyishi Girls and Boys under Non-Formal Educational System in the Study Area

It is revealed from Table 5.2 and Diagram B that the total number of both boys and girls partaking education under the non-formal education system, viz., Open school, IGNOU, Distance Education, correspondence courses and other means of continuing education is on the increase. However, the overall rate of increase is found higher among girls than among boys, indicating a better position for girls than for boys in non-formal education. As observed through Diagram B, girls have always been in a better position than boys in non-formal education with the exception of 2006, where boys were equal to girls. The highest and lowest number of girls pursuing education through non-formal institutions is 43 and 21 in 2009 and 2005 respectively. The maximum (29) and minimum (18) number of boys are found to

Table 5.2: Nyishi Girls and Boys under Non-Formal Educational System in the Study Area

Year	*Girls (in number)*	*Boys (in number)*
2005	21	18
2006	22	22
2007	26	22
2008	31	24
2009	43	23
Total	143	109

Source: Field Survey.

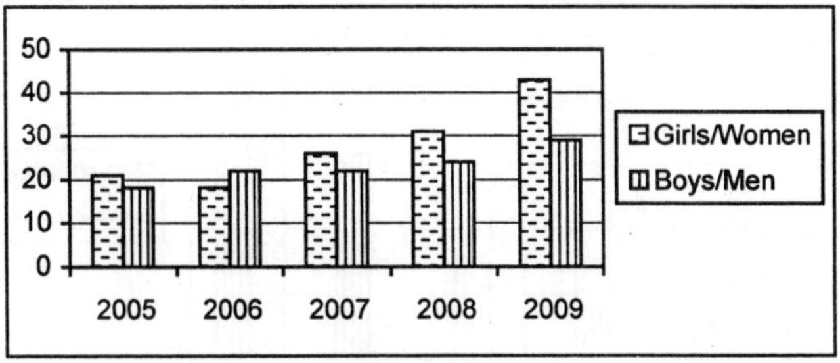

Diagram: B

have been educated under the non-formal education system in 2009 and 2005. During 2008-09, the highest annual growth rate in terms of the number of girls throughout the reference period is found which exhibits an increase of 38.7 per cent. However, the recent scenario of boys pursuing education through non-formal means shows attainment of a 'plateau', as no significant growth in the number of boys has been observed. Altogether, 143 girls and 109 boys are found to have undertaken education in non-formal educational institutions.

C. Average per Family Spending on Education between Nyishi Girls and Boys in the Study Area

It can be observed from Table 5.3 and Diagram C that altogether, the study area has shown an increasing trend with regard to spending on education (both boys and girls) with the exception of 2006 in the girls' case. It has been revealed that, throughout the study period, the average per household spending on girls by their parents is higher than for boys with the exception of 2008. Interestingly, the maximum amount of spending on girls and boys' education has been evident in the year 2009, amounting to Rs. 22,218 and Rs. 16,239 respectively.

Table 5.3: Average Per Family Spending on Education Between Nyishi Girls and Boys in the Study Area

Year	*Girls (in Rs)*	*Boys (in Rs)*
2005	13180	5720
2006	12140	7720
2007	13290	7890
2008	14438	15832
2009	22218	16239

Source: Field Survey.

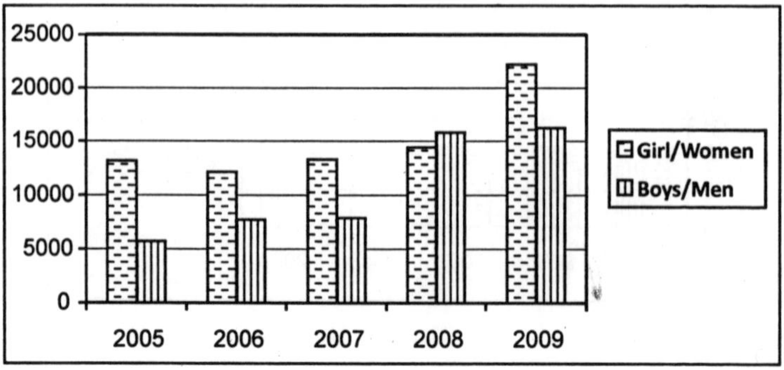

Diagram: C

Looking at the present position with respect to the amount being spent on children's education, the dominance of girls over boys in future in the educational arena can be safely predicted in the study area.

Findings and Results

From the above analysis, the presence of discriminatory tendencies between girls and boys in the field of education among the Nyishi community in Doimukh circle can be summarized under the following heads:

A. *Boys and Girls at different stages of formal education:* A discriminatory attitude against girls' education prevails at the pre-school and primary school levels in the study area amongst the Nyishi community, as boys have outnumbered girls because of their higher enrolment at an early stage of education by their parents. This enrolment pattern has ensured that boys are in larger numbers than girls in higher education. Interestingly, girls continue to dominate at the secondary school level. This may be because of greater consistency, sincerity and lower dropout rates among girls during adolescence. However, lesser number of girls tend to enroll for college and university education, which is probably due to early marriage. Lesser number of girls in elementary education can be due to greater amount of domestic 'responsibilities' and poor sex-ratio in the study area.

Nevertheless, the annual growth rate in terms of number of girls enrolling in educational institutions is more than the boys during the study period, which is very encouraging.

B. *Boys and Girls under the purview of non-formal education:* It is revealed from Table 5.2 and Diagram B that in the study area, amongst the Nyishi community, there is no discriminatory tendency against girls' education under non-formal education, as girls have always been better than boys. This phenomenon could be akin to the need for continuing education of girls despite having been married early and other engagements. So, no prejudice against girls is evident amongst the Nyishi tribe in non-formal education in the study area.

C. *Spending on education for boys and girls:* It evident from Table 5.3 and Diagram C that parents have made no discrimination in terms of spending for their girl children, as throughout the study period, the average spending per household on girls by their parents is higher than boys with the exception of 2008.

Suggestions to Place Girls at Par with Boys in Education

Keeping the importance of girls' education in view, the Nyishi tribe of the Doimukh circle in Papum Pare District in particular and the state in general, need to stress on the following aspects to bolster girls' education:

- Parents should allow their daughters to get married only after they have attained maturity (at or above 18 years). This will ensure that girls have enough time to devote to learning and education. Therefore, early marriage of the girl child has to be kept in check.
- Parents falling under the study area should take a stance that the girls will get married only after they complete their education at least up to the matriculation level.
- Reduction in girls' daily chores and other workload at home and in the field will go a long way in promoting girls' education in the study area.

- Parents should open bank accounts and adopt insurance policies and other financial plans for their daughters to enable them to pursue higher education and continuing education through non-formal means even after marriage.
- Emphasis on qualified and skilled tutors at home for girls should be given so that, despite being laden with work at home and the field, they can catch up with boys in education.
- Parents should give effective counseling, guidance and moral support to their daughters so that they an compete with boys at an equal level.
- There is a need for an attitudinal change in parents. Parents must start believing that girls are equal to boys in all fields including education.
- Large number of girls drop out of the formal educational system due to marriage or employment. To address this phenomenon, the government should increase the number of non-formal educational centres including adult education, distance education, Open school and Open university education enabling girls to have continued education.
- Parents should avoid child marriage and early engagement of their children.
- The educational policy of the state should attempt to incorporate aggressive plans, policies and programmes to promote girls' education in the study area in particular and the state in general.

Conclusion

To reiterate, promoting equality in education between girls and boys is essential for greater economic prosperity. Recognition of, and addressing discrimination against, girls and women in education would make success more likely and more lasting in the fight against all forms of discrimination—colour, class, race, ethnicity and age. In fact, entire societies develop when girls and women are reasonably educated. Thus, prevalence of discrimination in terms of girls education at primary level among the Nyishi tribe members of the Doimukh Circle can be changed through attitudinal change among parents and also by a few policy changes by the state government. Such changes will ensure that the Nyishi tribe will enjoy highest literacy levels not only in India but also in the world.

Notes

1. Official website of The Directorate of Information and Public Relations and Printing, Government of Arunachal Pradesh, Naharlagun,. 2009.
2. *Population and literacy in Papum Pare district of Arunachal Pradesh*, 2001 Census.
3. *Statistical Handbook of Papum Pare District (2007-08);* Economics and Statistics Department, Papum Pare District, Yupia, Arunachal Pradesh.
4. UNFPA, "Gender Equality: An End in Itself and a Cornerstone of Development". United Nations Population Fund, February 2006, http://www.unfpa.org/gender/.
5. UNICEF, "Gender Equality", http://www.unicef.org/gender, May 12, 2008.

6

Negotiating Modernisation

Challenges and Response[1] *in Arunachal Pradesh*

Tajen Dabi

Modernisation[2] has brought about tremendous change in Arunachal Pradesh[3]. Though contact[4] with the world outside has been there in some form or an other, the nature and degree of contact and the consequent impact has changed dramatically in the post-Independence period; since the beginning of the 1960s all the tribes of Arunachal Pradesh have come under the scope of state-sponsored development[5]. The state boasts of an assortment of rich and diverse culture[6] and a plurality of ethnic communities distanced from each other by language[7] and geography. Evolved gradually[8] into a full-fledged state from the remnants of a colonial past, the experience of varied ethnic groups under a single and uniform political setup has been a remarkable story of (re)discovering[9] itself; recognising and accepting the other[10] as part of a given political identity[11]; and negotiating a secure[12] and honourable[13] place in the cultural and political space of the emerging nation. The article makes a modest attempt to capture the dynamics of the recent episodes—socio-religious movements, language initiatives, and the changing socio[14]-cultural climate in the context of modernisation. The emphasis will be on the central belt[15] of Arunachal Pradesh, the so called *Tani belt*[16]. In many fora[17] there have been observations as to why there is no insurgency in Arunachal Pradesh [18] (!). The Arunachal Dragon Force (ADF) is one reported outfit based in Lohit; there has been no report of its activities in recent times[19]. In the recent past there was the National Liberation Council of Taniland (NLCT)[20]. It is all too obvious that there will be enquiries given the presence of a plethora of insurgent outfits present in the Northeast: there are 36 in Assam, 39 in Manipur, 04 in Meghalaya,

03 in Nagaland, 30 in Tripura, 02 in Mizoram, and 01 in Arunachal Pradesh, totalling 115,[21] an average of one outfit for every three and half lakh population against the country's' average of one crore seventy seven lakh. It would not be improper to surmise that the logistics and social climate necessary for insurgency to take root and emerge has simply been absent in the state.

One possible reason lies in the way statehood was achieved; there was no prolonged democratic movement for the same. Consequently, any scope for germination of a common identity corresponding to the political boundary, based on which a common linguistic identity[22] might have evolved, or any issue(s) which in succeeding years could become a possible agenda for a separatist outfit to exploit—like in neighbouring Assam[23]—was seriously negated. If the history and experience of the other regions and communities of the Northeast is any indication, one most plausible explanation would be the absence of state-formation in this frontier. Second, the space that was created with the coming of statehood was enough, initially at least, to absorb the steadily growing educated youth in government jobs and related contract assignments. This, added with the cushion of the Nehru-Elwin policy[24] and continued enforcement of Inner Line Regulation, made sure that forces and circumstances for the growth of insurgency did not find a pasture in Arunachal Pradesh. Consequently, we do not find any informed group of people venting their voice against the state as such. The possibility of a section of people having a perception of being 'alienated' by the Indian[25] state is thus negated.

Third, the natives being distanced by geographical and language factors, did not portray an ideal picture from where a common agenda could evolve to inform their collective consciousness to fight for, if necessary, against the state, for a separate state or sovereignty, as is witnessed in the rest of the region. This brings us to the issue of how the natives perceived the modern democratic system and responded to it, so as to, one, further compliment the absence of militancy in the state, and two, thereby to carry forward the narrative of response to development.

The New 'Democratic'[26] Space in Elwin's Sanctuary[27]

With the coming of electoral politics, the process of democratisation has been accelerated. This has been followed by a liberal grant[28] from the Centre from time to time, post-1962, in this strategically important frontier state. The protective territorial and civil rights embodied in the Inner Line Regulation 1873, continues to 'protect' the cultural and economic interests of the natives. There is reservation for natives in the state Assembly[29] and in public employment. Almost all business/contractual activities are carried out by locals, at least on paper.[30] There is a plethora of new economic avenues available to the locals. There has been increasing engagement of the natives with the people from across the country of varying shades, people from neighbouring Assam, Bengal, north India, even the south, petty shopkeepers, Marwaris, etc.

Consequently, the state became the major source of employment. The architecture of the state itself became the rallying point of a new-found political articulation in which respective groups sought to stake their rightful claim to power and governance. The emergent leadership thus became the leader of his/her group/community; the scope for a leader to command popular support beyond his/her ethnic constituency did not emerge[31] . This probably explains why horse-trading and an unstable pattern of political behaviour is acutely marked in the state; larger ideological aspects (of national political parties, including that of the People's Party of Arunachal [PPA]) do not find resonance with the emerging socio-political preference of the varied ethnic group. The lure of power and concomitant benefits that follow, takes an ethnic dimension insofar as participation in governance is concerned; the chain goes down to clan and related kin networks.

The overall process may be identified by what Roy Burman calls *infra-nationalism*[32] and *proto-nationalism*[33]. There is simultaneous reinforcement and reinterpretation of traditions[34] to forge a common identity among certain cognate groups within and across tribes. Roy Burman cites the example of the moving closer of the *Gallong, Padam, Minyong,* etc. to forge a larger *Adi*[35] identity in the late fifties and sixties[36]. It was around the same time that the apex tribal council of the Adis-*Bogum Bokang* was constituted, partly as a response to the promulgation of the Assam Frontier (Administration of Justice) Regulation of 1945[37] . In fact, it was during this period that festivals began to be celebrated at the community level; this could be taken as the beginning of community level celebrations of native festivals in the entire Tani belt, if not the whole state. *Solung,* the agriculture festival of the Adis, was celebrated first in 1966 at Pasighat and Pangin[38].

The proto-nationalistic[39] tendencies manifested with the passing decades. The most notable issue that contributed to this seems to have been borne out of the nomenclature debate. One of the stated objectives of the early *Bogum-Bokang* movement was the substitution of the word '*Adi*' in place of '*Abor*', which was and is considered derogatory[40]. Another notable movement of a similar nature was that of the '*Dafla*' issue. The *Nyishi Elite Society* (NES) and the *All Nyishi Students Union* (ANSU) had been engaged in a prolonged movement to replace the derogatory '*Dafla*' with the endoethnonym '*Nyishi*'[41]. It is interesting to note that the term 'Abor' continues to be in use legally[42] and there has been no persistent movement in recent years to get it 'rectified'. The derogatory '*Dafla*' has since been repealed and properly substituted with '*Nyishi*'.

Language and Religion

The democratic space so created has led to an unprecedented intercourse with new group of people the natives had never experienced before. The level of interaction is at two levels—one within and among the various ethnic groups themselves, and two, between the 'tribals' and the 'non-tribals'. The issue of language takes its seat in this context. Absence of a commonly[43] accepted language has necessitated the indigenous tribes of the state to adopt Hindi and Assamese as their contact language[44]. Due to its close proximity and historical reasons, Assamese continues to be spoken by a significant number of people[45]. Though English is the official medium of instruction in schools and universities, and in government correspondence, what is recently emerging as a popular mode of communication across the state is Hindi. Polyglot that the state is, the language fits into the growing cosmopolitan space; it is the emerging mode of communication in secular establishments (offices, banks, shops, transport, public gatherings, etc). The linguistic diversity of the state is complemented by an equally diverse migrant population,[46] widely spread business community, people from 'outside' in public establishments, businessmen, daily wage earners. Besides this, there are military and paramilitary personnel in large numbers—for internal security in the eastern districts of Tirap and Changlang, and for external security on the Chinese border.[47] Thanks to rapid urbanisation, it appears, the spread of Hindi owes more to the huge popularity of cable/satellite TV, Bollywood and aforesaid factors than the mere adoption of Hindi in place of Assamese as the 'second language' in public schools.[48]

Various community organisations, of late, are bringing out 'dictionaries' of local languages; attempts are on to teach the same as a 'third language' in government schools in respective areas to 'protect' and 'preserve' the native dialects. However, there is an element of irony in such efforts; it targets the rural students only, who in any case learn the native tongue. Not every child joins the school in their locality; almost all the salaried and affluent classes send their children to private schools and those run by reputed NGOs, where the above-mentioned 'third' language scheme does not exist. It is from this middle class that much of the debate is emerging because of their varied experience: the sense of urgency to relate to one's 'pristine' past after having had a taste of 'confusing' forces of modernisation, the inspiration drawn from similar movements in other parts of the country and the world, an urge to assume a position of leadership thanks to new-found status, etc. This brings another dimension to the issue of 'preservation' of native language(s). Contrary to the much publicised slogan of *Loss of Culture, Loss of Identity* by some NGOs running schools across the state, they actively discourage use of any local language among the students.

It is in the realm of religion that the attempt to re-define[49] and give a proper shape is most evidently manifested. Out of the numerous Gods and Goddesses, attempt has been to identify one of them as being the representative of the entire well-being of the humankind and thereby elevate them to a position of prominence and divinity, the 'almighty superintendent of the universe'[50]. There are instances where such native Gods and Goddesses are seen to have been incorporated into the larger Hindu pantheon[51]. This calls for an investigation into the nature of the native faiths and religious practice and juxtaposes it with the current Hindu faith.[52] Insofar as the popular aspect of Hinduism is concerned, there does not seem to be any conflict with the underlying philosophy of the tribal/native religious practice[53]—legends of mythical[54] heroes, cosmology, catholicity of rituals, institution of priesthood, absence of doctrines or a regular religious order, etc.– the list of commonalities is endless. These elements of native faith appear to be quite an integral part of the larger and heterogeneous tradition of the subcontinent, particularly when contrasted with Christianity. While public reception to this reformist-revivalist movement has largely been sympathetic, there are reservations among some quarters against the overtly Hinduised way in which these religious reform initiatives are being undertaken.[55]

There is a particular pattern in the articulation of these neo-religious movements. Their target has primarily been (the spread of) Christianity. The other agencies of change are neglected. Therefore, we do not find any serious attempts at reforms at the social level[56] – polygamy, child marriage, etc. Given the wide momentum and enthusiastic investment in religion, the absence of a similar counterpart in the social arena is conspicuous. The economic and psychological aspect of conversion has not been explored; focus is only towards 'preserving' the native faith, if possible, by re-inventing it, as is being done. The potential for genuine reform is becoming a casualty in the process. For example, in the case of the Nyishis "the dominating factor for the spread of Christianity…is undoubtedly, the perennial nature of rituals and sacrifices that are involved in tribal religion. Spirituality has never been a driving force behind the conversion…"[57]

Conclusion

The broad contours of modernisation that emerge thus, are suggestive of the fact that the ethnic assertions and religious movements seek to create a niche in the broader space of the Indian nation[58] -state rather than an attempt to create an independent and differing ideology as posited against the latter. It is the nature of the participation that offers an array of competitive ethnicism, and some semblance of collective imagination at times. Dynamics of underlying fissures and constant re-adjustment emerges in-between. Given the experience from other states in the region, (relative) peace—within and beyond the state—for long is neither argued.

Notes

1. The phrase is borrowed from B K Roy Burman's 'Challenges and Response in Tribal India' in M.S.A. Rao (ed.); *Social Movements in India: Studies in Peasant, Backward Classes, Sectarian, Tribal and Women's Movement*, Manohar, New Delhi, 2006, p. 317.
2. In using the term *modernization* I follow Giddens standard definition.
3. *Arunachali* is the term presently being argued to be used to refer to the people of the state, in an apparent attempt to build a common identity. Local dailies are the medium of this emerging debate. This paper also avoids the suffix 'Pradesh' for sake of brevity, as is being done by other researchers and commentators.

4. The customary projection of the contact the people of the state had with outside world has been to look at it in the nature of hill-plain economic 'symbiotic' relationship. For a discussion on external trade routes see Sudatta Sikdar, 'Cross-Country trade in the Making of British Policy Towards Arunachalis in the Nineteenth Century', NEIHA, Dibrugarh, 1981, pp. 210-220.
5. 1947 is an indiscriminate choice; recent scholarship emphasizes more on 1962, Chinese invasion, which seems more appropriate. See S.N. Mishra, 'Arunachal's Tribal Economic Formation and their Dissolution', *EPW*, Vol. 18, No 43 (Oct 22, 1983), pp. 1837-1846 where the subsequent increase in plan outlay after the Chinese invasion has been shown.
6. Verrier Elwin has classified the tribes into three cultural group viz. first, those practicing or influenced by Buddhism (in the west); second, the *Tani* group of tribes, the *Mishmis* and 'sundry tribes' in the central portion and; third, the Noctes, Tangsas and the *Wanchos* in the east. Quoted in M L Bose, *History of Arunachal Pradesh*, Concept, New Delhi, 1997, p. 22. With reference to the area of study in question, there doesn't seem to be much difference in religio-cultural practice. As Amartya Sen argues in the context of the larger Indian picture, "...the contrasts are not quite as they are depicted..." (*The Argumentative Indian*, Penguin, New Delhi, 2005, p. 138)
7. 'Language...does not serve as a unifying factor among the tribals of Arunachal', see Nani Bath, *Electoral Politics in Arunachal Pradesh: A Study of Assembly Elections (1978-99),* unpublished PhD thesis, Arunachal University, 2002, p. 146.
8. The state, at the time of India's independence, was a centrally administered area, the responsibility of administration being given to the Governor of Assam. See J B Bhattacharjee, *State and Society in Post-Colonial North-East India*, NEIHA, Dibrugarh, 2008, p. 491. For the larger picture of the evolution of the state of Arunachal Pradesh *see* P.N. Luthra, *Constitutional and Administrative Growth of NEFA*, Shillong, 1969.
9. The term is used to refer to ethnic and religious movement which while drawing on traditional forms and practice, unmistakably incorporates values and idioms brought about by modernization. This process of re-discovery is more akin to the phenomenon of 'staged authenticity' (D. Mac Cannell, 'The Tourist: A New Theory of Leisure Class', New York, 1976 quoted in Rajesh Dev, 'Narrative Claims and Identity Impass: the Experience of the Nowhere People' in Sukhapa Bhattacharjee, and Rajesh Dev (ed.), *Ethno-Narratives: Identity and Experience in North-East India,* Aushah Pub., Delhi, 2006, p. 79.
10. The term is used to refer to ignorance about one's neighbour rather than

an abject identification about the latter as being the 'other'.

11. I use *political identity* in constitutional sense. It was more the geographical and cultural factors that guided in creating a separate state of Arunachal than a consistent movement by the natives for the same. Therefore, the state as part of the larger body-politic of the emergent nation-state itself was a *fait accompli* for the natives in which they were expected to co-exist.
12. I use the term *secure* in the sense of economic security. The contact and the nature of relationship between the natives (the Tanis of Central zone) in the hills and the Ahoms and the British in the plains have largely been revolved around the issue of *posa* and related economic aspects. Therefore to project a relationship beyond this frame would seem to be an exaggeration. For a detailed exposition of this dynamics during the colonial period please see, Braj Narain Jha, Colonial Intervention and Tribal Response in North-East Frontier of India, unpublished PhD thesis, Arunachal University.
13. Constitution is one arena where many ethnic/identity movements are centered. One is on the change/renaming of respective nomenclatures of the tribe/group, and the other in securing constitutional safeguard under the Sixth Schedule. There are at least two such demands for autonomous region in the state viz. the *Mon Autonomous Region* in the western Buddhist-dominant part, an office for the same exist in the heart of the town of Tawang; the *Patkai Autonomous District Council* for Tirap and Changlang district in the eastern part of the state (*Constitution of Patkai autonomous District Council,* Naharlagun, 2007). Lately, one more similar demand has been reported in the local media: *Ziro Valley Autonomous Council* (*the Arunachal Times*, 29 August 2010) for the Apatani plateau. The Nyishi Elite Society (NES)-the apex community body of the Nyishis, the largest tribe in the state, is also demanding a separate 'Department of Nyishi affairs' (*Echo of Arunachal*, March 18, 2010). Earlier the Akas (*Hrusso* is the name being preferred by the locals now) and the Mijis of west and East Kameng district also moved for creation of a separate district for them—*Bichom* district. See Chaudhary, Sarit Kumar, *A Tribe in Transition: A Study of the Mijis of Arunachal Pradesh,* unpublished PhD thesis, Arunachal University, 1999 pp. 217-233. For the broad perspective of such response in India see B.K. Roy Burman, no. 1, pp. 317-337.
14. The economic aspect of the recent change has been discussed in S.N. Mishra, no. 5. A more recent work on the aspect is found in N.C. Roy and P.K. Kuri, *Land Reforms in Arunachal Pradesh*, Classical Publications, New Delhi, 2001. Focusing on typologies of communal agrarian rights and related reforms, the book throws light on theoretical

aspects or the lack of it on the agrarian institutions of the state. The book also discusses relevant books published till then on the economic aspects of the state.

15. Three cultural zones as proposed by Elwin, discussed above, are followed here.
16. The central region-so called *Tani belt*—extends from the eastern bank of Kameng river in the west to western bank of Dibang river in the east, covering almost half the geographical area of the state, inhabited almost, except in few cases, by tribes who trace their 'origin' to a superhuman mythical male ancestor *Abotani* (literally, 'father of man'). The tribes, from west to east, with districts they inhabit in parenthesis, are: the Nyishis (East Kameng, Papum Pare, Kurung-Kumey, Lower Subansiri, Upper Subansiri), the Apatanis (Lower Subansiri), the Tagins (Upper Subansiri), the Galos (Upper Subansiri, West Siang, East Siang), and the Adis (West Siang, East Siang, Upper Siang, Lower Dibang Valley).
17. I encountered this on two occasions: first in a symposium at Teen Murti, New Delhi on 20th January 2000, and another during a seminar on 30 March 2009 at OKDISC, Guwahati.
18. The NSCN (both factions of which are reported to be active in the state in the eastern districts of Tirap and Changlang which claims it under 'Greater Nagalim' scheme) as is known, does not originate in the state. Centre for Development and Peace Studies reports that every government employee and businessman in Tirap is forced to pay nearly 25 per cent of his or her gross income as a tax for the outfits (source http://cdpsindia.org/arunachal_insurgency.asp accessed on 25th Oct, 2010). There are reports in media that informs arrest of cadres of organizations (NLCT) named after legendary forefather *Abotani*. These are limited to a cadre base of few individuals only, and does not represent a full blown insurgent outfit who commands a wide public support or enjoy even a modest influence.
19. http://www.satp.org/satporgtp/countries/india/terroristoutfits/index.html accessed on 28 August, 2010. All the data related to the number of insurgent outfits in North-East and India is derived from it. Of the 34 organisation banned by the Govt of India at least 13 are from North-east, source http://www.mha.nic.in/uniquepage.asp?Id_Pk=292, accessed on 15 Oct, 2010,.
20. http://www.sentinelassam.com/northeast.php?sec=2&subsec=9&ppr=1&dtP=2009-10-18, accessed on 28 August, 2010.
21. *Ibid.*
22. There is a movement to popularize *Tani Lipi* (literally, 'Tani script') developed by Toni Koyu. *Echo of Arunachal*, the first English daily of the sate, regularly publishes relevant lessons on it. This however seems

to have found no significant popular, academic, or institutional support. Tianshin Jackson Sun, in his PhD dissertation (unpublished), *A Historical-Comparative Study of the Tani (Mirish) Branch in Tibeto-Burman*, University of California, Berkley, has put forward the term *Tani* to identify these cognate language group, thereby initiating a possibility of regrouping of these ethnic groups under one umbrella. Though linguistic aspects can not be commented upon since the paper lacks competence in the field, the movement for a common Tani Lipi (script) itself shows a tendency-at least among some few—towards bridging cultural gap which is ironical when contrasted to the identity movements within the Tani group.

23. For the issue of Assamese identity and its close link with language please see Udayon Misra, *The Transformation of Assamese Identity: A Historical Survey*, H.K. Barpujari Endowment Lecture (4), NEIHA, Shillong, 2001.
24. Elwin, Verrier, *A Philosophy for NEFA*, Directorate of Research, Government of Arunachal Pradesh, Itanagar, 2006.
25. Since many insurgent outfit in the North-East are waging a war-with ideological dimensions—against the Indian state for perceived notions of injustice, 'Indian' has been prefix before the 'state'. Researches and debate on this issue is too well known be repeated, mention however may be made of: Sanjib Baruah, *Durable Disorder: Understanding the Politics of North-East India,* OUP, New Delhi, 2007; Sajal Nag, *Contesting Marginality: Ethnicity, Insurgence and Sub-Nationalism in North-East India,* Manohar, New Delhi, 2002; Udayon Misra, *The Periphery Strikes Back*, IIAS, 2000.
26. Democracy is claimed to have been in existence since 'time immemorial'. For a critique of liberal use of such phrases and other colonial constructs in writing community history in North-East India, see Sarah Hilaly, 'Representation of the Ethnic Communities of North-East: An Overview', NEIHA, Dibrugarh, 2008, pp. 415-419. Elwin's book, *Democracy in NEFA,* Government. of Arunachal Pradesh, Itanagar, 2007 (published first in 1965) seems to have influenced liberal use the term 'democracy' in relation to the various quasi-judicial tribal courts, where actually it is the decisions that are taken in a democratic manner, rather than the adjudicating body itself being *democratic*. The better known among them is that of the *Kebang* of the Adis. See Bani Danggen, *THE KEBANG, A Unique Indigenous Political Institution of the Adis*, Himalayan Publishers, Itanagar, 2003 for a sympathetic view on its mythical origins and the evolution of the system. The 'BUNGO' (*Banggo*) system—the complementing unit (a village being the basic unit in the Kebang set up) within the larger Kebang structure is said to

have been started and instituted by a British official to divide the people of Siang when the Congress movement had spread! See B.B. Pandey, *Arunachal Pradesh: Village to Statehood*, Himalayan Publisher, Itanagar 1997, pp. 92-93. Recent research on the introduction, working and effects of democracy in Arunachal may be found in: Pura Tado, *Political Transition Among the Tribes of Arunachal Pradesh: A Case Study of the Apatanis*, unpublished PhD thesis, Arunachal University, 2001; Suparna Bhattacharjee, *Political Parties and Political Modernisation: A Study of the Functioning of Political Parties in Arunachal Pradesh (1975-1995)*, unpublished PhD thesis, Arunachal University, 2000; Rejir Karlo, *Emerging Patterns of Leadership in Arunachal Pradesh*, Commonwealth, New Delhi, 2005; Nani Bath, no. 7; Milorai Modi, *Kebang as a Traditional Democratic Institution of the Adis of Arunachal Pradesh*, unpublished PhD Thesis, Arunachal University, 2000.

27. The term may sound offensive. I have deduced it-though not literally— from the three respective schools that evolved with respect to policy adoptions with regard to tribes of North-East viz., the Assimilationists (GS Ghurye), the Isolationist (Elwin), and the Acculturationists (DN Majumdar). For this please see T B Subba, Joseph Puthenpurakal and Shaji Joseph Puykunnel (Eds.) *et al.*, *Christianity and Change in North-East India*, Concept, New Delhi, 2009, pp. 8-9.
28. S.N. Mishra, no. 5.
29. The Supreme Court has kept in abeyance the last Delimitation exercise in the state. There was perceived sense of possible ethnic disturbance because of the impending re-drawing of electoral boundaries. While some section would have become 'minority' in the new electoral constituency so created/re-adjusted, the fear of 'loosing' electoral seats added to the pandemonium that was there; others hoped to 'gain' seats.
30. Though 'trade license' are given to locals, it's the migrant population that conducts the chunk of these activities by virtue of 'power of attorney'. No regular/official statistics on this aspect is though available.
31. Nani Bath, no. 7, p. 154.
32. B.K. Roy Burman, no. 1, p. 332.
33. *Ibid.*
34. *Ibid.*
35. The *Galos* (listed as 'Gallong' in the ST Order as a separate tribe) have since 'separated' from the larger Adi identity with the establishment of *Galo Welfare Society* in 1999. The 'separation' is most noticeable in the function of the apex *Kebang* (*Keba* in Galo): the *Adis* sit together in the *Adi Bane Kebang* while the former meets in the *Galo Bane Keba*, each with separate functionaries and agenda. It is noticeable that the apex Adi council/convention, the *Bogum-Bokang*, held since 1949, met last

in 2000. Thereafter, the above schism seems to have taken place (the proceedings of the last Bogum-Bokang reflects this) rendering thereby 'Bogum-Bokang' itself in oblivion. Pl see Bani Danggen, no. 26.

36. *Ibid.*
37. Bani Danggen, no. 26, p. 74.
38. Igul Padung, no. 26. p. 193.
39. B.K. Roy Burman, no. 1.
40. Bani Danggen, no. 26.
41. For the debate on the nomenclature issue see Tana Showren, *The NYISHI of Arunachal Pradesh: An Ethnohistorical Study*, Regency Publications, Delhi, 2001, p. 62. Please see Nabam Tadar Rikam, *Changing Religious Identity of Arunachal Pradesh: A Case Studies of the Nyishi since 1947*, unpublished PhD thesis, Arunachal University, 2003 for the growth and role of community orginisations among the *Nyishis.*
42. Scheduled Tribe (ST) certificate continues to display so. Names of respective 'sub-tribe' are prefixed before '*Abor*'. With respect to the *Gallongs* (the suffix 'ng' is not used by the people in question themselves), there appears to be variation; while in some case the above pattern is followed, in others merely the '*Gallong*' is mentioned as 'tribe'.
43. Early in 30s of the last century, there was an attempt to develop an *Adi* primer (*Adi agom lupo sinane*) which was opposed by certain other section of the tribe in question. Copies of the primer were burnt in protest. See Egul Padung, *Emergence of Pasighat: A Case Study of the Dynamics of Urban Growth*, unpublished PhD thesis, RGU, 2006, pp. 194, 196. Efforts to evolve a common script/language, even among the cognate groups within the Adi tribe do not seem to have been seriously explored thereafter. The *Galos*—some members belonging to this community participated in the protest in the primer issue—have since emphasized on a separate identity than on the larger *Adi* identity. This is a contentious issue; the author is currently undertaking an independent research on the issue.
44. Nani Bath (2002), no. 7, p. 146.
45. There seems to be difference of opinion regarding the date of change in the medium of instruction from Assamese to English and Hindi. One source puts Assamese as the medium of instruction till 1950, when Devnagiri script was introduced in the state (*Arunachal Review*: May-June, 1991, p. 7 quoted in Egul Padung, no. 43, p. 195). Another date is 1972, when after the movement in support of English and, Hindi as second language in place of Assamese, by the students of Jawaharlal Nehru College Pasighat in May 1970, Assamese was done away with when policy changes were made when the then NEFA became the Union Territory (Anjan Saikia, *A Comparative Study of Elementary Education*

in Assam and Arunachal Pradesh, unpublished PhD thesis, Arunachal University, 2002 pp. 38-39). It is notable that 'NEFA' was christened as Union Territory with a pronounced Sanskritic name '*Arunachal*' during this time. There are quite a few writers from the state in Assamese of notable distinction. Mention may be made of Sh Lummer Dai: *Paharor Shile Shile (*Upon the meadows of hills*)* being his first novel, *Prithivir Hanhi* (The Laughter of the Earth), 1963 earned him critical acclaim; *Mon Aaru Mon* (Heart to heart), *Koinar Mulya* (The Bride Price), *Upor Mohol* (In the High Places). Another writer of prominence is Yeshi Dorjee Thongchi, his *Mouna Ounth Mukhar Hriday (Silent Lips, Murmuring Hearts)* earned him a Sahitya Academy Award. For a critical appraisal of the works of these two authors, see Juri Dutta, *Tribal Life and Society in Select Novels of Lummer Dai and Yeshi Dorjee Thongchi*, unpublished PhD dissertation, Arunachal Institute of Tribal Studies (AITS), 2007.

46. According to 2001 census 37.78 per cent of the total population of the state is comprised of non-ST population, the bulk of which comprises of the people of the said category. Moreover no proper enumeration of so called floating population, most of who engage themselves as daily labourers—in urban areas has been done.
47. Personal visit to some of the areas show that army personals are visible mostly in two regions: Bhaluking-Tenga-Bomdila-Dirang-Tawang sector in the West Kameng and Tawang district respectively; and Basar-Aalo-Mechuka sector in the West Siang district. It is in these two sectors that Hindi seems to be the exclusive mode of communication-if we exclude the local languages/dialects-in day to day life. In the eastern districts of Lohit, Changlang and Tirap, Assamese seem to be more frequently used; this may be because of the long history of engagement with the neighbouring Assam by the people of these areas. In other 'foot hill' areas of the state, there seems to be a mix of both the trend; while older gentry are more comfortable in Assamese, younger generations are tilting more towards Hindi. No proper statistics/research/survey could be collected/done though I have visited and met with people of all these areas.
48. Local dailies in the state air respective views on the emerging language issue; the apparent perception is the 'threat' to native tongue and call for 'preservation' of the same. This may be seen as part of the larger identity and religious movement, some aspects of which are revivalist in nature.
49. These movements are largely centered in non-Buddhist areas: for example, *Donyi-Poloism* in the *Tani* belt, *Rangrafraism* among *Tangsas* in Changlang etc. One such temple dedicated to Lord *Rang-Fra* has come up in the campus of Rang- Frah Government College Changlang.

One can be easily forgiven for mistaking the image of Lord Rang-Frah as that of Lord Shiva. (Personal visit to the temple).

50. D.H. Killingley, 'Vedant and Modernity' in C.H. Philips and Mary D. Wainwright (eds.), *Indian Society and the Beginnings of Modernisation c. 1830-1850*, London, School of Oriental and African Studies, 1976, p. 132. Quoted in Kenneth W Jones, Socio-Religious Reform Movement in British India, Cambridge University Press, New Delhi, 2003, p. 31
51. This is most evident in calendars and bills published by NGOs like Vivekananda Trust etc. Tribal gods and goddesses are resuscitated from folklores and myths, given a new life and meaning, and incorporated into the larger Hindu pantheon.
52. I use 'faith' in contrast to 'religion' to emphasize on the popular aspect of Hinduism that is apparent to the followers of native faith. Also, it avoids the rigours of having to enter into the debate of explaining the nature of Hinduism itself as a single religion, which is beyond the scope or competence of this paper.
53. This aspect is most noticeable in the words of *Golgi Bote* Talom Rukbo-considered as the father of *Donyi-Polo* Movement: *In this world, there are many types of religion. In our quest to find the origin and source of these different religions, we usually take two important characteristics of the religion into consideration. They are the conventional and the organizational nature. The conventional religion are those religions, which have been in existence since the evolution of human beings. They are like Hinduism and Donyi-Polo religion... The conventional religion trace its origin from the beginning of the world itself; for instance the Hindus believe in 'AUM' as the beginning of all life in this world and the Donyi-Polo in 'KEYUM', i.e. dark-age as the source of evolution of the universe.* (Source: Igul Padung, no. 43, pp. 210-211). The apparent attempt to bridge the cultural gap only adduce more credit to the argument that the tribals are 'backward Hindus', as claimed by G.S. Ghurye (quoted in T.B. Subba, Joseph Puthenpurakal and Shahji Joseph Puykunnal, no. 27 pp. 8-9)
54. See Verrier Elwin, *Myths of the North-East Frontier of India, Directorate of Research, Government of Arunachal Pradesh*, Itanagar, 1993 for an extensive reading of tribal/native folklores of the state
55. Some recent research on the issue includes: Nabam Tadar Rikam, no. 41; Ashan Riddi, *Traditional Institution of the Tagins*, Continuity and Change, unpublished PhD thesis, Arunachal University, 2003; Hage Naku, *Beliefs and Practices of Apatanis—A Study in Continuity and Change*, unpublished PhD thesis, Arunachal University, 2006, etc.
56. Instances such as child marriage are still reported from remote areas. Polygamy is still practised—in rural areas, and by neo-rich in urban

areas. Apart from some women rights group no serious effort has till been done to curb such practices.

57. Nabam Tadar Rikam, no. 41, p. 241.
58. 'Indian nation-state' implies that 'nation state' which has emerged during the two hundred years of British colonial rule, and hence it should not be confused with state of the identities existing prior to the colonial period.

7

Igus of Arunachal Pradesh

Relocating Indigenous Healing Tradition of a Frontier Tribe of India

Sarit K. Chaudhuri

"Shamans as mediators create order and reestablish balance with in their groups such that their role is socially embedded in their cultures." (cf. Hoppal. 2002: 93).

"The shamanic state of consciousness (SSC) is the very essence of shamanism, and critical to the premise that the shaman is the past and present master of the imagination as healer." (Achterberg 2002: 108)

Arunachal Pradesh, the erstwhile NEFA, one of the seven sister states of Northeast India, consists of 26 large tribes with more than 100 smaller tribes or sub-tribes.[1] Amidst admirable cultural heterogeneity, most of these tribes reflect a very strong healing tradition practiced by their indigenous priests or shamans. However, Idu Mishmis represent one such tribe who have carved out a special niche for themselves within such a healing tradition because of the presence of the *Igus* (shamans) who are still very central to the traditional social system of the tribe.

The Idu Mishmis

The Idus Mishmis are considered one of the major tribes of Arunachal Pradesh. Their total population strength is around 10,000 people and they are located in the Upper and Lower Dibang Valley districts of Arunachal Pradesh. They are sometimes included as part of the larger constellation of the Mishmi group, which also includes Digaru and Miju Mishmis.[2] Culturally, Idus are largely distinct from the other two, which is reflected in various aspects of their day-to-day life and social structure as well as their value system. The Idu Mishmis are commonly known as Chulikata Mishmis because of their distinct hairstyle. Perhaps this nomenclature was given by the people of the plains (Bhattacharjee 1983: 13) with whom the Idus used to trade. In a few documents of the colonial era, some Idus were wrongly identified as a separate tribe called Bebejiya who were negatively portrayed (Needham 1900, Allen 1905, Cooper [1873] 1995).[3] Dalton (1872: 18) reported them as being Midhi people and mentioned that they were intensely detested and mistrusted by their neighbours—the Abors and Tains, and they were much dreaded by the Saudiya[4] population because of their tendency to kidnap women and children.

Bhattacharjee (1983) and Baruah (1960: 13-33) tried to textualise their origin and migration on the basis of various elements of oral narrative, while in his recent publications (2003-2004, 2005) Blackburn touched upon this area and critically discussed their memories of migration and their journey compared to some of the tribes of Arunachal Pradesh.

Traditionally *igu* represents the central icon in the arena of religious beliefs and practices in Idu society. Almost every major aspects of life of the Idus pivoted round their *igus* and their importance is reflected even beyond the sacred boundary, as they are involved in profane activities. The key concept of spirit (*khinu*) rules their world of the unknown, which may be benevolent or malevolent though they have the concept of supreme creator known as *Inni:* "The Supreme God *Inni,* embodies the highest ethical conception reached by the Idus. Besides being Supreme Creator of all things, He is the impersonal principle of justice and the upholder of moral order of creation" (Barua: 1988. 69).

Bhattacharjee (1983: 117) writes, "An Idu constantly haunted by the spirits (*khinu*) who abound in jungles, hills, shadowy recesses, rivers, gorges, cliffs as well as in the house and the village. They are dreaded, as no one knows when and where one may fall into the trap. The spirits are real masters of their fate. Any calamity befalling them is attributed to spirits". Idu mythology also reflects that syndrome.

Since the origin of the universe man and spirits were the progeny of the same forefathers. As per their beliefs, even in the world of the unknown, hierarchy remains within the variegated deities who were responsible for the creation and survival of the moral order of things (Linggi and Mathem 2000: 23).

It is the *Igu* or shaman who works as the mediator between the Idus and their world of the unknown through performance of various rituals, supernatural, religious acts and mostly importantly, by unique dances with the help of some team members who join or assist the *Igu*. Therefore, the *Igu* occupies the most significant social status in their society. The *Igu* has such a pervasive influence in the whole social system that even today, when their society is passing through the process of transformation, most of the people have a strong cognitive perception about the divine power of the *Igu*s; an institution which is gradually fading from society. The study of shamans or issues related to shamanism are at the core of the anthropological study of religion and later paved the way for interdisciplinary frames. Even with the development of science, technology as well as the subsequent changes in societies all over the world due to modernization or globalization, there is a renewed interest in the study of shamans in spite of heterogeneous contested notions, as it still holds meaning for many communities across the world beyond the primitive or modern stereotypic divide (Hoppal 2002, Halifax 2002, Houston 2002).[5]

However, the fundamental question that remains is that, how an Idu becomes an *Igu*? This issue is dealt with elaborately by Chaudhuri: 2008, pp. 84-106). In brief, as per their popular belief systems, no one can become an *Igu* just by wishing for such spiritual power transmitted as the gift of God, which may be reflected by some symptoms; mostly through some abnormal activities. So, any son or daughter of *Igu*s cannot become an *Igu* automatically; rather a son of a non-*Igu* (*minga*) may become a powerful *Igu* by God's grace. The hymns which an *Igu* chants cannot be understood by common Idus except by a few. The process of becoming an *Igu* is quite varied and numerous popular beliefs can be traced to describe such unusual events, such as, sleeping on tree leafs, consuming human excreta and many other such acts. Some of the *Igu*s have narrated their own unique experience of becoming an *Igu*.

The most significant process of becoming an *Igu* is called *Alomo*. The very first instance of an Idu experiencing divinity in his or her life is reflected through some abnormal acts which are beyond the comprehension of an Idu individual, as mentioned earlier. Such acts go on for a few hours and such a period of divine transition is called *Atombo*. And only then does one establish oneself as an *Igu* and is empowered to act as a mediator between human beings and the Gods, Goddesses, spirits, etc. who control the world of the unknown.

A few narratives of the *Igu*s are mentioned here out of the many cited by Chaudhuri (Ibid). Narrating his experience of becoming an *Igu*, Yango Mow of Angrim Valley said that when his mother fell ill, instead of calling any other *Igu*, he took a *kalih* (herbal medicine/ root used by an *Igu*) and sat outside his house on the verandah and began chanting hymns in a very low tone lest passersby should hear him. As he began chanting, many men and woman passed by asking him what was he muttering about. As they came near him, he would hide the *Kalhi* between his lap. So in this way, with *Aanyongo* he cured his mother. It was because of the wish of God that he became an *Igu*. But after this incident he made no further attempt to perform *Igu* because he felt shy that if anyone heard him they would ridicule him. Once he went with his friends to construct Ganyo Milli's new house. After the construction of the house when the need of an Igu was felt, his friends told the owner that Yango was an Igu. On hearing this, the owner asked him to perform the ritual *Thruh* (protection of new house by sacrificing hens). He was very nervous and felt shy and was sure that he would be laughed at. He suddenly began with a very loud voice so that everybody was startled, and burst into laughter. After a few minutes, everything was smooth. He was not aware of what he was saying. After the ritual everyone applauded him for his strong hymns. In this way he turned into a professional *Igu*.

Smti Imuno Linggi of Anini narrated her experience of becoming an *Igu*. She said that her father was a renowned *Igu* but he never encouraged his daughter to become an *Igu* though the villagers talked to her father about her behaviour. When she came to stay with her husband she began developing some peculiar habits like eating mud from the toilet which was the sign of becoming an *Igu*. Seeing that, the grandmother of her husband who herself was a powerful *Igu* encouraged her. The grandmother started taking interest in her but she didn't teach her any hymns, nor chanting, because she herself had the spiritual power to chant the hymns. The chanting of hymns came to her mind spontaneously. According to her, self-acquired knowledge or wisdom is more powerful than learning it from any senior *Igu*. Her husband's grandmother made her an *Igu* by insisting that she perform *Amraseh* (giving protection to all the family members of the house for peace) for the first time at their home. So *Amraseh* was the first ritual in her life that she performed. Her next ritual performance was *Rehguh* (ritual performed at *Reh*). She was called for *Rehguh* by Ashalo Elu at his *Reh.* She was nervous because it would be her first great ritual and she never expected there would be many great *Igus* to hear her. And the *Igu* she feared most was Towshi Miuli who said that she would not be perfect in the chanting of hymns, especially the *Shacha* (hymns chanted when mithun [*Sha*] is to be sacrificed). Before sacrificing of the mithun the hymns on the origin of mithun are chanted by taking the soul of mithun to its place of origin).

On her way to the village she was nervous. She could not cut the bamboo properly which is taken by an *Igu* to perform *Reh,* called *totho*. She could not speak nor look at the face of her followers. When she began the ritual and the chanting of hymns all those present were amazed. After hearing her hymns Toshi Miuli praised her saying that she knew all the hymns and rules of the chanting of *Reh*. In this way she has till now conducted 23 *rehgu*s and 15 *Yah*.

Rano Mihu who is one of the seniormost *Igus* of Mihundo village said that he had no teacher nor had training under any *Igu;* rather he listened to *Igu*s at rituals though he didn't understand the chants. He believes that it was due to the wishes and blessings of the Almighty that he became an *Igu.* He began his performance with *Anyongo. Aanyongo* is of two types, '*Kaliwooh*', where Kali (herbal medicinal root) is given to the person with hymns and power chanted on it, and '*Machi Wooh*', where water is given instead of *Kali*. In *Machiwooh,* small pieces of *Kali* are cut and put in the water. This is meant for the children who cannot chew the *kali*. After he was successful in *Aanyongo* his friends encouraged him to go for *Ayiih*; after *Ayiih* he conducted the ritual *Ekularuma*, then *Amrasey* and then *Brocha* which are countless, Mihu added.

So it appears that though ideally shamanism is perceived as the gift of God but a few Idus had achieved the same by their sustained interest and it was even reported that one may becomes an *Igu* by assisting powerful *Igu*s for a long period. However, Idus believe that generally such *Igu*s are less powerful and cannot perform all the rituals. Bhattacharjee (Ibid: 121) reported: "Not anyone can become a shaman even if he tries to be so. He must show some indication of being possessed by spirits and definite sign of communication and understanding with supernatural elements, which dominate the world of the Idus. He should also be well conversant with legends and the history of the tribe from the beginning of creation and should have detailed knowledge of various ceremonial rites, otherwise his standing as an *Igu* will be held in ridicule".

Healing Mechanisms

Various types of sicknesses or diseases are broadly classified into six basic categories and such classification is part of the community's collective notion as well as shaman's belief system (Mitapo 2000: 38-39) which are given below:

1. *Arru*—The diseases which are acquired through contact, are air-borne, water-borne, and are acquired through droplet infections are called Arru. Idus suffering with such diseases are generally advised to take medicines by their Igus.
2. *Khinnyu Meko*—Any disease caused by the spirits of dwelling house and such diseases can be cured by the Igus as per the general perception of the community.
3. *Assa(ng)*—Diseases which are caused by the spirits of the forests and need to be treated by the Igu.
4. *Achu-cho-a-aanggra*—It includes serious diseases which are believed to be caused due to the non-observance of necessary rituals and these diseases can be cured by the Igus only.
5. *Manu-mara*—This includes skin, eyes and internal diseases caused by the manu (spirit) and acquired from the paddy field or paddy storehouses.
6. *Apomo*—It indicates swelling with itching in different parts of the body, which can be treated with the help of the Igu or by using plants (leaves) as medicine.

Beyond these six varieties another category which does not figure under the category of any disease but also causes suffering because of a variety of reasons is *Naa*-du, which includes injuries and even accidents where the *Igu* as well as medicines are effective.

It is evident that a variety of plants and animals are used for treating different kinds of diseases and such ethno-medicinal wisdom is part of the community knowledge base rather than knowledge system of the shamans or the priests. However, as per the belief system or the worldview of the Idu Mishmis, a majority of the diseases or sicknesses are caused by the spirits (*khinus*) which dominate their surroundings or the world of the unknown. Mitapo and Umpo (2000: 32) classified the traditional healing system of the Idus into two broad categories—preventive and curative—and in both the areas *Igu*s have very special roles or act as the central figures in traditional healing mechanisms. Umpo (2000: 32-37) gave some information regarding preventive healing practices especially the variety of ritual practices, mainly performed by the *Igu*s to protect the Idus from disease or sickness-causing spirits. A few rituals can be mentioned here as mentioned by Umpo (ibid):

Ah-tareh/Yu-aru: This ritual is performed at the time of birth by the *Igu*s in order to protect the new-born baby from the effect of the evil spirits and only select people are allowed to enter the house for upto ten days for the boy and nine days for the girl child. The mother is not even allowed to cross rivers, mountains or hills till the new moon.

Reh: This is the most popular ritual which every Idu dreams to perform to bring prosperity in the family in terms of both wealth and health. It is performed by the *Igu* for 5 days where all kin, clan members and neighbours gather in a household. During Reh an *Igu* performs a ritual dance and chants for all these days which is very special and unique to the sacred life of the Idus Mishmis.

Areh-bi: The Idus believe that when an individual attends a funeral of a person who has died an unnatural death, or mediates a murder dispute, or tries to cure a person having nightmares, then the *Igu* needs to be called to perform rituals to protect him or her from evil spirits.

Alo-thru: This ritual is performed by the *Igu* to protect every individual who comes to attend a funeral of a person who has died a natural death so that the evil spirit responsible for death cannot cause any harm.

Omen-do: This is performed by the *igu* after the construction of a new house so that household members are protected against fire or other calamities.

Apeh-shu: This third ritual is performed in different contexts, such as, seeing persistently bad dreams, facing accidents, bringing fined money in to a house etc.

Yu-meu-ru: This is performed to prevent the ill-effect of the spirit of the land in which one is residing or cultivating and even for a successful hunt (ibid).

Curative or Therapeutic Measures

Besides these ritual performances, the *Igus* also take recourse to various other options where, besides using living or non-living objects, they adopt various spiritual healing mechanisms depending on their perception of the symptoms or spirits or other supernatural elements which they relate with the causes of the disease or physical ailments.

Barua (1988: 78-80) mentioned about the *Ai-i* which is a ceremony performed by the *Igu* to ward off evil spirits causing sicknesses. In such cases, at first, the *Igu* collects the history of the sickness and then holds a piece of turmeric (*Kalih*) in the right hand and invokes the tutelary spirit thus:

> 'You have been receiving sacrifices from the days of my father, grandfather and, great grandfather. Whenever I have summoned you, you have been helpful to me. When a tree grows big, if it is not wanted, it is to be cut; if dirt accumulates on the body, it is to be removed. So also, if a man falls sick, he is to be cured. So and so has fallen sick. Let this piece of turmeric prove a good medicine, and cure the patient from his ailment. Be satisfied with the fowl which I am offering you as sacrifice.'

Barua (ibid) added that after this chant the *Igu* blows on the piece of the turmeric three times and then hands it over to the patient to eat and then he or she has to remain inside the room for a few hours.

Similarly *Amrasea,* is a ceremony which is performed by an *Igu* when a person is suffering from a serious illness. When leaving the house for treating such a patient, the *Igu* first offers a sacrifice to his or her own tutelary spirit so that it accompanies him or her. Here also, the collection of the history of sickness from the patient is mandatory in order to ascertain the identity of the spirits who are responsible. Barua writes (ibid: 80), "For this ceremony, a large number of sacrificial offerings such as fowls, pigs, rice-beer, sometimes *mithun* are needed. The priest asks the tutelary spirit to drive away the evil spirit. The tutelary spirit is believed to be half-witted, and thus requires to have everything explained, such as whether the illness was caused for breaking some taboo or by the malice of an evil spirit to ward off the powerful spirit causing illness."

According to Umpo (ibid: 35), an *Igu* has to perform *Tama-ela* while dealing with wounds, burns, injuries and incurable diseases, such as leprosy (*chedeh*) where an *Igu* has to send his power in favour of skylark (*Payu*) and Eagle (*drinki*) to bring medicine from a place called *Mudugoito* or *Kandigoito* which is located in heaven (*Mudumbru*). In the meantime, an *Igu* appeases all other spirits in the neighbourhood to prevent the ill-effect on the patient. When any of those birds returns, the *Igu* keeps his stretched hand towards the sky standing at the corridor, obtains the medicine, and then gives that to the patient. The whole process takes an hour and the *Igu* receives cash, chicken, *dao* (big knife made of iron) and rice beer as remuneration from that person and both the *Igu* and the patient have to observe taboo for five days when they should avoid taking onion and ginger.

In case of acute pain (*Ah-oh*) the *Igu* chants hyms (*Anyoko*) using wild banana groves followed by *Aphu* where an *Igu* sucks out the poison from the effected side. It is commonly believed that some spirits shoot arrows fixed with poison (*Ambo*) which leads to sudden pain (ibid).

During my field work I had the opportunity of seeing an *Igu* from the Desali area in action curing a lady suffering from acute back pain along with pain in the abdominal area. Hearing of this, I reached the house at night along with some Idu schoolteachers and I stayed there for 3 hours sitting just next to the *Igu* while I recorded his chanting for an hour. On entering, I found that a good number of young and middle-aged Idu Mishmi males and a few females were sitting in a circle playing cards. And next to them just by the hearth was one Idu lady who was lying fully covered in a blanket. Her daughter, along with some other ladies, was sitting at her head and an *Igu* was chanting while beating his sacred instrument (*ripu*) in a rhythmic way. From time to time the *Igu* took a plant in his hand. All the while the lady was screaming in pain. She would touch some water kept in a small bowl near the fireplace, and then rub her abdomen to bring some relief. After almost 40 minutes of chanting, the *Igu* took a break and sipped their local liquor from a mug. Then he started repeating the same chant. He did not have an assistant. He did not perform a dance or even wear a typical *Igu* costume. But he sat in a particular spot and chanted continuously, taking a break from time to time. He was trying to drive out the evil spirit which had caused such sickness. On one occasion, the lady sat up comfortably for a few minutes, then lay down again and took up her previous posture. Some elderly Idus from neighbouring houses called in and sat besides the *Igu* for some time and shared the local liquor. After almost two and half hours I left the house though this scene went on until midnight.

Bhattacharjee (1983: 126-128) gave a graphical description of the healing method which is used in case of severe suffering due to disease, which helps to understand the various stages of complex healing methods, which needs to be supported by his or her associates specially in case of the healing dance.

"The *Igu* arrives with his companions. He brings along with him bamboo twigs from his village or from the way. One of the twigs is struck near the steps and another taken inside the house. Before he starts, the owner of the house will offer him beer and money—the payment being already negotiated earlier.

One large cock will be kept near the porch in full view of the *Igu*. The Igu will take out the K(Ng)ali (plant like object) and after grinding a little in his teeth blow it out in front and at the back of the house. Then he proceeds with his incantations. The inmates of the house squat on the floor in line, starting from the entrance in the front room. The men sit alternately with the women.

The Igu continues his chanting along with rhythmic dance, moving back and forth within the room followed by drummers. One man carries a cock, swings it over the heads of the persons assembled. The *Igu* then takes out his sword and one of the bamboo twigs. He touches the heads of all those sitting on the floor one after the other saying that the sword is the most powerful and the bamboo will drive away the obstinate spirit from the house and the blood of the cock will wash off the evil.

The fowl is then cut by the *Igu* with his sword. The blood is then sprinkled in front of the people and the dead fowl is held over the head of all—the blood being allowed to trickle down to the floor. After that *Igu* will sit and have a little rest. He sips beer and may eat his food but no meat.

He starts his incantations with the rhythmic dance. He narrates his power to hold and challenges the spirit to face him at once. Often he peeps through the open door to see if the spirit has come.

The *Igu* then hands over his drum to one of his companions and goes to the afflicted person, removes his garments, identifies the place where the illness started. With the edge of the sword he draws out the imaginary object, goes to the door, stretches out his hand and blows this off through the door. His companions simultaneously beat the drum and the blow the trumpet, feet stamping loudly to drive away the spirit.

The *Igu* does not talk at this time. He carries a cock and touching the drooping portion of his head gear (tail) (*A-ye-to*), makes a sweeping motion over everybody. A feather of the fowl is given to each person who stick it on the head.

The *Igu* then takes out his sword. Holding out the sword in his right hand and the cock in the left hand, he runs to the door, crosses the door, jumps to the ground below, pierces the cock through the heart and throws it away; but soon a man who lies in wait catches the fowl, holds back the *Igu* who tries to run away and brings him back to the house. The *Igu* is now in full flow. He again takes out his sword, strikes first at the roof over the side door and opposite wall and continues his dialogue with the spirit. After that he repeats what he has seen and announces whether the patient could survive or not and the chances of obdurate spirit leaving the body.

After this phase a shaman leaves the house and while moving out of the village, he needs to perform some symbolic acts including sacrifice and he may even need to spend five nights in the forest before entering his village. If disease persists, then the same shaman or even other shamans may be called for help.

Healing Chant

Chanting is one of the major instruments, which an *Igu* uses for healing diseases/sicknesses, though the content, tune, and mode of application differs according to a shaman's perception of the cause of sickness. As shamans use a language, which is not understandable for a common Idu and most of the time, it continues for hours. Moreover, they never chant out of context; that is taboo for them. Naturally, it is very difficult to record and textualise the content of actual chants, though some parts of such chanting are transcribed and translated, in order to have a basic understanding of the content associated with the healing method.

Ayi Ritual Chanting

Inilo Selo Lango Midi, Apomeh Iduyee Yachemu
Lango Midi Ayaga, Loko Ambrigi Gadoma

Dambre Adane Gadoma, Zahi Witirow Koko Ye
Anuli Sudu Koko Ye.

At the place of dawn and dusk of the sun and the moon, the Alita (a ginger like plant used by the shaman for the treatment of the patient) has sprouted.

Diseases have come out from the place of dawn and dusk of the sun and the moon and entered the Idu world.

In that direction the Zahi, place of Beka (an evil spirit), is destroyed.

In that direction the Anuli, place of Manu (a spirit of forest), is destroyed.

Niyawa Aloli Rutowe, Ambu Iridi Koko ye
Aami Atoru Koko we, Ipiru Yunipru Koko
Mimu Apoli Achuli,

Aloli gave birth to all diseases.

So the dysentery (Ambu) has to be cured

Pain in the body which is caused by Aami (an insect/worm) has to be cured

Paralysis-like disease (Epiru) has to be cured

So the Alita at the place of dawn and dusk of the sun and the moon, have started growing.

Cheto Niyala Ambruli Apo Iduliya Achu Ye
Anjo Apeya Achu Ye, Apo Iduyi Achu Ye
Adeya Achu Ye, Aka Adepe Abrabi
Bruta Amaro Apuma Yochime,

One after another, at different Mrabas (heavenly places) i.e., from Cheto, Niyala, Anjo, Apeya, Adeya, Bruta, the Alita was brought and grown and finally reached the dwelling of Idu people who have the power of treatment and cure.

Short Summary of Ayi Ritual Chanting

It was Alonjuru, a legendary Idu shaman, who first introduced the ritual called Ayi which is meant for diagnosis of sickness. The chanting above is the mythological story chanted out by the shaman referring to how diseases and their preventive medicine, the Alita, originated and was used for the cure and treatment of a sick person. In the end, chanting the above, the shaman seeks the blessings of the Almighty Alonjuru, to cure the patient using the turmeric Alita (may be rubbed/ sprayed on the whole body or worn on the neck by the patient or eaten in little portion by the patient). To drive out the evil spirit, fowl is sacrificed and its blood is offered to them for not harming the patient anymore.[6]

Indigenous Healing Wisdom of the Community

It is evident across the Idu Mishmi inhabited areas that though the *Igu* remains the central figure in the domain of health and healing, there are some healing methods or knowledge which is part of the collective indigenous wisdom of the community which passes from one generation to another. Some information about such common healing plants and animals are also given by a few scholars (Mitapo: 2000, Pulu: 1988 etc.,), some of which are given below.

Herbs Used as Medicine

1. *Jarimu Naa*—leaves used for cut injuries.
2. *Eyawe Naa*—do- Leaves are crushed and juice is applied
3. *Ero* (coptis tita)—Direct intake for stomach ache (*Khepo Yaaso*)

1. *Jarimu-Naa*

2. *Eyawe- Naa* (Creeper)

3. *Tayu-Anjimere, Anjita*—These plants are used for cough (*Massu*).
4. *Kadra-bra, Metodo-ru*—These are used for treating asthma (*Ithri*).
5. *Arukhimuru, Ero(ng)*—These are used for bacillary dysentery (*Khiyu*)

6. *Marsa chie, Aposhru chee*—Used in case of worm infestation (*Anjipo ashu*).
7. *Tayu-naa, Anjikhi-naa*—Used in case of headache (*Ikuji*).
8. *Omrita, Ajibru, Tambre*—Given to anemia (*Iyupu nga*) patients.
9. *Rupoto, apperekasi*—Used for treating jaundice (*Jonta-mi*).
10. *Ero(ng), Ethrumbo*—Used in case of urinary track infection (*Thethu*).
11. *Andey ripri, Kamusi Mbo kopra, Seteka ripri*—Used for treating toothache (*Nta-na*).

Animal Parts Used for Medicine

1. *Aahu Immu* (Bile of beer)—Directly taken for curing stomach ache.
2. *Pra-ah-so* (fats of bird, i.e., of hornbill (Potho, Pandro, Thomu)—Used to heal burn injuries.

Bhattacharjee (1983: 4-5) mentioned that the valley and the hills of the Idu-inhabited areas are dotted with medicinal plants which are known to the people. He has listed ten such known medicinal plants and their common uses.[7] All Mishmi tribes were famous for the trade of *Coptis Tita* which is popularly known as Mishmi Tita, a plant belonging to the family *Ranunculaceae* located at an altitude of 7000 feet which contains a high percentage of *Alkaloid berbarine*.[8] One aconite plant, locally called '*Mra*', found in the snow belt, is highly valued by the Idus as it is still used for hunting animals. But in case an individual swallows this poison then a little quantity of yeast (*Pa*), fruits of the '*Anachi*' tree, and bamboo shoot (*Aposhu*) are mixed and forced down to the throat of the victim which induces vomiting by which the poison comes out. However, an *Igu* may also be called to cure such toxic effects[9].

It is evident that such indigenous healers (*Igus*) are fading fast because of many reasons which Chaudhuri (Ibid: 104-105) mentioned, adding the polyphonic voices of the shamans. One such opinion was expressed while dealing with the plight of shamanism among the Idu Mishmis (ibid); that of Rano Mihu, one of the seniormost legendary shamans, that shamanism is losing its hold from the society and he is sad about what is happening around him. He prays to the Almighty to give birth to more *Igu*s because *Igu*s are now diminishing. He encourages the youth to listen to an *Igu* carefully so that they can learn the language and tell others what *Igu* says and does. He is even ready to teach if anyone asks him to. With regard to the organization, he would like to take initiatives because he feels that *Igu*s do a lot for the society. He was one among the persons who gave ideas of the first celebration of *Reh* as a community festival under the leadership of the late Ita Pulu. But sometimes it is difficult to bring all *Igu*s to a common platform for a common cause because the ideas of *Igu*s would clash and ultimate result in the destruction of innocent human life, Mihu appends.

Conclusion

This study revealed the existing status of the indigenous healing tradition as well as the dilemma about the future of the institution of Igus. Many Idu elites, those who run the ICLS, are apprehensive about the future of such institutions and as a sequel to that, they are planning to textualise the whole genre of oral tradition related to the *Igu*s so that they can use those documents to train new *Igu*s, or at least, can conduct their Reh festival or other rituals and ceremonies. So far, the role of *Igu*s as healers still has a pivotal role both in the preventive as well as curative domains. It is true that some of the basic healing methods are part of the indigenous knowledge base of the community, but ritual healing or healing through the propitiation of spirits or driving them out through complex ritual performances, is a more dominant form prevalent among the Idu Mishmis. In addition, *Igu*s are still deeply regarded across the length and breath of the Idu-inhabited areas, though many such healers are not shy of accepting modern medical facilities in order to address diseases or sicknesses. They themselves are not averse to opt for such healing methods, which were alien to them before the expansion of state-sponsored medical facilities. The majority of the tribes of Arunachal Pradesh having their own indigenous healers are facing a similar situation. However, as long as village life will exist, the shamans or indigenous healers will continue to live; this institution may go through some modifications keeping in tune with the ongoing process of transformation and developmental initiatives which this frontier state has been experiencing since independence.

Note: This chapter is an outcome of a 5-year (2002-2007) collaborative project on "Tribal Transitions in Arunachal Pradesh" by Rajiv Gandhi University, SOAS, British Museum and CCRD of Arunachal Pradesh. Being one of the key members of the project, the author did extensive fieldwork among the Idu Mishmi tribe of Arunachal, India. Stuart Blackburn of SOAS, University of London, directed this project.

Notes

1. The number of constitutionally recognized tribes are much less as many tribes are yet to receive scheduled tribes status in Arunachal Pradesh.
2. The Miju Mishmis are now commonly known as Kamans, whereas Digaru Mishmis are called Taraons. However, one distinguishing feature of the Mishmis is their hairstyle (Dutta Chaudhuri, 1978).
3. The Intelligence Branch of the Division of the Chief of the Staff, Army Headquarters, India, reported (1907: 181) that the Chulikattas are the largest and boldest tribe, while the Bebejias, occupying more remote areas, are known to be the least civilized and the source of violence in the plains.
4. During the colonial period, Saudia was a famous trade centre in the plains of Assam near the Brahmaputra River. This was the place where hill tribes of NEFA (North-East Frontier Agency) used to come down along distinct trade routes to barter, sell or exchange their indigenous products with the people of the plains. During the return journey they used to take back whatever they needed, such as salt, beads, clothes, iron implements, etc. Most annual administrative reports from Assam during the colonial period contain detailed accounts of such trade activities which British administrators encouraged and for which they had to draw up a distinct policy regarding trade in Saudia.
5. With the passage of time the definition of shamanism is reexamined which Hoppal (2002: 93) narrated in his paper under the sub-heading 'Towards a New Definition'. He mentioned that the earlier definition of the term "shamanism" was based on the assumption of ecstasy whereas new definitions looked it from the social perspectives, as an institution which serves to construct a meaningful semantic universe by the process of symbolic mediation.
6. Transcription and translation of *Ayi* ritual chanting is done by Tarun Mene, an Idu doctoral research scholar of AITS, Rajiv Gandhi University, Arunachal Pradesh, India.
7. For example, *Amugi* is a small herb found over 4000 feet altitude. Leaves of this harb are used as vegetables and pickles, as well as medicine for stomach trouble especially indigestion. Scientific names

of such plants are hardly given but local names are mentioned along with their habitat.

8. Many colonial documents reflect about the trade of Mishmi Tita both with neighbouring people of hills and plains. Even Cooper (1989) mentioned about this highly valued medicinal plant traded by the Mishmis of Lohit valley.
9. Such aconite is collected from a shrub where aconite is formed in winter in the form of tuber. Person who prepares the paste out of such tuber has to follow some food taboo. After preparation the paste is smeared in arrow heads with the help of a twig not touched by hand. Big games including elephant can be killed by using arrows smeared with such poison. Because of high toxic effect this tuber is kept secretly and not given to a stranger.

Bibliography

Achterberg, J. 2002. The Shaman: Master Healer in the Imaginary Realm, *Shamanism: An Expanded View of Reality* (compiled) Shirley Nicholson, Pilgrim Publishing, Varanasi.

Allen, B.C. 1905. *Assam District Gazettiers*, Vol. 8, Lakhimpur, Calcutta: City Press.

Baruah, T.K. 1960. *The Idu Mishmis*, Itanagar: Directorate of Research.

Bhagabati, A.C. 1998. "Indigenous faith and customs: Some Observations". In *Indigenous Faith and Practices by the Tribes of Arunachal Pradesh*, edited by M.C. Behera and S.K. Chaudhuri, Itanagar: Himalayan Publishers.

Bhagabati, A.C. 2002. "Social Structure in Arunachal Pradesh: An anthropological Overview". In *Arunachal Pradesh: Environmental Planning and Sustainable Development, Opportunities and Challenges*, edited by R.C. Sundriyal, Trilochan Singh and G.N. Sinha, pp. 47-50. Almora: G.B.P.I.H.E.D.

Bhagabati, A.C. and S.K. Chaudhuri. 2008. Social Transformation Process in Arunachal Pradesh, *Bull. Dept. Anthropology*, Gauhati University (Spl. Issue) 10.

Bhattacharjee, T.K. 1983. *The Idu Mishmis of Dri valley*, Directorate of Research, Shillong.

Blackburn, S. 2003/2004. "Memories of migration: Notes on legends and beads in Arunachal Pradesh, India". *European Bulletin of Himalayan Research*, 25/26, pp. 15-60.

——2005. "The journey of the soul: Notes on funeral rituals and oral texts in Arunachal Pradesh, India". In *Der abschied Von den Totem. Trauerrituale im kulturvergleich,* edited by Jan Assamann, Franz Michaels, pp. 1-35 [as per original English version] Gottingen, Wallstein.

Chaudhuri, S.K. 2008. Plight of the igus: Notes on shamanism among the Idumishmis of Arunachal Pradesh, India, in *European Bulletin of Himalayan Research*, 32. Spring. pp. 84-108.

Chaudhury, S. and D.K. Duarah. 2004. "Religious beliefs and Institutionof priesthood among the tribes of Arunachal Pradesh". In *Understanding Tribal Religion*, edited by T. Mibang and S.K. Chaudhuri, pp. 19-34. New Delhi: Mittal Publications.

Cooper, T.T. 1995 [1960]. *The Mishmi Hills*, New Delhi: Mittal Publications.

Dalton, E.T. 1872. *Descriptive Ethnology of Bengal*, Calcutta.

Dutta Chaudhuri, S. 1978. Arunachal Pradesh, Lohit District Gazetteer, Shillong: Government of Arunachal Pradesh.

Dutta, P and S.I. Ahmad. 1995. *People of India: Arunachal Pradesh.* Vol. 14. Calcutta: Seagull Books.

Eliade, M. 1964. *Shamanism: Archaic techniques of ecstasy.* London: Penguin books.

Elwin, V. 1957/1999. *A Philosophy for NEFA.* (4th reprint), Itanagar: Directorate of Research,.

Halifax, J. 2002. Shamanism, Mind, and No-Self, *Shamanism: An Expanded View of Reality* (compiled) Shirley Nicholson, Pilgrim Publishing, Varanasi, pp. 213-222.

Hoppal, M. 2002. An Archaic and/or Recent Belief System, *Shamanism: An Expanded View of Reality* (compiled) Shirley Nicholson, Pilgrim Publishing, Varanasi, pp 76-100.

Houston, J. 2002. The Mind and Soul of the Shaman, *Shamanism: An Expanded View of Reality* (compiled) Shirley Nicholson, Pilgrim Publishing, Varanasi, pp. vii-xvi.

Intelligence branch, A.H.Q., India. 1907. *Frontier and Overseas Expeditions from India,* Shimla: Government Monotype Press.

Lingi, M. and T. Miso. 2000. "Rituals practised by the Idus and and role of an Igu", in Seminar report on *Traditional systems—Change and Continuity among the Idu Mishmis*, Roing: The idu Cultural and Literary society.

Mitapo, S.J. 2000. "Traditional healing by use of herbs, plants and animal products in Idu Mishmi community", in Seminar report on *Traditional systems—Change and Continuity among the Idu Mishmis*, Roing: The idu Cultural and Literary society.

Needham, J.F. 1900. *Report of the Bebejiya Mishmi Expedition, 1899-1900.* Shillong.

Stirn, A. and P. Van Ham. 2000. *The Seven Sisters of India,* Ahmedabad: Mapin Publishing.

8

Tibetan Buddhism as a Culture and Way of Life: Focus on the Indian Buddhists Living in the Borders with Tibet

Jayanti Alam

It is important and necessary to acquaint ourselves with the basic tenets and philosophy of Buddhism and with the "way of life", prescribed by the Lamaism of Tibet; this kind of background will facilitate our understanding of the Buddhist societies of the Monpas and the Sherdukpens, bordering Tibet in the extreme North-west of Arunachal Pradesh and more or less, all over Sikkim and a few others found along Northeast India's border with Tibet. Their mind, way of thinking and way of life, including the architecture and the choice of colours in the paintings on the exteriors and the interiors of the mosques and the temples are almost inseparably similar to those of the monasteries of the Tibetans in India and in Lhasa. The monasteries in Tibet and within parts of China which were partially damaged during China's "Cultural Revolution", are now fully renovated with typical Tibetan architecture and the colours/paints.

The tenets of Buddhism are broadly as follows:

A. Suffering (Duhkha)

This is regarded as the first noble truth or the truth of the nobles, meaning those who have noble virtues within them. This awareness and the experience makes one conscious of the (i) source of suffering, (ii) cessation of suffering and (iii) path (marga) leading to "dharma". Each noble truth has three aspects. [*Three aspects will be covered at the right place, i.e. when I am discussing a particular "noble truth*]. The first is characterised by (a) the misery of suffering, (b) the misery of change (because all pleasures are temporary and are inevitably followed by pain) and (c) the misery of motivations (because "karma" inevitably is followed by "klesha" or suffering. The typical prayer-wheel of the Tibetans has sets of 12 turnings, symbolically representing 4 truths, 3 aspects.[1]

The miseries, for example, are birth, old age, sickness, guarding one's valuables, not possessing valuables, etc. And, to dispel the pain of hunger there is food, to dispel the pains of heat, cold and shame there are clothes, for sleepiness beds, for commuting vehicles, and for illness there are medicines. Human beings belonging to any religious group believe that 'duhkha'and 'klesha' made Prince Gautama leave the comforts and power of royal life and go into deep meditation and serious questioning for years and when he got the answers, he started preaching his deep realization and beliefs and thus came to be known as the "Buddha", the most knowledgeable or the wisest.

B. Karma

Karma, naturally, is the second noble truth because without that we cannot possibly win over "duhkha". The notion is quite similar to the Hindu belief of Karma. Karma, however long-lasting, can ultimately come to an end. "As to the maturation in this life the fruit of Karma matures. At the time "Siddhi"(success) is attained, the evil effects of Karma are warded off and the vicious cycle of the causes and the inevitable effects are then abandoned. . . .

Life, then, becomes like the sky." (Translated from Tibetan, meaning perhaps, "as endless/vast and free as the sky"). During the 38 weeks of pregnancy the "winds of Karma" are said to influence foetal progression.

I found that this belief about pregnancy is rather strong and universal among both the educated and the illiterate women; and the reasons for the weak and anemic mothers/would-be-mothers and/or under-weight or premature babies are ascribed to wrong Karma. But, luckily and strangely, the mother is not abused, nor punished, unlike in the highly 'patriarchal' major religious societies of India. Such a rare humane value is found in spite of these societies, like all other tribal societies of Arunachal, being patriarchal! Let me also mention that all the societies of this state are basically patriarchal and patrilineal, without being oppressive to their girls and women — very much unlike almost all the other religious societies of India. By "patriarchy" they mean that the owners of property, particularly immovable property, are always the males and the lineage is also from the father. Yet, there is no crude and cruel form of 'son-preference' and absolutely no female infanticide, nor foeticide! Above all, the woman is never blamed for not bearing male children; though, I don't think that the men are aware of the scientific fact that it is the "Y" chromosome, found only in men and never in women, that determines the sex of an unborn. The level of literacy is not that low or far above than what we find in the so-called "BIMARU" states of India; but, education above the school level, particularly in the rural areas, is not satisfactory. Besides, like in the educationally developed states of India, this important knowledge about the significance of the "Y" chromosome is absent even among the university students near the capital Itanagar. In any case, in most of the oriental societies, patriarchy, ably supported by religion, where the God, the prophets and the scriptures or dicta writers are invariably males, and the feudal-capitalist system of oppression of the many by a few, it is not all that rare to find eminent scientists, judges, scholars, etc. believing in female foeticide and even dowry, along with all the evils associated with it.

C. Seed Consciousness

Seed Consciousness is the third noble truth. Thought of enlightenment is like the father-seed and insight-intuiting non-self is like the mother-womb. The act of creating seeds is a characteristic faculty of human consciousness.[2] We must not miss the striking fact or the observation of the women activists that in reality a woman, particularly a mother, has greater insights, strong intuition and of course, selflessness, particularly in case of her child/children. A father, in general, is more knowledgeable, though not always 'enlightened" also, by virtue of being a male; he gets all the opportunities he needs or seeks for self-development. An overwhelming majority of the societies or social systems are deeply patriarchal and therefore, all the privileges and benefits are constructed by a few powerful males, who have managed to have socio-legal rights over all the natural and man-made properties.

The source of origin of life, viz., the seed, is the father, quite similar to the Hindu belief of the "male" as the creator. From the mother the child derives "all essential substances", i.e. all the physical and mental characteristics and features. The mother enjoys a very special position of honour and reverence in Tibetan thinking; the mother's love is glorified as "boundless love and boundless compassion" and she is regarded as the Parent No. 1. But it is widely and genuinely believed that the mother cannot protect or rescue and only the father or the other males in the family can. That is why, widowhood is discouraged, widows though, are not despised.

D. Dharma

Dharma, is the fourth noble truth. It leads one to the path, leading to the end of suffering. Three instructions need to be followed, viz:

(i) morality (adhishila)
(ii) mind-training (adhichitta)
(iii) insight (adhipragna)

Dharma, thus, guides and regulates our Karma and is, therefore, "good in the beginning, good in the middle and good in the end.......a continuum."[3] We must not fail to notice and realize that "Dharma" here is like the etymological meaning of the word in Sanskrit; the "root" is the sound "dhri", meaning something that holds or controls one from going astray. Thus "dharma" in the unadulterated Vedic religion, which later came to be known as "Hinduism", does not indicate various rituals and the do's and don'ts that divide humanity into numerous categories of "the superiors" and "the inferiors", and gives "immoral" power and decision-making rights to those, who have cleverly vitiated the true or the etymological meaning and significance of this noble word. It actually means "morality" or "ethics", for which insight and mind-training are absolutely necessary. That is why interestingly, the remnants of the Buddhist societies like Tibet, Bhutan, Sikkim and the extreme West and the extreme East of Arunachal Pradesh, bordering Tibet, have remained relatively gender and class equal with greed, temptation and jealousy — the chief causes behind discrimination, violence and injustice that are destroying most other societies or eco-political systems — being almost absent.[4]

The reciprocal duties of each unit have been discussed, at length, in the Sigalovada Sutta.

A child towards parents — once supported by them, it should, now, be support for them and it will transfer merit in due time. It is compulsory for the adult children, whatever the sex, to take care of their aged parents, grandparents. It is a law even in non-Buddhist Communist China.

Parents towards children — restrain them from vice and exhort them to virtue; also, hand over their inheritance in due time.

Pupils towards teachers — eagerness to learn and attentive learning.

Teachers towards Pupils — training them well and making them masters of what they have already learnt. The teacher should also praise his students to their friends and companions.

Husband towards his wife and wife towards her husband as well as employers towards employees and employees towards employers — duties of mutual fulfillment of goals, i.e., complementary duties towards each other and towards the society. Has any other society (or religion) been able to talk of duties as 'complementary?' In all other societies —even in the so-called 'democratic' and 'socialistic' forms of governance — the duties between man and woman, ruler and ruled, and so on — are never 'complementary'; a sense of 'superior' and 'inferior' or 'more' capable and 'less' capable inevitably and unavoidably exists. The Buddha himself was against women monks or nuns and when he finally conceded to his favourite disciple Ananda, he saw to it that the nuns are not allowed decision-making powers. He too, like all other prophets and gurus – may be with the exception of Christ – regarded women as seductresses and less intelligent or less sensible!

Laity towards community of monks — treating them with affection in action, speech and mind, keeping one's house open to them and supplying them with their temporal needs.

Community of monks towards laity —restraining them from evil, exhorting them to do good and loving them with kind thoughts, revealing to them a way to a heavenly state.[5] Individual health of each unit contributes to the society as a whole; the welfare of the individual and of the society is closely interdependent.

The theory of Karma also gives a lot of importance to the "death experience". Since rebirth is inevitable, "death consciousness", "death vision" and "death-time act" to determine the next life are of equal importance. "The Munis do not wash away defilements of the stream of consciousness with water as though it were a matter of washing away dirt; do not remove suffering with hand as though it were a matter of pulling out a thorn.......they liberate the beings from the cyclical flow by the teaching of the truth of real nature, i.e., the absolute truth; the beings got to meditate on its meanings." [Tibetan annotated commentary].

The next vital belief of the Tibetan Buddhists is in *Virtues* or *Perfections.* The Bodhisattva's first perfection is in *Giving.* Whether or not there is concrete/actual giving, what is important is the volition of giving. In Tibetan philosophy, therefore, there is no conception of "more" or "property". That is why perhaps, in spite of property being owned by only the males of a family among the Arunachal tribes along the Tibetan border, there is no oppression of their women — married, unmarried, widowed or deserted – in the slightest. Deserted women are almost absent as there exists a strong belief in family ties and decision-making by the entire family of all generations and a powerful pressure from the community seldom allows that to happen. They enjoy as much or as many freedoms as their men and all the women I met, of various ages and performing different household duties, looked totally relaxed and happy, so much so that when asked if they get equal share in the family's food, clothes, etc., they stared at each other, trying to understand what that type of a query meant, just as the Tibetan women in the Tawang district of Arunachal Pradesh and the Darjeeling district of West Bengal were extremely surprised when asked about the rate of, or the propensity towards, sexual abuses by their men or in their society.

The second perfection is of *Striving,* the *third* of *Insight* and the *fourth* of Common Pursuits. [Ibid]. The stress is on the word "common"; unlike in Hindu theology, there is no discrimination/ distinction of high or low, superior or inferior. The emphasis on this word or the concept of "common", meaning "for" or "of" each and everybody, without any discrimination whatsoever, in concept or behaviour or social custom is of great importance among the Tibetan Buddhists, who have deeply and comprehensively influenced the thought and belief process of the overwhelming majority of the inhabitants of the Tawang and West Kameng districts of Arunachal Pradesh, surrounded topographically, much more by China, including the Tibet Autonomous Region, Bhutan and Myanmar than by India, of which it is a state.

Buddhism, born in the kingdom of Pataliputra or present Bihar, can be, and actually is, regarded as an Indian religion, like Jainism, Sikhism and Sanatan Dharma or Hinduism; but, its essence or ethics have spread much more outside the political boundaries of India. It is considered the least 'divisive' religion or faith, particularly because it does not talk of caste or any other unfair division/discrimination that unfortunately a majority of the world religions do. And, there is no denying the fact that the Buddhist societies say, for example, of Tibet and Sri Lanka, are far less discriminating among human beings of whatever sex and class. Yet, we cannot ignore the excessive racial and religious biases of the Sri Lankan ruling classes. But definitely, gender bias is much less there, as a striking contrast to Kerala, where we find much less patriarchal torture compared to any other state. Even in West Bengal gender and various other biases are stronger than in Kerala and far stronger than in Sri Lanka. Even the utterly feudal society of the Tibetans, where the land-and-power-holding lamas were only 2% of the population living in the luxury of the monasteries and a huge 98% were the "serfs", living a sub-human life in utter deprivation and tortures of the worst kinds, Buddhism was the religion!

But, an unbelievable transformation in the life, belief, rituals and mindset had taken place in among the Tibetans, who had settled in the Himalayan regions of India, bordering Tibet. A unique sense of equality and no differentiation even on the basis of gender is found among the non-Tibetan tribes or racial groups, which, due to geographical proximity and climatic similarity, appear to be no different from their next-door neighbours, viz., the South-eastern part of China's Tibet. "Dharma" or Theravada Buddhism has engulfed them in every single aspect of their life – living, beliefs, thoughts, the auspicious signs found on the hand-woven silk, silk made in China scarves, tea-mugs, windows, walls, front-doors of their houses, monasteries, guest houses, etc., apart from the wooden, finely carved tea-tables, the very warm home-made carpets and other woollens. The choice of colours are so typically Tibetan – mostly bright yellow, bright red and soothing green and natural/organic colours. Nobody knows for sure if the Tibetans of both sides of the international border were influenced by the Indian Buddhists of Arunachal Pradesh and Sikkim or was it the other way around. Folklore and folk songs fail to indicate clearly who influenced whom; nor do the extensive conversations with the women of these tribes help us to unravel the mystery. Only one thing I could gather for sure, that the international border between the Buddhists of the feuding nations has made no visible or discernable effect on the unquestionable similarity in culture and beliefs between the people of the region; it is almost impossible to ascertain, unless one sits with a map.

Buddhism came to Tibet in the 7th and 8th centuries AD and got smoothly and peacefully amalgamated with the existing Bon religion. Mahayana Buddhism entered Tibet, possibly from Kashmir in 7th. century AD and again found its way back to India among the Monpas and the Sherdukpens of the Kameng District of Arunachal Pradesh via Bhutan.[6] Guru Padmasambhava, popularly known as Guru Rinpoche or Lopon Rinpoche had come to Tawang area in the 8th century, not directly from India but, through Tibet and the world-famous Tawang monastery, known as Gamden Namgyal Lhatse Ling, meaning 'Celestial Paradise of the Divine Site Chosen by a Horse', got established in as late as the 17th century, by the fifth Dalai Lama, Lodre Gyatso. Oral history says that Tawang and its adjacent areas, extending up to the foothills of the Himalayas, were under Tibetan rule since many centuries. The Tibetan culture, along with its religion, had 'infiltrated' this region to the West of Bhutan and South of Tibet through the trade route; a similar story is true of the Tibetans in the Darjeeling district of West Bengal.[7] According to K. Gupta in his book *The Hidden History of the Sino-Indian Frontier*, Tawang was a part of the Tsona district of Tibet". In 1950, the matter had been raised in the Parliament that the Tibetans were forcibly collecting money from the devotees of the Dalai Lama for the Drepung monastery in Lhasa. In India's pre-independence days, every family in Tawang had to pay a certain amount of grains, as taxes or 'Khrai', to the monastery officials. And, in 1683, the 6th 'incarnation' of the Dalai Lama was born in this region.

This successful blending, as Lobsang Lhalungpa says, was a strong indication of Buddhism's ability to adapt beautifully to the local conditions while retaining its innate doctrinal purity. For example, the Tibetan symbols of four elements, viz., tiger, lion, eagle and dragon, are used in Tibetan Buddhism. Prayer flags on the roof-tops, etc. also indicate the continuation of Bon practices incorporated in Tibetan Buddhism. This religion is also unique in having embraced the essentials of both Theravada and Mahayana Buddhism. *Vajrayana,* typically Tibetan, contains Indian Tantric beliefs and practices, but is based on the Mahayana concept of Nirvana. Buddhism received active encouragement from king Khri-Srong-Idebstan in the late 8th century, when the Tantric master Padmasambhava was invited from India. There was a debate, around the same period, to decide if the Indian or the

Chinese form of Buddhism should be adopted in Tibet. Needless to add, the Indian form of Buddhism was adopted. Ateesha Deepankara, the Mahayana master from Bengal, gave a profound impetus to Buddhism in Tibet and he is, ever since, placed in the rank of the Five Great Religious Masters— a position and honour much above that of the Dalai Lama. [8]

The understanding and belief that Man is composed of six elements, viz., earth, water, fire and wind...plus...space (akasha) and perception or understanding (vijnana) are common to both Buddhist and Vedic philosophies. "One cannot become enlightened through a contrived mind. Rather, the basic mind is to be identified, in relation to which all phenomena are to be understood as the sport of the mind". [Dalai Lama, Nov.23, 1990]. That may be the reason why the Tibetan and the Arunachali Buddhists have such strong adherence to everything "Natural". As mentioned earlier, both the communities on two sides of the international border use nothing synthetic or artificial in their food, clothes, and jewellery including man-to-man and man-woman relationships. Women occupy a special position in the family because their bodies nurture life before and after childbirth. That is why, a woman is the sole decision-maker with regard to: (i) how many children she wants, (ii) of what sex, (iii) at what intervals and even (iv) whether she wants children at all or not! This "Natural" or "Nature-given" freedom or human right that a woman in these societies enjoys characterizes these societies as dramatically different from any other society that we know of. Such 'just' freedom, which is Nature-given, is not allowed to the females even in a matrilineal society —say, for example, amongst the Khasis of Meghalaya or a few extinct ones in Kerala! What is most astonishing is that the Indian followers of Tibetan Buddhism belong to a patriarchal family/society and yet, their women enjoy this vital right! This is where these women enjoy a true identity of their own, which is not dependent on the identities of their male relatives like the father, father-in-law, husband, son/s and even brother/s.

Patrul Rinpoche, "the wise man" in Tibetan language, in his "The Words of My Perfect Teacher", says "there is nothing so uniform as water, nothing so creative as the wind, nothing so far-flung or elevated as error and nothing so correct as the measuring rod"– a rather interesting way of reminding us of the hard realities.

The next important concept is of the *Teacher.* Teaching is the "great vehicle" and time is the ever-revolving wheel of eternity. The teacher embodies the essence of all the Buddhas. Notably, a curious belief among the Tibetan Buddhists is that there is not only one Buddha, meaning approximately "the one who has reached the ultimate in knowledge and realization", but many. This kind of concept or belief becomes possible in Buddhism because there is no concept of God, the supernatural; this 'ism' is only about ideal Karma and ethical life. That is why the particular Buddha is the union of three Jewels; his body is like Sangha, his speech is like Dharma and his mind is like the Buddha. The Teacher or the 'Rinpoche' therefore, tells all his followers of 'an ethical life the way the Buddha has shown'; he says,

I've shown you the methods
That lead to the liberation (of your mind and actions),
But, you should know
That liberation depends upon yourself or your ethical 'karma',
The way the Buddha has prescribed.

He further adds, "unless you practice Dharma according to Dharma, Dharma itself can become the cause of evil (rebirths). This is the most fascinatingly eye-opening guidance from a guru (teacher)! (How I wish the religious bigots of all other civilisations understood this!) This explains why the Tibetans have an unquestioning trust in and obedience to their religious-temporal leader, the Dalai Lama's wisdom and also why they honestly endeavour to do what has been explained to them as good and virtuous, including their superbly democratic Constitution given to them by their government-in-exile. Without a law for "reservation" of seats for women, the Parliament (in exile) has almost equal number of women 'law-makers'. Once again, it can be mentioned that that there is no gender or class distinction or differentiation in their society—not even in "China-occupied" Tibet. It is a wonder how a thoroughly feudal, oppressive and fundamentalist civilization could turn into such an ideal one and also notwithstanding the fact that the so-called 'Socialism' and stringent beliefs in 'classlessness' of Maoist China are still a strong believer in male superiority! If nothing else, female infanticides in the villages and foeticides in the cities are practiced ever since the Han rulers are not allowed to have more than one child; the ethnic and cultural minority groups are not prohibited, though.

As mentioned earlier, the Monpas and Sherdukpens and a few other tribes, insignificant in their numbers practicing Tibetan

Buddhism or the Dalai Lama's Buddhism, belong to a social system which, like all other Arunachali tribes, believe in the immovable property being in the hands of the senior-most male of the family or the extended family. But, the concept of or belief in "patriarchy" begins and ends there. In everything else, like the Tibetan Buddhists, their socio-economic system is as egalitarian and even gender-equal like the Tibetans'. The family head or the custodian of the family property takes all the decisions in consultation with all the members including adolescent children. Can anybody from amongst us wishfully belonging to an emancipated family imagine that a Monpa, Sherdukpen or Tibetan (there are many Tibetan families both in Bomdila and Tawang) husband/father cooking with his baby tied securely to his back, while the mother is away for some business or money-earning activity? Therefore, it is needless to point out that there is no son-preference and not even any strict 'division of labour'; man or woman, husband or wife does whatever is necessary at a certain point of time or as the situation demands. Interestingly again, the would-be-bride starts working in her in-laws' and the would-be-groom in his in-laws' household! There is no strict marital migration and of course, no dowry. There used to be "bride price" like most of the tribes in Arunachal, the Northeast and even in Central India, but, with the advent of economic 'globalisation' and change in attitudes or mindset, formal/religious/ritualistic marriages are becoming more and more uncommon and the boy and the girl just decide to live together. There is no back-biting or condemnation, unlike in the non-Buddhist tribal societies of Arunachal Pradesh and of course in "mainland" India. Sex obviously, is not a taboo because the incidence of non-consensual sex or rape is something 'foreign' to them and the child born to an unmarried mother is as much welcome to the families and the society. Another man (and not the biological father) may happily accept the child while marrying or living with its mother! The Monpas' and any other tribe believing in Tibetan Buddhism, are quite prone to joke around 'free and uninhibited sex and usually the man and wife or the man and the woman are of the same age.

"Bless me and the foolish beings like me
That we may attain the very essence of
The freedoms and advantages,"

The teacher truly means it and the pupil strives best to keep up to this prayer or the "blessings" he/she receives.

The next significant feature of Tibetan/Vajrayana Buddhism that strengthens the Tibetan mind further is their deep belief in *Impermanence.*

Impermanence of the outer universes in which *Beings* live,
Impermanence of the beings, living in this universe,
Impermanence even, of the Holy Beings, i.e. of so many Buddhas,
and Impermanence of those in positions of power.

This is where this religion is so pragmatic and egalitarian. In contrast, Hinduism and most other religions talk of absolute power in the hands of the "guru" or the priest or the "murshed", who represents a particular God as the interpreter and the performer of the rituals (on behalf of the credulous) and clear-cut power-hierarchies. Emphasis on the theory of impermanence in Tibetan Buddhism is laid thus:

Causes of death are numerous,
Causes of life are few
And even those may become causes of death.

The Buddha said, "to meditate persistently on impermanence is to make offerings to all Buddhas, and to be guided, inspired and blessed by them."[9]

The following are the "wrong doings", which causes suffering, re-birth and further suffering:

1. Taking life, i.e. (a) killing out of hatred; (b) killing out of desire, e.g. animals (for eating); (c) killing without knowing if it is right or wrong. The most condemnable killing is of father, mother and teacher; even creating schism within Sangha is considered a crime equal to "killing".
2. Taking by force, trickery or stealthily what is not given. Business or commercial activities are looked down upon because these involve "piling up" and "corruption". This explains why Tibetans, in general, are quiet, soft-spoken, amiable and peace-loving. Though they are successful traders and shopkeepers, they are generally honest with their

customers and do not aim at lots of money or a very high profit, which is possible only by malicious intent. They like good living, but feel ashamed to get marked out as rich and different from others. There are no forced divisions on the basis of occupation (which was prevalent in pre-1951 feudal Tibet), class or gender. They believe that greed leads to property, property to corruption, and these together lead to power. (The 'shastras' of the Hindus also say that; but, the powerful interpret the way it suits them; besides, there are too many books and laws and their interpretations.) Power can survive only on division, hatred and oppression. But these cannot happen if people are devoted followers of the "Teachers" and their teachings.

The other "wrong-doings" are—

3. Sexual misconduct
4. Lying
5. Sowing discord, particularly among the members of a Sangha.
6. Harsh speech
7. Worthless chatter
8. Covetousness
9. Wishing harm to others
10. Wrong views, i.e., to think that the Buddha's words, Teacher's instructions or the texts of the learned commentators are in error or to doubt and criticize them. (Such an injunction can easily become anti-freedom and source of orthodoxy, by giving unspecified power or freedom to the gurus/teachers and superstitions among the followers.)

The severest of the sins are "taking life" and holding "wrong views". The Buddha said:

"The joys and sorrows of beings
All come from their actions."
"Do not take lightly the small misdeeds
Believing they can do no harm;
Even a tiny spark of fire
Can set alight a mountain of hay."
"Do not take lightly small good deeds,
For drops of water one by one

In time can fill a giant pot."
"When the moment comes to leave, O King,
Neither possessions, nor friends nor family can follow;
But wherever beings come from, wherever they go to,
Their actions follow them like their own shadow." [10]

How I wish all of us, Hindus, Muslims, Christians, Sikhs and the tribes believing in their own religion/faiths/rituals or way of life had followed these precepts like the Tibetans try to (at least).

The next important advice to the people is about arousing *Bodhichitta* or training the mind for Four Boundless Qualities, viz:

(i) boundless love
(ii) boundless compassion
(iii) boundless sympathetic joy
(iv) boundless impartiality.

The last quality is regarded as the most important and binding, because love, compassion or joy tend to be one-sided and therefore, impure. Besides, honest adherence to the principle of 'equality' becomes possible only if one and all are truly 'impartial'. It is, also, advised that the best method to arouse compassion within oneself is to imagine *Oneself* to be the tormented person and true impartiality is achieved when one is able to give up hatred of foes and infatuation for friends. This height of noble mentality, which appears rather unattainable, can be reached when one is not only able to put oneself in another's' position, but also considers others more important than oneself. All these are results of true *Wisdom,* which can be attained through (a) hearing, (b) reflection and (c) meditation. No hearing is worthwhile unless the brain "reflects" on what has been said through the sensory organ of hearing. Let me make my readers conscious of the thoughtful/careful choice of the adjective "sympathetic" with "joy"; it is important because in our normal 'self-centered' lives, we seek joy or happiness or well-being only for ourselves and our family, not the extended family of our earlier generations. But, what is ideal as a virtuous human being is to feel happy for and with the happiness of others; that is what, I feel, is meant by the word "sympathetic".

Merit and wisdom are regarded as two rich "accumulations" and one needs four *Powers* to accumulate. They are:

i. power of support (from teacher, teachings, one's faith, understanding, determination, etc.). It is through faith that absolute *Truth* can be realised.
ii. power of regret (for negative actions)
iii. power of resolution (against negative and for positive actions and feelings)
iv. power of action (i.e., positive action as an antidote to negative actions) [11]

Patrol Rinpoche says:

Being born in the hell, in the "preta" realm,
As an animal, long-lived god or a barbarian,
Having wrong views, being born when there is no Buddha,
Or, being born deaf or mute
Are the eight states *without Freedom.*

Pretas are the bodyless spirits; but in this context they are the evil spirits. The Gods have no opportunity to practice Dharma, because they spend their time in a state of mental blankness. This could have been taken as a dig at Hinduism or idolatry, found prominently also in many tribal faiths, because a majority of the Gods have no power, but are "long-lived" in the psyche of the ignorant and the superstitious; but, inimical attitudes towards others – whether thoughts, beliefs, cults, etc.—is totally against the basic tenets and teachings of the Buddhas or Rinpoches.

Note the word "freedom" and the importance attached to it! Can we think of or search out any other religion, which talks of "freedom"? Isn't the very first casualty of any religious belief or way of life is the concept of freedom, because how else can the self-styled interpreters and "protectors" of a religion impose, inflict, deny or scare? True freedom and an in-depth notion/belief in freedom will negate the very purpose of the invention of a supernatural and inscrutable power called "God". Freedoms and advantages do not come by chance or coincidence; they are the results of an accumulation of merit and wisdom.[12]

A human life can be called a "precious human life" only when it is complete with all the virtues; and that is not possible without freedom. One must not therefore, overlook the vital importance given to 'freedom' in "The Words of A Perfect Teacher" , since no other known (or major) religion talks of "freedom". On the contrary, the worst enemy of 'freedom' is religion and its endless dicta. Therefore,

> To find this precious human life
> Is more valuable than finding a precious jewel, and
> To meet a perfect teacher
> Is more valuable than gaining a kingdom.
> To see the real nature of mind
> Is more valuable than meeting the Buddha.

What a sacrilegious statement even for a Buddhist! But, the true virtue of this 'way of life' or 'ethics' and no belief in anything supernatural like God lies in this!

There are two important books of Law. The first contains 10 Commandments for the Holy Order and 16 Articles for the laity. The second book is composed of 13 Commandments from Gyan-ch'u Gye-tsen (14th century). It is elaborate, covering everything from petty thefts to the conduct of a ruler. The gist or the significant messages from these are —

All human beings are born free and equal in dignity and rights. They are endowed with reason and conscience and should act, with one another, in a spirit of brotherhood. One, who is deprived of inner peace, will not be able to propagate peace in society. If man is to survive on this earth, peace has to be sustained. Peace is an art of survival without which we cannot speak of happiness on this Earth, or of human rights and values, nor of the achievements of human civilizations. Buddhism, preaching the unity of mankind, unfolds a way of life for the betterment of the quality of life here and hereafter. But, this rich, remarkable socio-ethical aspect of Buddhism, particularly of Tibetan Buddhism, has not been adequately emphasized.[13]

'The Words of my Perfect Teacher', by Patrul Rinpoche, is constantly recommended by the Dalai Lama and other eminent teachers as a manual of practical advice for anyone sincerely wishing to practice Dharma: It was written in a style that could convey as easily to the nomads (Tibet having been a dry and cold plateau there were hardly any farmers) and the villagers as to the lamas and the monks. The writer was a firm believer in Ateesha Deepankara's dictum that the "best spiritual friend is the one who attacks your hidden faults." Ateesha was the first monk and a "wise man" to travel to Tibet from India and is still revered as one of the five most venerated

wise men. Khu, Ngok and Drom, the three main disciples of Ateesha, were told that:

The best scholar is one who has realised the meaning of *no-self*
The best monk is one who has tamed his own mind
The best quality is a great desire to benefit others
The best remedy is to know that nothing has any inherent reality
The best accomplishment is a steady lessening of negative emotions
The best sign is a steady decrease of desires
The best wisdom is not to grasp at anything at all.

The Buddhist societies that I have encountered do, in general, carry, quite noticeably, the tenets "a great desire to benefit others" and "not to grasp at anything at all". The rays of the evils of "privatization" and "globalization" have, no doubt, entered these self-contained societies so remote from so-called 'mainland' India and thus, modern consumerism, Hindi film songs and jeans, etc. have unavoidably entered these cultures; yet they have remained true to the "steady lessening of negative ideas" and happy and cooperative/ helpful. Tibetan religion places primary emphasis on maintaining harmony in both the realms of "outer" and "inner" experiences. Political ideologies advocate peace from without, i.e., world peace through economic re-adjustments, equitable distribution of wealth and, ultimately, a classless society. But, can that bring stable and permanent peace unless man's craving impulse remains controlled. Inner reform has to be effected; peace has to be established from "within", viz., in the mind. The right mode of thinking, therefore, is the best method/approach to peace. The principle of non-violence is the basic concept on which the ideal of peace is founded. Non-violence exists only in a mind which is totally free of craving, greed, lust and a sense of superiority (ego) and when wealth is not an end in itself: it is only a means to fulfill social and religious obligations. There is a need for two accumulations *only – Merit & Wisdom.* [14] Another Teacher, Rigdzin Jigme Lingpa, said,

"Wisdom is the self-liberation from grasping and clinging;
In it there is neither thinking nor a thinker,
"It is free from false convictions".

This rich, remarkable socio-ethical aspect of Buddhism, particularly of Tibetan Buddhism, has not been adequately emphasized. The Tibetans believe that in order to practice true Dharma one must, first, seek an authentic spiritual friend – a teacher who has all the necessary qualifications. They believe that Dalai Lama is that "teacher-friend", who is there forever as long as he is kept away from "inordinate negative" influences and feels able to work *for* and *on behalf of* his people and all other sentient beings. The same is the case with the Buddhists on our side of the border, viz., in Tawang and West Kameng districts of Arunachal Pradesh. I perhaps, don't have to remind you all about the fuss China created over Dalai Lama's visit to the monastery at Tawang (this was his entry point to India in 1959) and the great ovation and respect that His Holiness received there; this indomitable spirit of devotion could get generated (even in a tensed political atmosphere, which could have, any moment, turned into violence) because the devout followers of the Dalai Lama and Tibetan Buddhism had for generations imbibed the fundamental essence of the "Words of My Perfect Teacher", along with the teachings of their highest spiritual leader.

The Monpas and Sherdukpens believe (like the Tibetans) that in order to practice true Dharma one must, first, seek an authentic spiritual friend – a teacher, who has all the necessary qualifications. Then, one should obey his instructions, praying to him from the depth of one's heart and considering him the real Buddha. It is only through faith that absolute truth is realized. Unlike the Upanishads or any typical Hindu scripture, Buddhist literature is not that of "Notes" of a "School", but that of sermons, delivered to a number of persons – very often a large concourse. Repetitions are wearisome, but they enable the faithful to memorise and thus, remember better and effectively.[15] Another significant reason why this religion or faith is so humane or people-oriented is that there is no general theory of "revelation" (unlike the Vedas or the Holy Quoran): the Tripitaka or the Jataka are "naturalistic human records. "

I lay no wood, Brahmin, for fires on altars;
Only within burneth the fire I kindle.

The way one listens to Dharma is very important, but even more important is the m*otivation* with which one listens to it. "Unless you practice Dharma according to Dharma, Dharma, itself, becomes the cause of evil. . . rebirth." (Dagpo Rinpoche).

Albert Einstein had, once remarked that Buddhism is a tradition that could fulfill the demands for a spiritual path adapted to the 20th century. Gender equality and genuine love for Nature and the environment in this culture should become a model for the 21st century. We in India, should strive to adopt that. It should not be difficult if we really want to. After all, a few tribes/communities in Northeast India and particularly, in the Northwest of Arunachal Pradesh have done it without perhaps, knowing that these values are very much in our Constitution.

Notes

1. Kunzang Lama I Shelling, *The Words of My Perfect -Teacher,* (translated originally by Patrul Reupoche), New Delhi: Harper Collins, 1996.
2. Ibid.
3. Ibid.
4. Ibid.
5. G.B. Upreti, *Early Buddhist World Outlook in Historical Perspective,* New Delhi: Manohar 1997.
6. Ananda K. Coomaraswamy and I.B. Harner, *The Living Thoughts of Gotama, the Buddha,* London: Gassell and Co., 1948.
7. G.B. Upreti. *op.cit.*
8. Ananda K. Coomaraswamy and I.B. Harner, *The Living Thoughts of Gotama, the Buddha,* London: Gassell and Co., 1948.
9. G.B. Upreti. op.cit.
10. Ananda K. Coomaraswamy and I.B. Harner, op.cit.
11. Kunzang Lama I Shelung, *The Words of My Perfect – Teacher,* (translated originally by Patrol Reupoche), New Delhi: Harper Collins, 1996.
12. Nirmal Chandra Sinha, *Considerations on Inner Asian History,* Calcutta: Firma K.L. Mukhopadhyay, 1967.
13. Kunzang Lama I Shelung, *op.cit.*
14. Nirmal Chandra Sinha, *op.cit.*
15. Bibhash Dhar, *Arunachal Pradesh: the Monpas of Tawang in Transition*, Guwahati: Geophil Publishing House, 2005.

9

Identity, Language and Cultural Transformation

Strategies for Consolidation

Moji Riba

As traditional cultures in Arunachal Pradesh are in transition in the face of development, globalisation, improved communication and the all-pervading media, the state is today at a point where even the very existence of the 'traditional' way of life and associated cultural values are threatening to fade away and God forbid, even die.

While we tackle these 'pressures' confronting fragile traditional indigenous societies, the question that has moved to the forefront of the dialogue on indigenous knowledge systems, is the idea of preservation of culture and the indigenous knowledge that these societies have. Fear has also been expressed about the decay of the native languages and mother tongues, as successive generations are discarding them in favour of languages of opportunity and lifestyles of acceptance. In the process, there is a definite loss of cultural continuity and social cohesion, necessary to maintain a meaningful cultural identity as 'language shift' takes place not over a century or a decade, but in just a few years.

At the core of the threat to knowledge and languages, is the fact that the repository of the traditional language lies with the older generation, whose numbers are fast dwindling. The challenge before us really is of how we can shift this repository to the younger generation. After all, the best way of preservation lies definitely in their continued usage.

No doubt that the documentation and protection of indigenous knowledge and languages *now* threatened, is vital, but it cannot be 'the only' solution. Preservation of this knowledge can at best be one of the many models that need to be concurrently taken up. There can be no one model to do this, but rather each must form parts of a larger process.

Living in the midst of one such society in transition, I am more and more convinced that preservation must now yield space to promotion—and that too specifically in the minds of young people. It is only when warrior tattoos become acceptable, when native language love songs become desirable and going to one's village to visit grandparents becomes fashionable, that indigenous knowledge and languages will survive.

Questions abound. Why are not the young people today interested in the rich tradition and cultural heritage of their ancestors, more so when the elders are lamenting the loss of a life lived, of an ethos forgotten? But then, questions are also asked on why these very young people, responding to a call to go into the future and the 21st century, should even be vaguely bothered about some quaint ritual observed by their forefathers? Counter-questions only add up to make the scenario cacophonic.

To my mind, with the experience of having worked for the last 12 years on documenting, archiving and disseminating this very rich repository of cultural knowledge and values, the 'why?' ceases to be problematic. What intrigues and motivates the mind more is 'how?' How can these youngsters be made to value these rituals, values and wisdom which deeply reflect and represent perhaps the only connect to the sense of a tribal/indigenous identity.

Not surprisingly, the answer lies hidden somewhere in being able to contemporise tradition, and to make it contextual to the changed lives these young people live today; very conspicuously having different motivations and different expectations. The question then becomes: 'How can these quaint rituals be relevant to their lives?'

To address this, we have begun to think of traditional knowledge and cultural heritage more and more as a kind of an elastic band, to stretch it as much into the future as we can through motivating young people to think about it, question it and understand it. It will snap one day; but if we are able to trigger interest in the mind of an 8-year-old today—we have effectively (given current life expectancy figures) ensured the survival of tradition for at least the next 58 years! It may not look a very long time, but if that child in turn is able to stretch the elastic band another 58 years, we see a replicating impact.

But how do we do this? Again, not surprisingly, education appears to hold the key to this challenge. Not only the pedagogic education as we know it, of culture being taught in schools through Central and State Board-prescribed text where chapters are included about festivals and peoples of the nation; but much more so, perhaps through experiential education, where young minds are given opportunities to understand and appreciate their cultural heritage better. But then, what are the tangible, 'do-able' things?

Shared below is a set of ideas, not a prescription for change, but definitely a pointer to what can be done—some already in practice and needing support, some that perhaps can be initiated:

Education-Centred Initiatives

- Promote mother-tongue learning;
- Ensure teaching of mother-tongues in the educational set-up;
- Creating and enable a body of teachers to teach this;
- Documenting, analysing and archiving;
- Creating contextual and participatory models of learning where, through experiencing, watching audio-visuals materials and sharing, children become more aware of their cultural heritage and their place in it;
- Giving space to expression where young people can interpret their heritage in the way they know it and not in the way we want to force them to know it. This can be done through youth festivals, school events and even holiday activity camps;
- Promoting and showcasing young talent that has been able to do this—in music, in art, in theatre, in dance and in writing, by organising performances and events;
- Bringing culture to classrooms by helping teachers themselves to understand cultural heritage better and then using it to expand the purview of classroom teaching into life learning. This is achievable by holding training workshops for teachers on incorporating cultural content in the teaching-learning process as value addition to the curricula;
- Give impetus for sharing resources, experiences and abilities across geographical and indigenous regions so that 'preservation' and promotion becomes everybody's concern. Networking, exposure visits and knowledge-sharing hold out promise to achieve this;

- Create, through youth-targeted competitions and challenges, avenues where young minds are provoked to take folk forms and idioms and create from them something contemporary that they will understand and appreciate;
- Create processes and systems where key stakeholders—in this case parents—tribe elders and culture-based organisations, are given avenues to contribute for instance, by creating school committees on indigenous knowledge and languages with them as partners and also engaging them in the teaching of mother-tongues.

Community-Centred Initiatives

Recognise that whenever a language disappears, that community starts to disperse and the habitat and socio-economic system that once supported a vibrant indigenous culture, disintegrates. For this, accept that strategies to save languages and cultures from threat are, in fact, the same actions that are needed to save biodiversity and promote cultural and ecological sustainability.

Encourage communities to know their indigenous cultural knowledge in the context of the world around them and create an appreciation of this, rather than 'rush' into everything modern. A market for this already exists—organically grown food, handicrafts, biodiversity conservation and traditional medicines. Only efforts need to be made to 're-popularise' them and make them accept it as a knowledge system at par with formal knowledge.

Empower cultural groups to use local resources in sustainable ways, to interact with global ideas using a repertoire of languages if needed, and to understand linguistic diversity as part of a larger system.

Strengthen traditional institutions and councils empowering them to engage with present-day state machineries like the NREGA and Panchayati Raj.

Create community-driven participatory documentation models where the communities themselves become both the documentarian and the repository of the knowledge. This can be achieved by training them in basic audio-visual documentation techniques. Local school and college students can also be engaged in the process.

10

Post-colonial Indian State and Indigenous Knowledge Systems in Arunachal Pradesh

A Case Study of the Built Environment

Jagdish Lal Dawar

Built environment is a loosely defined concept which includes most aspects of the physical environment and especially the spheres of building, architecture and planning. The long association of the people of Arunachal Pradesh to their natural surroundings had given them an understanding of the value and use of the various natural resources. Important social and religious elements in their life were reflected in their domestic buildings and usually symbolically expressed in their design and decoration. Their construction technology and household materials took care of the predominant physical features of land including the seismic factor. The rituals performed during different stages of construction, the seasons of collecting materials, direction of house, etc., were significant from the point of the maintenance of the ecosystem. However, after independence, changes started taking place in the building environment as a result of intrusion of the state, market and education. This article is an attempt to understand the nature of this change.

Nationalist Discourse of Modernity

The Nehruvian elite had 'succeeded in establishing its pre-eminence in national politics' soon after independence and defined the terms of national discourse for independent India.[1] The 'national integration' was an important aspect of this discourse. In order to achieve this goal the 'Nehruvian modernizing elite' had set the agenda of secularism, welfare and development. However, this agenda was sought to be performed through the agency of the State.[2] However, for the Statist model of modernization, Nehru 'relied on the bureaucracy as the central state agency for modernizing India.'[3]

In the context of NEFA, the exponents of the nationalist discourse were: Sir Akbar Hydari and Jairamdas Daulatram (both of whom were governors of Assam), Jawaharlal Nehru, and Verrier Elwin, the adviser, Tribal Affairs to the Governor of Assam. However, Elwin played the key role since 1953 and largely molded the Government's policy towards NEFA. The policy pursued during this period is generally known as Nehru-Elwin policy. The essence of this policy was 'integration' by means of exercising cultural hegemony.[4]

One of the most prominent strategies adopted for exercising cultural hegemony was through 'appropriation' of tribal cultural practices. The development of the tribes along the lines of their 'tradition and genius' formed part of this appropriation. It was aimed at creating a sense of legitimacy. By 'appropriation of culture' in this context, I mean the bureaucracy, as the State agency becomes the custodian of tribal cultural traditions.[5] This discourse of protectionism is summed up in the words of Verrier Elwin:

> "Our policy is to develop the tribes along the lines of their own tradition and genius. The whole stress of NEFA policy is on change. We are all aware that very great changes, which we hope will be enriching rather than impoverishing, will come, not as an imposed break with the past, but by a natural evolution from it... There should be no forcible imposition of another culture and... the old culture should be helped to grow and develop into the new one".[6]

The protection of indigenous knowledge systems was part of this agenda of exercising cultural hegemony. 'Local knowledge' was perceived to be significant from the conservation and sustainable development perspective. The protection of 'Built environment' formed an important agenda of this policy.

The Post-Colonial State and the Built Environment

The officials decided to follow the indigenous architectural designs in the construction of public buildings (Government buildings, schools, hospitals, museums, etc.) It was accepted in principle that buildings should "grow out of the landscape."[7] As the Prime Minister himself pointed out, "a building has to fit in with the surroundings and with the purpose in view."[8] The use of "brick and mortar" in buildings was cautioned against because firstly, it was costlier and secondly these "do not fit in at all with their surroundings."[9] Moreover, it was believed that the cement houses and CIG roofs in villages would "create a gulf" between 'officers' "and the people."[10]

Before utilising the traditional architectural designs it was kept in mind that the pattern was not to be uniform throughout NEFA. Since this region constitutes heterogeneous cultures it was suggested that the designs were to be adapted taking into consideration the specificity of the cultural traditions of the tribe concerned. For example, at Tezu it was decided to "use some Khamti temple design for the roof."[11] In the Siang district it was suggested that buildings be constructed along the lines of the *dere, moshup* or *bango*: "Long buildings with hearths down the centre, raised on platforms, with a sitting platform at each end, and a small veranda all around."[12]

In the senior officers conference held in 1954 it was recommended: "The architecture of the Educational Institutions should be adapted to the local pattern and some representation of the structural art of the local people should be made to fuse with the construction plan of our buildings, particularly, the school buildings".[13] It was suggested by Elwin that in "all school buildings" and also in all other official buildings, "the floor will be raised off the ground and will be made of bamboo in a style designed by official architects."[14]

Another important feature of 'indigenous' architectural design proposed to be appropriated in the official buildings was the 'sitting platform'. It was believed to enable "the people to sit and warm themselves in the sun."[15] If constructed in front of Political Officers' and Assistant Political Officers' bungalows, it was imagined to serve the practical purpose: "The tribal visitors would be quite happy to sit smoking or talking on it while waiting for an interview."[16] In addition to the official building 'The sitting Platform' was considered crucial for schools, hostels or staging-huts.[17]

The officials were apprehensive that the alien system of modern education might make the students misfits in their community and therefore it was important to create a familiar physical environment in their hostels: "Students, whether in our schools or CITPC's, who live in hostels that are totally different from their own, will be less likely to return to their villages and may well become misfit in them".[18]

Therefore, in order to create the same environment as in their homes, it was suggested that central hearths be created in the school buildings, especially in the hostels as they are accustomed to such type of fire-places.[19] This was believed to create a homely feeling among the boys and they "would be healthier"[20] It was tried in some of the inter-village schools.

The Improvement of the Existing Architectural Designs

However, it was found that many of the tribal architectural adaptations which were utilized in *Bash type* buildings were not suitable in H.T. type buildings. Thus in a note dated May 18, 1960 it is indicated: "If we are going to have chairs, tables and beds in a room there is not much point in having the central hearth which does not fit in very well with the furniture".[21] The note further clarifies how it was not possible from practical point of view: "The buildings designed on the general plan of a Mishmi house do not work out very successfully in a HT building. The Mishmi house, with its low roof and six or eight small rooms, opening out of a corridor, is a very different thing from a building containing two rooms and a small veranda which is shut in by a low or high wall which does not come up to the roof."[22] Hence, the corridor was dropped from the plan. Therefore, a process of rejection, selection, and modification of the forms was involved to suit the altered conditions. Here the question of hygiene was given the utmost importance: "The tribal houses themselves require some modifications because they do have a number of un-hygienic disadvantages which in the interest of health must be removed. We, therefore, must give attention to housing and here again evolve designs which would certainly retain the existing attractive features of the tribal houses but also suitably modify them to ensure that the layout lends itself to health."[23]

The concern with modern conceptions of hygiene seems to be responsible for rejecting a few other elements too: "The sitting platforms attached to schools and other buildings are most important, but the walls or railings surrounding them are not popular. In Tezu the boys hardly use the sitting platform and use walls or railings to hang up their linen to dry".[24] Therefore, it was suggested that any idea of surrounding these sitting platforms with walls or railings be given up. In fact, the people were persuaded to "recondition their houses under hygienic conditions."[25] The officials' emphasis on the question of sanitation and health speaks of the language of modernist nationalists.[26]

The officials emphasized the importance of the concept of 'self-help'. It was believed that "a school building constructed by the villagers and maintained by them as their own", would make "the people proud of their institution".[27] Consequently, it would "wipe out the wrong impression" that "Administration is forcing education on the people."[28] However, it was also realized at the same time that: "There is a tendency among the tribal people when asked to put up buildings on self-help basis to make them of very inferior specification with badly woven tarza walls, thin layers of thatching and on kutcha ground".[29] The officials' attitude to buildings constructed by the tribals on self-help basis evokes, at least, implicitly the image of modernity confronting a backward, static, and traditional society. This is implied in the following passage: "The general quality of the buildings in the interior is deplorable and there must be a fantastic waste of public money in erecting at the cost of thousands of rupees these miserable hovels in which our men are condemned to live. Where their building is entrusted to the tribal people, they are often put up in the course of a single day and it can readily by understood that if a contract of Rs. 1,000/- or Rs. 1,500/- rupees is completed in eight hours it will not be very sound. Moreover, the tribal people are having (sic) to build in a style they do not understand and accordingly do it badly"[30]. It was, therefore, felt that if a teacher had to be provided in a village the definite specifications as laid down by the official experts were to be adhered to by the tribal people while carrying out the work on self-help.[31] The political officers and their staff were directed "to convince the villagers by intensive effort, of the psychological advantage of this new arrangement."[32]

The improvement of the existing architectural designs was the hallmark of the policy. For this, certain models of 'attractive houses' incorporating various tribal elements were designed by the architects.[33] In fact, improvement is the general policy in all aspects of the tribal economy and society. There was emphasis on the improvement of taste of the natives as regards beauty of form and finish in the articles of daily use among them. Their aesthetic judgment was of course wholly derived from Indian and European concepts of beauty. Architectural designs formed part of this larger discourse of improvement, betterment or in other words, of overall developmental process. The categories of 'improvement', 'progress', 'inspiration', 'inducement' formed the leitmotif of their writings. These words mean more than their literal meaning. It reveals attitudinal biases which were shaped by the 'modernization' model.

Thus Verrier Elwin felt that "the tribal people themselves should be made to improve their houses under the guidance of NEFA officers."[34] The remarks made by the Development Commissioner, NEFA, Shillong, Colonel P.N. Luthra, as far back as March 1, 1957 are very revealing. He suggested: "We make some posters illustrating how houses can be improved. For example, we could show somebody falling through a bamboo floor and side by side a nice plank floor with the housewife cleaning it with a broom. We could similarly show the interior of a house pitch-dark with children rubbing their eyes as result of the smoke and everyone looking very dirty and beside it in another interior showing a house with food windows and a chimney with everybody clean and bright-eyed children and so on. I suggest that this might be more effective method of achieving what we want".[35] A note in Elwin's paper states: "It is important that when NEFA people erect Basha type buildings on a self-help basis and of course always when they work on contract they should be induced to follow not what they have come to imagine to be appropriate for an official building, but the new specifications that we are now making".[36] Therefore, it was decided to train the tribals in the line of new specifications.[37] It was suggested to give "great importance to improve the technique of thatching throughout NEFA" and "every attempt" was "made to induce the people to improve the roofs"[38] It was also recommended to create the double roof system.[39] In case of use of CIG sheets, it was advised to paint these in "a suitable green or dark red colour."[40] Because paint "preserves the sheet" and "adds enormously to the aesthetic appearance of administrative centers."[41] In case the people buy CIG sheets at their own expense, "it might be made a rule that these should not be permitted unless they undertake to paint their roofs."[42]

The adviser to the Governor put forward a point that "knowledge and experience gained in experimentation of new ideas must be utilized" in effecting changes in the construction of tribal houses by providing a double roof, additional ventilation, separation of latrine blocks by passages, etc." for future developments.[43] In fact, hegemony was also exercised in creating the model villages. Thus, it was discussed at length that the CITPC (Cottage Industries Training cum Production Centre) might be planned as a model village.[44] The local style would be incorporated in these model villages but "the whole settlement would be planned in such a way that it would inspire not only the trainees but all tribal visitors with ideas about planning and building their own villages."[45] For instance, in a note dated July 23, 1958 it is stated: "The whole point of this is that the CITPC should be a model village and that the buildings should not be of the ordinary OB type put up by our own tribal contractors but that they should be real model tribal houses which would be an inspiration to the local people and to the trainees themselves."[46]

Forces of Change

While conceiving themselves as participants in the ongoing traditions of tribal architecture, the policymakers made an effort to hegemonise those traditions with the values of modernity and thus created a space for national integration. The overall policy was beset with contradictions. On the one hand, it was advocated that the indigenous knowledge system be 'protected', while on the other hand, the changes as a result of 'imposition' of modernity from 'above' brought about the gradual erosion of the traditional knowledge system. This process was accentuated after the Indian debacle in Sino-Indian border conflict in 1962, and the demise of Nehru and Elwin in 1964. The exercise of cultural hegemony now took a different direction. Less attention was paid to the 'appropriation' of tribal culture and more to exercising 'mainstream' cultural hegemony.

Gradually, the Nehru-Elwin policy of protection of indigenous knowledge systems started getting diluted as a result of rapid development activities and the intensification of the process of integration of the tribes of Arunachal Pradesh with 'mainstream' Indian culture. Consequently, there was a process of change in the manners, morals and tastes of the people. There were many forces responsible for generating this change and for creating a social base for change in the attitude to indigenous knowledge systems. To mention a few such forces: (a) Institutional changes in agriculture; (b) various changes in traditional occupations; (c) the developing urbanization; (d) the migration, internal as well as from outside the state;[47] (e) Gradual abandonment of the so-called Nehru-Elwin policy; (f) super-imposition of the 'mainstream' political structure over traditional autonomous socio-political institutions, thereby bringing about a series of changes in tribal polity.[48]

It is worthwhile to discuss in brief the two forces which brought about change in the manners, morals and tastes of the people of Arunachal Pradesh thereby affecting their attitude to the indigenous knowledge systems. These are: (a) Modern Education and (b) Hindi Cinema.

Modern Education: Modern education seems to be one of the major actors for bringing about change in attitude towards indigenous knowledge systems. Investigating the process of change in agriculture in the three districts of Arunachal Pradesh—West Siang, Lower Subansiri and Papumpare, N.C. Roy and P.K. Kuri argue that it was the centrality of education, which was the major actor in bringing about a series of changes in agriculture.[49] In fact, it is education which seems to have brought about the change in attitude towards indigenous knowledge systems among the first generation of educated persons of Arunachal Pradesh. Thus, Oshong Ering, who had been pursuing his education in Shillong and belonged to the first generation of literates of society, expressed his disagreement and dissatisfaction over Elwin's proposal to construct hearths (fire-places) in inter-village schools.[50] He wrote this letter after his visit to the inter-village school in Sile in Pasighat division. He was shocked to see some hearths inside the hostel building of the institution. He protested against this decision on the grounds of: (a) Discipline, (b) Hygiene, and (c) Tribal traditional practice. According to him, the construction of hearths violated all the above-mentioned norms.[51] Oshong Ering argued that it was a new element. "So far we know hearths have not been constructed in Pasighat and in High Schools. If small boys and girls can study in these high schools without having hearths, why will boys and girls in inter-village school not be able do the same.[52] These grounds reveal how the elites had been hegemonised by means of education. What the letter speaks is the language of modernity, of civic consciousness, of health. It speaks of certain ideas of beauty, an order of aesthetics from which the ideals of public health and hygiene cannot be separated.[53] It is also the language of a modernist nationalist. It speaks of liberal democratic construction of reality and it may also be the product of a particular kind of domination.[54] Even among the illiterate persons I perceived a change of tastes as a result of the impact of 'second Orality'[55], that is, Hindi cinema.

Therefore, it is worthwhile to discuss in brief the impact of Hindi films in Arunachal Pradesh.[56]

Hindi Cinema: Hindi cinema was introduced by the officials of the state during the 1950s, '60s and '70s. Thus, films gained popularity among the tribes of Arunachal Pradesh and the NEFA officials started publicizing it.[57] However, it was the percolation of video technology which really popularized Hindi cinema.[58] VCRs started to 'percolate rapidly after the Asian Games in 1982, when Doordarshan's broadcasting went colour, and when the Indian government liberalized import duties on TV sets. [59] In Arunachal Pradesh, video cinema was introduced in 1983. Since then, it became very popular and the Directorate of Information and Publicity, Government of Arunachal Pradesh has issued large number of video licenses. Thus, the figure up to May 21, 1996 was 717 [seven hundred and seventeen].[60] I conducted interviews of a cross-section of viewers of different age groups, gender, social, educational and economic backgrounds. An analysis of these interviews has brought out an important fact to me that Hindi cinema has played an important part in exercising nationalist hegemony in terms of law, language and taste among the people of Arunachal Pradesh.[61] The central thrust of entertainment is 'utopianism', that is, it projects imaginary solutions to real problems as the only available ones. As Richard Dyer points out: "Entertainment offers the image of 'something better' to escape into, or something we want deeply that our day-to-day lives do not provide. Alternatives, hopes, wishes—these are stuff of utopia, the sense that things could be better, that something other than what can be imagined and may be realized."[62] Sudhir Kakar, eminent psychoanalyst approaches Hindi cinema as a 'collective fantasy, a group daydream'. [63] Hindi films emphasize 'the central features of fantasy'; the fulfillment of wishes.[64] Sudhir Kakar does not use 'fantasy' in the ordinary sense of the word, 'with its popular connotation of whimsy, eccentricity or triviality',[65] but as another name for that 'world of imagination which is fuelled by desire'.[66] Fantasy, 'the stuff that dreams are made of' is the bridge between desire and reality; 'spanning the chasm between what is asked for and what is granted' and well 'deserves the paean' in its praise as 'the vehicle of hope, healer of trauma, protector from reality, concealer of truth, fixer of identity, restorer of tranquility, enemy of fear and sadness, cleanser of the soul'[67] The creation of utopia among the filmgoers is evident in the way two of our respondents replied to the question, 'what constitutes a good film'. Or 'what type of films do you like most'? A good film is one which represents stupendous efforts of a person to achieve 'greatness.' By 'greatness', he meant a rich person who saves a lot of money and constructs a big house.[68] A desire to own big houses similar to the ones represented in Hindi films was expressed by another respondent also. [69] These are real needs created by capitalist society. That is, while entertainment 'is responding to needs that are real, at the same time, it is also defining and delimiting what constitutes the legitimate needs of people in this society.[70] It is apparent from the above account how Hindi films created a desire among my respondents to be opulent as represented in Hindi films. It reveals the changing attitude of the people to the indigenous knowledge system including the building environment.

Summing Up

To sum up, while conceiving themselves as participants in the ongoing traditions of tribal architecture, the policymakers made an effort to hegemonise those traditions with the values of modernity thus creating a space for national integration. The overall policy was beset with contradictions. On the one hand, it was advoçated to 'protect' the indigeneous knowledge system and on the other, the resultant changes as a result of 'imposition' of modernity from 'above' brought about the gradual erosion of the traditional knowledge system.The exercise of cultural hegemony. This led to the influx of 'alien' cultural practices, thereby leading to the erosion of indigenous knowledge systems which in turn led to environmental degradation.

Note: This is a revised version of the Paper presented in the conference on "Local Livelihoods and Global Challenges: Understanding Human Interaction with the Environment," Copenhagen, Denmark, August 4-8, 2009, as part of the first World Congress of Environmental History, 2009.

Notes

1 D.L. Sheth, "The Great Language Debate: Politics of Metropolitan versus Vernacular India" in Upendra Baxi and Bhikhu Parekh, (Eds.) *Crisis and change in Contemporary India,* Sage, New Delhi, 1995, p. 192.

2. D.L. Sheth, "Movements, Intellectuals and the State: Social Policy in Nation-building", *Economic and Political Weekly*, Feb. 22, 1992, p. 428; also see D.L. Sheth, "State, Nation and Ethnicity: Experience of Third World Countries", *Economic and Political Weekly*, March 25, 1989, pp. 619-626.

3. Bhikhu Parekh, "Jawaharlal Nehru and the crisis of Modernization" in Upendra Baxi and Bhikhu Parekh, (eds.) *Crisis and change in Contemporary India,* no. 1, p. 22.

4. I am influenced Gramsci's concept of hegemony. See Antonio Gramsci, Selections From the Prison Note Books, (Ed. and trans.) Quentin Hoare and Geoffrey Nowell Smith (New York, 1971), pp. 12-13, 53, 55-60, 238-39, 261-64; also see Antonio Gramsci, *Selections From Cultural Writings*, ed. David Forgas and Geoffrey Nowell Smith, (trans.) William Boel Hower (Massachusetts, 1985), pp. 164-65, 172-73, 220-21, 342-43.

5. For the concept 'culture as appropriation' see Roger Chartier, 'culture as appropriation: Popular cultural uses in Early Modern France' in Steven L. Kaplan, (ed.) *Understanding Popular Culture*, Mouton Publishers, Berline, 1984, pp. 229-253.

6. Elwin papers, File No. ATA/G/55, Secret, serialized (listed) as File No. 96, p. 2. The manuscript section of the Nehru Memorial Centre for Contemporary Studies, Teen Murti, New Delhi; also Nehru's Note on His Tour of the North-East Frontier Areas in October, 1952, p. 5. (Emphasis added).

7. Elwin Papers, File No. ATA/G/42, p. 18.

8. Prime Minister of India to the Chief Minister of Assam, copy of letter No. 496-PMO/59 dated 1stAugust, 1959, in Elwin Papers, File No. ATA/G/42 serialized as File No. 73, p. 14.

9. Copy of the Prime Minister's Note dated 25-5-55 in Elwin Papers, File No. ATA/G/42 serialized as File No. 73 p. 16.

10. Elwin Papers, File No. ATA/G/42 serialized as File No. 73 p. 19.

11. Elwin Papers, File No. ATA/G/4, p. 94.

12. Ibid. p. 31.

13. P.N. Luthra to Superintendent Engineer, NEFA, Letter No. Ed. 12/54/47, 12th July 1955 in Elwin Papers, Ibid. p. 2.

14. Note dated 15.3.58, File No. ATA/G/4, p. 33.

15. Ibid. p. 19.

16. Ibid.
17. Ibid.
18. Ibid. p. 26.
19. Superintendent Engineer's note dated 30-6-60 to Elwin, in Elwin Papers, File No. ATA/G/4, p. 96.
20. Ibid. p. 31.
21. Ibid., p. 91.
22. Ibid.
23. P.N. Luthra's comments dated 19.7.55 on the various paragraphs of the note by ATA. File No. ATA/G/4, p. 2. Emphasis mine.
24. File No. Ibid. p. 91.
25. Ibid. p. 50.
26. See Paul Rainbow, French Modern: Norms and Forms of the Social Environment, Cambridge, Mass,1989, pp. 33-34; also see Peter Stallybrass and Allon White, The Politics and Poetics of Transgression, London, 1986. Both these reference have been cited by Dipesh Chakravarty, 'Of Garbage, modernity and the Citizen's Gaze', *Economics and Political Weekly,* March 7-14, 1992, p. 542.
27. Minutes of the Meeting held in A.G's (Adviser to Governor) Room on the 22nd April 1960 in Elwin Papers, File No. ATA/G/4 p. 89.
28. Ibid.
29. Ibid. p. 29.
30. File No. Ibid. p. 19.
31. Ibid.
32. Ibid.
33. Ibid, *pp. 26-27.*
34. See minutes of the Meeting Held in A.G'S Room on the 22nd April 1960, op. cit., p. 90.
35. File No. ATA/G/4.
36. Ibid. p. 29. Emphasis added by me.
37. In the Elwin Papers I came across a note titled 'Architecture in Tirap' but it has not been signed anyone. The date on this noting is not indicated. But it must be before 15th May 1958, because the note in question is paginated as No. 19 while a letter p. 32 of this file is dated 15th May, 1958. In this note (p. 19) the writer is shocked to find "the deplorable" quality of the buildings in the interior areas. He seems to be doubtful whether the tribals would be able to construct buildings meant for the use of others, *unless they are trained.* (Emphasis mine).
38. Elwin papers, File No. ATA/G/4, p. 28.
39. Elwin's note dated 4-5-60, File No. ATA/G/42, p. 53.
40. File No. ATA/G/4, p. 28.
41. File No. ATA/G/42, p. 53.

42. File No. ATA/G/4, p. 28.
43. Minutes of the meeting held in A.G's room on the 22nd April, 1960, File No. ATA/G/4. p. 90.
44. File No. Ibid. p. 56.
45. Ibid.
46. Ibid. (23-7-58).
47. For a detailed empirical work on the process of migration in Arunchal Pradesh see A. Mitra, *Internal Migration and Economic Development in the Hills,* Omson Publisher, New Delhi, 1997, pp. 50-73.
48. See Atul Chandra Talukdar, *Political Transition in the Grassroots in Tribal India*, Delhi, 1987, pp. 91-159.
49. N.C. Roy and P.K. Kuri, *A Study of Land Reform in Arunachal Pradesh,* Report of the Project Sponsored by ICSSR, New Delhi, 1997, pp. 160-61.
50. Letter No. Do-1/60-61/dated 29th September, 1960, Elwin papers, File No. ATA/Cor/19, listed as File No. 39, p. 26.
51. Ibid.
52. Ibid.
53. See Dipesh Chakravarty, *op. cit.* also Paul Rabinow, *French Modern: Norms and Forms of the Social Environment.* Cambridge, Mass, 1989, pp. 30-34; Peter Stallybrass and Allon White, *The Politics and Poetics of Transgression,* London, 1986.
54. See Douglas E. Hayes, *Rhetoric and Ritual in Colonial India,* The Shaping of Public Culture in Surat City, 1852-1928, Oxford University Press, 1992 p. viii (Preface).
55. The concept 'second Orality' has been Walter J. Ong, *Orality and Literacy: The Technologizing of the Word.* New Accents. (Ed.) Terence Hawkes. (New York: Methuen, 1988).
56. Jagdish Lal Dawar, " Nationalist Discourse and Cultural Hegemony in North East—Arunahcal Pradesh(NEFA) and the Indian Mainstream since 1950s" in Tamo Mibang and M.C. Behera, (eds.) *Tribal Studies-Emerging Frontiers of Knowledge,* Mittal Publications, New Delhi, 2007 pp. 51-74.
57. See Tour diary of Shri T. Haralu, dated 26-11-54, in File No. RTD/8/55 [code 5/55] p. 7 in Arunachal Pradesh State Archives, Itanagar; Tour diary of Shri T. Haralu, dated 30-11-54, [Daporijo], Ibid., pp. 13.17; *The NEFA News letter*, in Broadcast on 2nd October,1960 in Elwin Papers, p. 2/45, para 6; *Arunachal News*, December, 1980, Vol. 9, p. 13.
58. See Jagdish Lal Dawar, 'Nationalist Hegemony and popular culture in Arunachal Pradesh: A case study of responses to Video-Cinema in Doimukh circle of Papum pare district', *Proceedings of North East India History Association,* 1998, pp. 291-302.

59. Arvind Singhal and Everett M. Rogers, *India's Information Revolution*, Sage, New Delhi, 1989, p. 85.
60. See Jagdish Lal Dawar, no. 58, pp. 291-302.
61. Ibid.
62. Richard Dyer, 'Entertainment and Utopia' in Simon During, (Ed.) *The Cultural Studies Reader*, Routledge, London, 1993, p. 273.
63. Sudhir Kakar 'The Cinema As Collective Fantasy' in Aruna Vasudev and Philippe Lenglet, (eds.), *Indian Cinema Superbazaar,* Vikas Publishing House Pvt. Ltd, New Delhi,1983, p. 89.
64. Ibid., p. 89.
65. Ibid., p. 90.
66. Ibid., p. 90.
67. Ibid., p. 91.
68. Interview with Tana Tei, Emchi village, Doimukh, Pappum Pare District, February, 27, 1998.
69. Interview with Tana Achi, Ibid.
70. Richard Dyer, no. 62, p. 278.

11

Development and Cultural Change

Dilemma of Arunachal Pradesh

Mrinal Kanti Chakma

Change is inevitable for every society. Contextually speaking, change is meaningful only when it is construed with a reference point in time. Thus, societal change of any kind needs to be examined in the context of a definite time-frame. Renowned anthropologist Christoph von Furer-Haimendorf, had considered the time-frame of thirty-five years for his study by revisiting the tribal community of Arunachal Pradesh in 1978. He found a significant shift in the society of Arunachal Pradesh from a rudimentary way of living to a high degree of sophistication, which he could have never imagined. For obvious reasons, he had appreciated the policy of the Government of India to protect and preserve followed in this region during that period of time. He extended significant credits to one such protective policy—the imposition of the inner line pass, to restrict the movement and inflow of people from outside. His appreciation went deeper when he compared the changes of some other tribal communities in other parts of India, particularly Andhra Pradesh, where he also carried out his studies almost in a similar timeline.[1]

Another recent study conducted by Wade P. Shepard, a scholar of Long Island University, credited the development strategy undertaken by the Government of India. Objectively, his study focused on the comparative development strategy followed by the Chinese Government in Tibet and the Indian Government in Arunachal Pradesh. He found a remarkable contrast in terms of approach and design of developmental plans in a geographically contiguous area with a population of the same stock of people and similar stage of development, but separated by an international border commonly known as the McMahon Line. In his critical assertion he commented that the protective initiatives that the Indian Government had shown towards the tribal population of Arunachal Pradesh is a far more peaceful, sustainable and productive mode of development than the militaristically, economically, and culturally coercive methods of China in Tibet.[2]

Whatever may be the good words said in support of the development strategy followed in Arunachal Pradesh by the policymakers of the country, a fresh and close inspection on the contributing variables of changes, and the matrices of loss and gain is essential to understand the true dynamics of our state-driven development strategy in this region. Such analyses of loss and gain are not an easy area to quantify and assess and much of its qualitative parameters need a different prism. Nonetheless, it is important to look into the dynamics of veritable social changes along a time-frame and to assess the true nature of their cause and effect.

At this transitional phase, a pertinent question that arises is, to what extent are the tribal people of Arunachal Pradesh able to retain their distinct cultural identity at the cost of so-called development that they have achieved. Is it essential or desirable to retain such various identity markers of their own culture in their original form? What is the course of direction that is emanating from continued and intensified influence from outside as the state policy has now taken a neo-liberal turn and getting ready for globalisation in the days ahead? Before making any attempt to find the answers, I believe a brief mention of the development policy adopted during the post-independent period and the dynamic of socio-economic and cultural changes in Arunachal Pradesh would not be out of place here.

Dynamics of Policy Change

For any society that comes into contact with a foreign or outside culture the spread of new ideas, beliefs, and techniques is inevitable. In this process of socio-cultural fusion there arises the dichotomy of an introducing society which is seen as dominant and a receiving society which is viewed as a subordinate one. In the context of the traditional communities of Arunachal Pradesh one can easily classify the whole initiative of the 'development' and 'modernisation plan' of the Government of India through its various agencies and administrative setups as introducer and the traditional communities as the receivers of this grand design. Prior to the initiation of this development process the prevailing conditions of the communities in Arunachal Pradesh were characterized by subsistence agriculture, a hierarchical social structure, and very low vertical as well as horizontal social mobility. The whole development process was undoubtedly a top-down one as underdevelopment of this region was considered a result of a large number of endogenous factors such as primitive mode of cultivation, lack of human skills with high degree of technological deficit, almost complete illiteracy rate and underdeveloped state of socio-political and institutional development. Hence, with such justification from the Government of India, the drive towards socio-cultural modernisation began to take shape in Arunachal Pradesh after independence. The first one-and-a-half decades of India's policy towards this region was marked by some hesitant but conscious steps which came to be known as the "Nehru-Elwin policy" as named after the framers of the same. The policy was evidently marked with gradual administrative expansion and the revivalist-protectionist approach towards tribal development in the hill areas. The major challenge faced by Verrier Elwin was: "It was not the question of reviving anything, it is more a problem of introducing change without being destructive of the best values of old life"[3]. In the subsequent years the Government of India's anthropological approach of tribal development for this area is viewed as "a phenomenally diverse mosaic of cultures which have to be preserved and enriched"[4]. But to what extent are we able to preserve and enrich the same? Before making an effort to find this answer, at this point I prefer to mention a few important policy shifts that were brought about after the Chinese aggression of 1962. The Nehru-Elwin policy which was followed during the first 15 years since independence came under sharp criticism after the setback of the Indo-China war. Thus, in the subsequent period, the earlier revivalist-protectionist approach that was dominated by an isolationist insinuation that drives a wedge between the tribals and non-tribals as well as hills and plains, was abandoned. In the post-1962 period, the political and economic policy of this region was found to be dominated by deeper administrative penetration guided by the security-centric approach. Although in the subsequent years there was remarkable expansion in the political and administrative setup in this region, it was not accompanied with the corresponding level of economic development. Of course, in the neo-liberal phase of recent times, development programmes fed with massive investment and excessive reliance on technology have been sought as a panacea of all the problems from underdevelopment to competing identity struggles of this region. Analyzing the impacts or changes resulting from implementation of a wide range of policies and programmes carried out in this region for more than 50 years is neither the intention of nor possible in this brief article. Instead, a humble effort has been made in the subsequent sections to highlight a few important developmental interventions carried out by the Government of India after independence that left a deeper impact in the life and society of this region.

Education Policy and its Impact

The first important step undertaken by the state as an 'introducer' was imparting education. During the beginning of the 20th century, Arunachal had no schools at all. The first primary school was established in 1918, at Pasighat, and the second in 1922, at Dambuk, during the British period. Most people in Arunachal Pradesh were not familiar with the written word until recently; many did not have a script of their own. The exceptions were the Buddhist tribes of the Kameng region in the west and the Lower Lohit Valley in the east. The Buddhist monasteries of the former provided religious instruction in the Bothi script and the Khamptis, belonging to the later groups, brought with them the tradition of reading and writing in the Tai-Khampti language from present-day Myanmar. As late as 1981, the literacy rate in Arunachal Pradesh was 25.55 per cent. One has to admit that this education programme is a successful one as Arunachal Pradesh can now boast of a literacy rate of 61.67 per cent (2001 Census), which a rise from almost illiteracy in just a couple of generations.[5] Presently, the medium of instruction in Arunachal Pradesh is English. However, as revealed by one of the academics in this region during my field study trip that, "on paper we find English as the language of instruction but in reality Hindi is the *de facto* language of instruction". The arguments behind opting for English and Hindi as mediums of instruction in education were that none of the major languages used by more than thirty varied linguistic groups in Arunachal Pradesh constitute more than 50 per cent of its population and none of them is found to be developed enough to carry the load of modern education. Of course, the cultural impacts of such state-introduced modern education in this region are too vast. Despite the fact of linguistic rights are protected both under the Indian Constitution (Article 29 (1) and Article 350-A) and by UN legislation including among others, Article 27 of International Covenant on Civil and

Political Rights (ICCPR) and International Labour Organization (ILO) Convention 107 (3), a large number of languages of this region are disappearing very fast. As a case in point, Apatani language, one of the major languages spoken in Arunachal Pradesh is listed as a "definitely endangered" language in the e-atlas of UNESCO with an interpretation that children no longer learn this language as their mother-tongue at home. This clearly suggests that language attrition has already paved its way into the life and society of Arunachal Pradesh. The most dangerous turn is perhaps, a high degree of co-relation between higher literacy rate and the list of endangered languages in the state. As noted in one report:

> "For instance, the Deori tribe has the highest literacy rate in the State (76.9 per cent) and their language, also known as Deori has been listed as 'definitely endangered'. This trend is true for 6 of the 10 tribal communities listed in the 2001 Census. So it could be that schooling is actually leading to language loss among tribal communities as more people aspire to learn Hindi or English in schools."[6]

It is also evident that education being a concurrent subject—meaning a joint domain of both the state governments and the Union Territories of India as well as the Central Government, the debate remains alive on the point of 'active and voluntary choice' versus 'imposition from Delhi' on the matter of the functional policy associated with a vital subject like medium of instruction that has a deeper underpinning on the identity aspect of its population. So far, the state government has officially a taken decision to teach nine tribal languages in school but barring a few such Monpa, Khampti, Mishmi and Singpho, others do not have books, no teacher and no fund for the same. Sachdeva, an academic associated with Central Institute of Indian Languages (CIIL) shares his own experience of promoting local languages in Arunachal Pradesh as: "There was a lot of enthusiasm to emphasise the importance of one's mother-tongue but somehow it was sidelined by the government's desire to integrate Arunachal Pradesh with the rest of India"[7]. Whatever could be the reason—active and voluntary choice or the impact of a well intended policy, the ground reality is that a good number of languages in this state are subjected to 'linguistic suicide'. Such prognosis clearly gives us a signal that the future of many endangered languages of this region is very grim. This further leads us to the fundamental question: What do we really lose or gain when people give up speaking one language and pick up a new one? Believers of cultural assimilation or homogenization may gain some pleasure by accepting it as direct approval of the Darwin manifesto of 'survival of the fittest', but for them, there is a word of caution. As pointed out by noted biologists like E.O. Wilson, each language death represents a significant erosion of human knowledge about, for example, local plant and animal life. He has argued that 'while modern science has been able to as yet classify only 20 per cent of the world's plant and animal life; much of the remaining 80 per cent is known, he believes, in the taxonomies of individual languages'.[8] In case of the indigenous tribal communities of Arunachal Pradesh who have been living so close to Nature in the Himalayan foothill region for so many centuries, this cannot be truer than the belief of E.O. Wilson.

Impacts of Change in Agricultural Production Technology

The second important step taken was change in production technology in the field of agriculture. With the economic modernisation drive, the region's shifting *Jhum* cultivators turned out to be on the forefront of the chopping block, as there have been massive efforts on the part of the government to introduce new higher yielding agricultural methods, settled farming and "better" agricultural practices. In the commission report, 'Transforming the Northeast (1995)', S.P Shukla wrote:

Hill farming in the Northeast is largely under *Jhum* though there are some excellent terraces in certain states and expanding patches of wet rice cultivation. *Jhum* farming is becoming less productive with a shrinking *Jhum* cycle and has caused erosion and forest regression in certain areas. Not all Jhumias resettlement schemes have worked well; nor can jhuming be ended all at once. The problem needs to be tackled sensitively as *Jhum* cultivation is also a way of life.[9]

As it is evident from the aforementioned statement in the context of Northeast India, adaptation of the new mode of production is not an easy solution. A synopsis of the tribals' initial reluctance to utilize the new agro-technologies is manifested in the government report that narrates:

Technology has been relegated to the back resulting in stagnation of growth. However, the state has gained much over the years, it is now necessary to consolidate the gains in order to make it sustainable and add new dimension during the coming years, so as to increase household income generation.[10]

The reasons for the technological lag in adaptation in the field of agriculture is understandable as it has a direct bearing on the life pattern of the community, culture, and diversity of traditions of the entire society of this region. So, giving up the traditional *Jhum* cultivation and adapting settled farming does not mean only acquiring a new technology of production (as viewed in pure economic sense) but for traditional society, changing of the whole way of life. It is in one way giving up the century-old accumulated knowledge that helped traditional society to survive for generations maintaining a symbiotic relationship with Nature. As all of their rituals, festivals, faiths and beliefs have a direct cyclic relationship with *Jhum* cultivation, hence, change of mode of production is tantamount to loss of their numerous cultural elements, identity markers and folk wisdom. There is no doubt that it takes only a single generation for a culture to forever lose its age-old lexicon of folk heritage.

When I pointed out about such loss of traditional society, one of my colleagues from West Bengal responded, "Nothing new, Bengali culture is now being dominated by Bollywood. Even *Ma-Durga* has now become fond of the Hindi movie song. Who cares about these as long as one has enough money to visit shopping malls with a new brand of car?" Obviously, it all depends upon the end receivers. Do the indigenous tribal people of Arunachal Pradesh really care for this change? Being a person having some generational connections with *Jhum* cultivation but without any training or study in the field of anthropology, I do feel the sorrows and joys of our older generations when I listen to our folk songs, read folktales or visit the *Jhumia* families living 'illegally'. So, I do care for it not only as reminiscence but due to my generational connections and sensitivity towards my earlier generation. Although I am aware of inevitability of such change, yet, for me, replacement of *Jhum* cultivation does not mean only change in the mode of production or economy of scale. Perhaps, it is something more than that which cannot be quantified with modern economic tools but can be related through experience only. Definitely it bears certain elements of spiritual consequences and cognitive functioning of faith system of human mind which is beyond the scope of assessment by technocratic tools of modern science. At this stage, I would like to mention about the process of replacement of institutions of governance similar to the case of technology of agro-production.

Impacts of Change in Governance Institutions

No society can function without a system of governance whatever may be its form and structure. It is an essential component of maintaining order in any society. The tribal societies of Arunachal Pradesh have a record of strong tradition of self-governing institutions. Among all its more than 30 major tribes and more than 100 sub-tribes, some system of a traditional self-regulating institution exists. There are as many types of traditional self-governing institutions in the state as there are tribes. The most prominent among them are the Kebang of the Adis, the Builiang of the Apatanis, the Nyele of the Nyishis, the Mele of the Hrussos, the Tsorgan system of the Monpas, the Jung of the Sherdukpens, the Abbala of the Idu Mishmis, the Pharai of the Kaman Mishmis, the Mockchup of the Khamtis, the Ngojowa of the Wanchos and Mungphong or Nockthung of the Tangsas. It has been observed by many anthropologists who had done extensive field work in this region that the traditional governance institutions do not represent any uniform pattern. Some of them are monarchical, while others are republics, some have a uniform pattern of direct democracy and others function through a Chieftain or small representative bodies[11]. Historical factors as well as geographical compulsion had encouraged many of these tribal groups to confine themselves to a particular area and also develop some isolationist tendencies. However, these traditional self-governing institutions have undergone certain changes in their operative mechanisms and the speed of change is gaining momentum in recent times with the introduction of the modern system of governance.

Of course, in this scenario the state impacted in a big way as an introducer of new ideas of modern participatory democracy. The modern representative democratic institutions were introduced in two phases in Arunachal Pradesh, namely, universal adult franchise and democratic decentralization. A three-tier Panchayati Raj system, namely Gram Panchayat at the village level, Anchal Samiti at the Block level and Zila Parishad at the district level, came into existence in 1969 in accordance with the provision of the North-East Frontier Agency (NEFA) Panchayati Raj Regulation, 1967. An Agency Council was also created as an apex body in the entire territory. It was later that the Agency Council was converted into a Legislative Assembly in 1975 and a five-member ministry was formed under the Chief Ministership of P.K. Thungan without elections to the legislative assembly being held. The first Assembly election in the state was held in 1978.

The introduction of Panchayati Raj brought about a significant change in the traditional village councils of Arunachal Pradesh. It gave a new orientation to politics in the state. The new electoral dynamics have initiated a process towards formation of an Arunachal civil society instead of a group of fragmented tribes and communities. It has also initiated a change in the outlook and created a prospect of broadening the political horizon of the people by forcing them to look beyond their community.

However, some observers of this region have noted that the phase of socio-political development in the state is still in the process of evolution and is characterized by certain transitional trends such as: localized nature of leadership; minimal participation of women in governance and failure of any regional party to create a reasonable political base in the state.[12]

In November 2009 during a field study, the majority of our respondents overtly revealed about the use of money power and direct buying of votes in the state Assembly election. Relatively small number of voters and close clan relationship also seemed to be the facilitating factors in this game. Hence, in a situation like this, electoral politics openly turns into the game of money politics thus undermining the democratic process of political formation.

Again some of our respondents who are officially associated with grassroots democracy opined that the success of the experiment to empower people through decentralized and participatory institutions of governance heavily depends on the actual devolution of financial and other resources to Panchayats and creation of a responsive support system in terms of technical and administrative skills, capacity-building as well as horizontal coordination among various governmental agencies.

Nevertheless, we were informed by majority of our respondents that even with lots of limitations and slow process of devaluation of power, Panchayat elections have made some positive impact on the political process through greater participation of women in politics. Outwardly, at some places though such participation of women appears to be a kind of proxy representation of their husbands or anyone of their close relatives just for the sake of maintaining reserved seats for women, but in the long run it may prove beneficial for strenthening democracy.

In this new scenario, the demand seems to be towards empowering the Panchayats with more power and delegation of responsibility for rural planning with necessary training, mobilization of resources and managing finance. Regarding such introduction of new governance structures at the grassroots level, one observer has mentioned that while the transition to the Panchayati Raj system has been relatively smooth, the simultaneous existence of a multiplicity of institutional mechanisms—both modern and traditional—at the village level without any clear cut demarcation of their functions, may lead to 'institutional crowding out'.

Upcoming Issues and Challenges

During our one month long field visit in November 2009 we have also come across a good number of issues pointed out by many of our respondents. Here, I would like to mention briefly some of the issues as a part of our exercise of understanding the direction of the winds of change:

Development disparity—the issue of development disparity in the spatial sense is nothing new. In the case of Arunachal Pradesh the spatially uneven process of development may pose new challenges and constraints in the days ahead. As per the 2001 Census, Arunachal Pradesh had been listed as the state with the highest urban-rural gap. It is evident from different developmental indices that there is a huge gap between the districts or the areas bordering Assam and the other peripheral districts of the state. Again, within the districts the areas near the urban administrative centres have better infrastructural facilities than the interiors. Such a generalized scenario becomes an issue when the range of deviation violates all the standard norms and accepted parameters; the case of spatial development disparity of Arunachal Pradesh is a similar case in point. As one development specialist of the region commented: "Inter-regional disparities in the state, therefore, have an additional implication—in many cases, it may reflect inter-tribal disparities."[13] Of course, such inter-regional disparity with an underpinning of inter-tribal disparity may lead to a new category of political demand formation, which is already visible in the state.

Demand for local autonomy—During our field study a good number of community leaders also spoke to us very assertively about their demand for autonomy, especially in the Monpa-dominated region of Tawang and West Kameang district. The tribal community of this region has been demanding the formation of 'Mon Autonomous

District Council' for a long time showing the cause of development disparity. Similarly, the tribal communities of Chanllang and Trip district located in the eastern flank of the state, are also demanding the formation of the 'Patkai Autonomous District Council'. As one local news report illustrated in August 2009:

At the floor of the state legislative assembly, the MLAs from Tirap and Changlang reiterated their demands for creation of Patkai Autonomous Council. The timing was perfect as the demand came when the state is gearing up for the assembly polls. Among many others, the promise of the creation of autonomous councils for Mon (Tawang and West Kameng) and Patkai (Changlang and Tirap) is believed to have been one of the issues that was crucial in the formation of the government led by Chief Minister Dorjee Khandu. The four districts have 16 MLAs of the 60 in the state. Since it is all about the numbers game, 16 is a decent number, capable of calling the shots. The demand for creation for autonomous councils had been there for quite some time. The state government even adopted a resolution way back in February 2004 for the creation of autonomous councils.[14]

It is important to note that both of these areas of the state are having international borders—on the western flank with China and on the eastern flank with Myanmar. Hence, geo-strategic implications of such demands may also turn out to be very vital in the long run, taking note of the prolonged history of insurgency in the adjacent states. One academic rooted in this region expressed to us in his interview that, creation of Autonomous District Councils (ADCs) in these areas may further lead to fragmentation of the whole state with various such demands on ethnic lines. As one local journalist analyzed, "It will soon be a birthday cake from where everyone will soon have a portion cut out even if there is no particular appetite."[15].

Issue of property rights and inefficient contract enforcement—The other area of constraint to economic development that one can find in Arunachal Pradesh is the lack of a market-enabling role for the state i.e., demarcation and safeguarding of property rights as an efficient contract-enforcement mechanism is not given due importance in this state. The tribal community seemed to be in a transitional state with regard to their property rights; i.e., from community ownership to private ownership. Hence, one section of the indigenous population has been able to use this institutional vacuum to their advantage. They have acquired wealth in the form of urban land, land for plantation, and cultivation purposes or have been able to use village forests for private benefits. Communal property has ultimately resulted in increasing concentration of income and wealth into the hands of a small section of the community as well as the weakening of traditional institutional mechanisms. The diverse customary laws of the tribal communities of Arunachal Pradesh are yet to be codified or well interpreted. Hence, the legal functional domain and its exercising mechanism within the social and economic sphere is not well defined. Such a transitional situation also provides immense power to the bearers of traditional institutions. As the old time egalitarian values of the earlier community leadership are gone with time so, the poor and the downtrodden turned out to be at the receiving end of all forms of exploitation. On the other hand, new forms of the social safety net or protective socio-political or organisational mechanisms are yet to come up to address the issue of minimum level of distributive justice. Such unchecked deprivation accompanied with high degree of unemployment among the newly educated young generation always bears the risk of potential conflict. It is pertinent to mention in this context that, the Indian income tax rules and regulations enforced in other parts of country are not applicable for the indigenous tribal communities of Northeast India. It is a total tax holiday for the whole indigenous tribal community, irrespective of the level of income or volume of assets and wealth accumulated by them. Hence, it is impossible to track down the level of asset accumulation or corruption in civil and political bureaucratic spheres in an indigenous tribal-dominated state like Arunachal Pradesh. Definitely, there is a need to call for a change in this aspect of financial governance of the states in this region.

Identity politics and the politics of inclusion and exclusion— The identity politics in terms of 'indigenous tribes' versus 'outsiders' as well as the competitive politics of ethnic differentiation among the tribes has initiated a complex multi-layered process of articulation of collective identity at various levels. Such fractionalization of the society on ethnic lines may also impact negatively upon the overall development process in the state in future. One of the most important factors of ethnic unrest in this state is the feeling of in-group-out-group and a perceived or socially constructed sense of marginalization propagated by the political actors of various genres. In many situations such a sense of marginalization orchestrated by the destabilizing political forces led to basic denials of human rights to many ethnic communities. The case of the 'Chakmas and Hajong refugees' can be referred as a case in point. In this case all the legal interpretations and directives of the Supreme Court for providing legal protection and granting citizenship and electoral rights to the Chakmas and the Hajongs have been played down by the state[16].

In recent times, the issue of granting Permanent Resident Certificates (PRC) to different ethnic communities such as Deoris, Ahoms, Morans, Nepalis, Lishus, Sonowal-Kacharis, Misings and Adivasis, etc. led to a violent clash between the so called "indigenous" versus "others" in Lohit district of the state which even necessitated calling for central forces by the district administration. It is pertinent to mention that many of these community members have been living in Arunachal Pradesh for many generations and demanding the PRC rights for decades. The decision of the state authorities regarding the status of nine communities in this region seems to be vacillating from one end to another. On June 24, 2010, the state government took a decision to grant them PRC but the same government revoked the decision after protests from All-Arunachal Pradesh Students' Union (AAPSU) that led to such a violent clash.[17] To narrate the situation one senior member of Deori community commented that, "The king (read as state authority) said you are right some days back and now saying you are wrong using the same tongue. To whom shall we appeal now"?[18] Such conflict may also have a dampening effect on the economy of the state in terms of frequent road blockades and strikes. It is important to count one strategic factor in this connection that the main lifeline of the state's economy, i.e., the national highway, passes through the areas populated by members of these communities. During the time of unrest and conflict, these communities may take advantage of this factor and create economic blockade as experienced by many other landlocked states in other parts of Northeast India. So far, many such social and ethnic tensions are mounting in Arunachal Pradesh over time, without any meaningful efforts at resolution from any quarter. The concern for the same grows deeper keeping in mind that the civil society institutions in the state are still passing through their initial stage of development.

Mega-dam development projects and concerns of the environmentalists—The immense hydro-electric potential of the state with a prospect of generation of more than 50,000 MW capacities has created a myth in this state that it is floating on hydro-dollars like the common saying about the Arab world, which is floating on "Petrodollars". Construction of any large dam is always a debatable issue due to environmental concerns, population displacement and downstream riparian rights on sharing of water, etc. In case of mega dam projects of Arunachal Pradesh such concerns of the environmentalists are getting louder because of fragile geological condition in the state due to young mountain formation, high seismic activities in this area and the need for preservation of its rich flora and fauna.

Again, the people in Assam and also in countries like Bangladesh remain deeply concerned that such mega dam project may impact them negatively by the way of taking control of Brahmaputra river water. It is now a general perception among the common masses that such mega dams result in scarcity of water during the dry season and cause floods during monsoon. So far the supporters in favour of the construction of dams are showing all the positive signs of adopting the high technocratic model of earthquakes resistant dams, less displacement of population and high possibility of economic growth in the whole region with ensured low-cost power supply. But the whole issue remains politically sensitive as opinion mobilisation by different quarters across the states of the Northeast bear the high potential of clashes in future. Civil societies of this region need to find ways and means to resolve such issues peacefully and initiate steps through dialogue with different stakeholders at the very outset before they take an ugly turn.

Conclusion

In conclusion, we can say that the development dilemma of Arunachal Pradesh is multifaceted in its characteristics. It reflects diverse patterns with heterogeneous impacts among the various tribal and non-tribal communities of the state. Development of this state in economic terms holds tremendous potential but preservation and enrichment of its diverse socio-cultural values, identity and customs, protection of its flora and fauna and its virgin forests with pristine beauty turns out to be equally challenging for the uevelopment planners and practitioners. As the traditional societies in Arunachal Pradesh are now in transition, the above-mentioned complexities and challenges seem to be a part of the process. In my simple understanding, the direction vector of the 'winds of change' with respect to their indigenous cultural identity remains very unstable and uncertain, as the state policy has now taken a neo-liberal turn and is preparing to go with the winds of globalization.

Notes

1. Christoph von Furer-Haimendorf. *Tribes of India: The Struggle for Survival,* University of California Press, Berkeley, Los Angeles, London, 1982, pp. 286-313.
2. Wade P. Shepard, *Development of Tribal/Nomad Populations in India and Tibet*, Senior Thesis, Friends World Program, Long Island University, pp. 1-14, http://www.vagabondjourney.com/90-usa-04-india-tribal-tibet-nomad-research.shtml, Accessed on September 1, 2010.
3. Elwin, Verrier, *The Tribal World of Verrier Elwin: An Autobiography.* Delhi: Oxford University Press, p. 295, 1988.
4. Ramesh, Jairam, "Northeast India in New Asia" Seminar, No. 550, June, 2005 cited in *India's North-East Policy: Continuity and Change*, Posted by Editor on Sunday, October 17, 2010. *ManipurOnline. Dealing With The Issues*, http://manipuronline.com/research-papers/india%e2%80%99s-north-east-policy-continuity-and-change/2010/10/17#ixzz1ChAnfkAm
5. *Arunachal Pradesh Human Development Report* 2005, Copyright 2006, Government of Arunachal Pradesh Itanagar, Published by Department of Planning, Government of Arunachal Pradesh, India.
6. Ali, Mehar, 'Mother Tounge endangered due to government neglect', *Hindustan Times*, December 9, 2009, accessed at http://www.hindustantimes.com/StoryPage/Print/484689.aspx (Date of accession: 2nd February 2011)
7. Jit Ray, Vulnerable Voices—Cover Story, published in Harmony—Celebrate Age, August 2010 Volume 7 Issue 3, Harmony for Silvers Foundation Printed at Thomson Press India Ltd, Plot No. 5/5A, TTC Ind. Area, Thane-Belapur Road, Airoli, Navi Mumbai-400708. p. 29.
8. Ayesha Kidwai, Managing Multilingual India, *The Marxist,* Vol. XIV, No. 2. April-June, 2008.
9. Ibid.
10. Ibid.
11. Dutta, P.C., Tribal Chieftanship, Himalayan Publishers, 2003, Itanagar and New Delhi.
12. Talukdar, A.C. and Pura Tado, 'Assembly Elections in the North East: A Case Study of Arunachal Pradesh', in Girin Phukan (ed) *Parliamentary Democracy in North East India*, South Asian Publishers, 1998, New Delhi, pp. 61-73.
13. Deepak K Mishra and Vandana Upadhyay, 'Governance and Development in Arunachal Pradesh: The Emerging Challenges', *Dialogue*, Volume 5 No. 4, April-June, 2004.

14. Are Autonomous councils the answer for Arunachal?, *Arunachal Times*, August 19, 2009, Accessed in: http://www.arunachaltimes.com/aug%2018.html (Date of accession 29 August, 2009)
15. *Ibid.*
16. 'Indian Human Rights Report-2006: Arunachal Pradesh' published by *Asian Centre for Human Rights*, Accessed in, http://www.achrweb.org/reports/india/AR06/arunachal.htm (Date of accession, 15 January 2011). And also see in: 'A Stateless Chakmas and Hajongs of Indian State of Arunachal Pradesh: A Study of Systematic Oppression' published by *South Asian Human Rights Documentation Centre*, accessed in http://www.hrdc.net/sahrdc/resources/stateless_chakmas.htm (Date of accession, 15 January 2011)
17. Correspondent's Report, 'Several Injured as Clashes rock Lohit', *The Daily Telegraph*, 24 October, 2010. Also available in http://www.telegraphindia.com/1101024/jsp/northeast/story_13092850.jsp (Date of accession: 18 January 2011)
18. An interaction with a senior Deori community member over phone two days after the Communal Clash in October 2010, who also prefers not reveal his identity to avoid retaliation.

12

Institutions, Identities and the Economy

Understanding Economic Transformation in Arunachal Pradesh

Deepak K. Mishra

Economic transformation is a multilayered process. While economists have often attempted to identify and analyse various dimensions of this transformation through the vantage point of the economy, economic anthropologists, sociologists and political economists, among others have contributed significantly to unravelling the social nature of economic change. Economics as a discipline, much to the discomfort of many economists, has gradually opened up to the consequences of ignoring the constitutive contexts within which 'actually existing economies' operate, particularly in the developing world. It is increasingly being realised that the idea that market is essentially an apersonal, atomist realm of voluntary transactions among free individuals guided by their enlightened self-interest, is far removed from actually existing markets. Hariss-White (2005) has termed this as the romantic idea of the market, which does not recognise the social context, historical and spatial specificities and the relations of trust, reciprocity and power that shape 'real' markets. 'To conceive economic phenomena as embedded', however, 'is not to renounce theory, certainly not, it is to start theorising differently' (Callie, 1994, cited in Harriss-White, 2005).

This article[1] attempts to describe the story of economic transformation in Arunachal Pradesh through the transitions in institutions. While the focus is on the 'economic' aspects of the transformation, the non-economic aspects of change have been incorporated, not just as examples of simultaneously existing diversities, but also as key determinants of the pace and nature of economic transition. A central argument of the article is the mutually reinforcing role of state, market and community institutions in generating this transformation. Contrary to theorisation of these diverse institutional forms as alternative and competing institutional forms, we argue that they interact and reinforce each other in creating the specificities of the process of economic transformation. This is a preliminary attempt to understand the multi-layered transformation in Arunachal Pradesh. The article is organised as follows: In the following section, the key aspects of economic transformation in Arunachal Pradesh have been outlined. In the next section, the roles of state, market and community institutions in the economic transformation have been discussed. In the section after that, the interconnections between identity politics and economic development have been explored. Concluding observations are placed in the final section.

Economic Transformation in Arunachal Pradesh

Due to its ecological and historical specificities, the trajectories of development in Arunachal Pradesh, are markedly different from the rest of the country. Home to more than a hundred tribes and sub-tribes, this thinly populated state, remained largely unadministered during colonial rule. The specificities of the state that remain crucial to the understanding of the process of economic transformation include the following aspects.

The relative isolation of the region during much of the colonial period and the subsequent establishment and consolidation of governing structures after independence by the nascent Indian state has left its legacy not only on the structure of governance, but also on the nature of development of the region, earlier known as North Eastern Frontier Agency (NEFA). This meant that the state assumed the role of the prime mover of capitalist transformation. It not only brought labour, administrators and traders from outside, it also played a leading role in the gradual monetisation and commercialisation of the tribal social formations. Being a border region also has added new dimensions to the process of development. The heavy military presence across the state, particularly after the 1962 war with China, has had many consequences for the local economy and society. Given the low levels of commercialisation of the economy, the army mostly depends on supply from outside the state even for basic food items. The army however, has influenced the local economy in a significant manner—by monetising transactions, by constructing physical infrastructure of diverse kinds, by creating wage labour markets, by giving supply orders and contracts to locals, by generating demand for local products and also, at times, by creating marketing infrastructures. But all this development has taken place in a context where the structures of governance have remained heterogeneous and fluid. As part of the Nehru-Elwin policy of tribal development, the state has not only recognised the customary rights to forest and agricultural land, but also has legitimised the customary laws of the tribes. Although, as will be discussed later, the introduction of panchayati raj has led to institutional crowding out at the grassroots, for the last few decades the formal and informal structures of governance have co-existed and have influenced each other in diverse and complex ways. This institutional plurality has important implications for the capitalist transformation of the state.

Further, specific legislations like the 'inner line permit', the restrictions on transfer of ownership of any kind of permanent assets including land and houses to persons not belonging to the Arunachal Pradesh Scheduled Tribe (APST), and the affirmative discrimination in favour of local tribal groups in allocation of business contracts, licenses and jobs, etc., has also shaped the development process in the state. The ecological specificities of the mountain region have influenced the development of the economy in important ways. Mountain specificities, such as inaccessibility, fragility, marginality and diversity, have been found to have significant implications for the local economies (Jodha 2001). The three most significant dimensions of the agrarian economy of Arunachal Pradesh, as mentioned above, are: the ecological specificities of mountain agriculture; the institutional complexity underlying the use of and access to the various forces of production such as land and labour; and the historical role of the state as the prime mover of agrarian transformation.

Institutional Plurality and Economic Change in Rural Arunachal

Social institutions refer to the rules, norms and governance structures to regulate relationships among individuals. Social institutions have been described as 'collective action in control of individual action' or a set of rules that order repetitive and interdependent activities among individuals and highlight what actions are required, prohibited or permitted. Institutions reduce transaction costs and facilitate in internalizing the externalities (North, 1990). Collective action, an action undertaken by more than one individual to achieve a common goal, becomes easier in the presence of institutions. The New Institutional Economics School (NIE) has attempted to bring in the role of such rules and ordered patterns of human interaction into the analysis of economic behaviour. However, in conceptualizing these institutional arrangements as outcomes of free negotiations/interactions among independent individuals, such an analysis de-emphasizes the structures of power in designing and sustaining institutional mechanisms. It is important to note that such an argument has also been advanced against the NIE perspective in general (Toye, 1995).

The political economy perspective on institutions, unlike the mainstream neo-classical school, has always conceptualized the economic processes as socially embedded. 'Institutions' were never treated as exogenous. Marxian political economy, in particular, treated such institutional arrangements being determined by the relations of production and productive forces in the society. After the 'rediscovery' of institutions in the New Institutional Economics (NIE) perspective, it will be worthwhile to 'bring in production relations' into the dynamics of institutions for natural resource management. The problem of resource allocation and management gets transformed into a political economy problem once there are multiple claimants to it, with differential access to productive resources (Nadkarni, 1989: 20). Markets are not apolitical, asocial phenomena. They are 'not only just socially embedded phenomena, they are sites of the exercise of power in ways which are not reducible either to the tool kit of the new institutional economics or to norms of social embeddedness' (Harriss-White, 2003: 486).

A well-functioning common-property regime is characterized by *efficiency* (low occurrence or absence of disputes and limited efforts required to ensure compliance), *stability* (capacity to cope with progressive changes), *resilience* (capacity to absorb surprises or shocks) and *equity* (shared perception of fairness among members with respect to inputs and outcomes) (Gibbs and Bromley, 1991: 26). One of the key problems in community-based natural resource management is to ensure collective action. Ostrom has identified the following features in institutional arrangements as facilitating efficient natural resource management: clearly defined boundaries, congruence between appropriation and provision rules and local conditions; collective choice instruments; monitoring; graduated sanctions; conflict resolution mechanisms; minimal recognition of rights to organize; and nested enterprises in case of multilayered CPRs that are part of large systems (Ostrom, 1990: 90). In a recent survey of literature on endogenous collective action, the following contextual variables have been identified as important determinants of collective action: the type of production and allocation functions; the relative scarcity of the good; the size of the group involved; the heterogeneity of the group; the dependence of the group upon the good; common understanding of the group; the size of total collective benefit; the marginal contribution by one person to the collective good, the size of temptation to free ride; the loss to cooperators when others do not cooperate; having a choice of participating or not; the presence of leadership, level of social capital, and a wide diversity of rules that are used to change the structure of the situation (Ostrom, 2000). However, collective action, social capital and trust operate within the structures of political economy. 'One person's social capital is another person's social exclusion' (Harriss, 2002: 117).

The property rights formations in Arunachal Pradesh have undergone substantial changes over the last few decades. The traditional form of land-ownership was collective, although animals, tools and implements were privately owned. Most of the villages had some institutional mechanisms like village councils to manage and safeguard property-rights in land and forests. While in some areas the institution of chieftainship was well developed and the individuals derived their rights of ownership from the village chief, in many areas the village-council, consisting of all adult male members was the basic institution of decision-making, conflict resolution and collective action (Das, 1995; Dutta, 2003; Pandey et al, 1999). The traditional shifting cultivation system was based upon elaborate networks of informal contracts, cooperation, and resource pooling, risk-sharing and mutual insurance mechanisms.

In spite of their low-productivity the shifting cultivation systems did provide a degree of insurance against non-covariant risks, access to various tangible and non-tangible assets through membership of the community as well as a scope for institutional reproduction. However, because of internal dynamics of the system such as non-coverage of covariant risks, absence of fairness in the distribution of agricultural land in terms of quality, lack of sufficient surplus generation and demographic changes as well as the mutually reinforcing interventions by the state and market forces, private property rights over land have emerged in many parts of the state (Mishra, 2001; Roy and Kuri, 2001: 53-59).

Although individualisation of ownership rights over land is the most widely noticed dimension of the transitional phase in Arunachal Pradesh, it is important to note that collective or communal property rights continue to have diverse context-specific *operational* meanings (Mishra, 2006). The land under shifting cultivation, generally described as communally-owned could also be owned by some specific clans or individual households. Similarly, our field survey revealed that in the case of privately-owned land, the rights of use, occupancy and inheritance are generally enjoyed by the owners, but the right to transfer is often conditional. In some cases 'limited transfer rights' (viz., temporary transfer rights under mortgage, use rights without inheritance rights etc.) and 'preferential transfer rights' (viz., transfer within family, clan or tribe) were found, along with unconditional rights to alienate. The transition to private property rights regime seems to be informal in the sense that even without explicit recognition from the state institutions, the land market operates on a limited scale. The specificity of the emerging private property regime lies not only in its weak institutional basis but also in the changing dimensions of collective ownership (Mishra, 2002a; 2006).

The emergence of private property over land is often preceded by the adoption of permanent cultivation, which in turn might have followed a gradual shortening of the shifting cultivation cycle or complete abandonment of shifting cultivation. Some of the important features of the agrarian structure in the study area can be summarized as follows: Firstly, the overall character of the agrarian relations in the study region is determined by the predominance of small holders. Secondly, the inequality in the distribution of land ownership, which was nearly absent in the traditional economies of the region, has been gradually increasing in the past decades. Thirdly, landlessness is an emerging phenomenon in the study region, but there may be different processes at work in the emergence of this landlessness; while in some villages it is largely because of customary inheritance laws, in others, along with that, indebtedness and rural-to-rural migration have played a role, while in some cases, it is largely caused by immigration from other states and countries. However, by and large landlessness is the feature of migrant non-Arunachalee households rather than that of the indigenous villagers. Fourthly, notwithstanding the description of the 'traditional' tribal institutions as more egalitarian, women are not the owners of the land although they are often found to be *de facto* managers of farm operations. Fifthly, transactions in the land market were found to be very few in number but they signify the direction of change in coming years. Transfer of land through mortgage, sale and informal contracts were found in all the sample villages but numbered a few. Community control over farm land does not simply disappear as a result of emergence of the land market. Thus, by and large the agrarian structure represents the characteristics of subsistence, and small peasant agriculture, although commercialization of agriculture has made deep inroads in the state.

It is important to note that in relation to commercialization, similar trends were found by Mishra (2004) both in the interior villages having settled cultivation and also in the villages nearer to an urban centre in West Kameng district. The findings broadly support the formulation of Demsetz (1967) that, as the value of common property resources increases, people are more likely to establish rights over it. However, while rise in the value of agricultural land might be linked with its better quality and productivity in some of the villages, the proximity to the urban centres and roads has caused increased demand for land in many others. The sale of land to outsiders (only to people belonging to APST communities, but not belonging either to the village or to the same tribe) is rare.

Important changes in labour relations have also been observed in rural Arunachal Pradesh. The traditional institutional arrangements like cooperative labour-sharing, collective-work and reciprocity have been on the decline. Emergence of the rural labour market and increasing occupational diversification has also altered labour relations in diverse ways. One aspect of these changes is the emergence of wage labour contracts in farm and non-farm activities. An important dimension of the livelihood diversification strategies of rural households is the increasing reliance on forest-based resources to take care of consumption snortfalls. Mishra (2003) in a field survey in the hilly district of West Kameng in Arunachal Pradesh reported as many as 30 different combinations of livelihoods at the household level.[2] So far as inter-village differences are concerned the developed villages show a greater variability in livelihood combinations than the traditional ones. Broadly speaking, two different kinds of livelihoods diversification strategies could be found in this mountainous region. The first one, which is mostly determined by the survival needs of households living in a high-risk, high diversity ecological setting, concentrates on diversification of livelihoods within and around agriculture. Households attempt to combine *jhum*, terrace and wet-rice cultivation with horticulture, animal husbandry, selling of forest products, casual employment in the emerging rural labour market and, in some cases, petty trading. The second kind of diversification is through increasing dependence on government service, trade and business and large-scale trading in forest products. The later kind of strategy is generally driven by an accumulative motive of relatively better-placed households. However, forest plays a central role in either kinds of diversification; in the first one as a source to mitigate risks and ensuring smooth consumption during seasonal shortfalls, and in the second, as a source of consumables as well as marketable products like timber, and a range of non-timber forest products including medicinal plants. While, historically, forest resources have played a vital role in the survival of rural people, the commercialization of forest products and use of wage labour for collection of forest products are relatively recent developments.

It is well-known that the extent of dependency on forests is particularly high among households living in the mountainous areas. A recent study conducted in 12 villages of Arunachal Pradesh concludes that on an average, 34.48 per cent of the consumption expenditure of the households of the study area was derived from the community forests. Further, around 37.93 per cent of the total consumption expenditure of relatively poor households was derived from community forests. On the other hand, 32.02 per cent and 31.06 per cent of total consumption expenditure was derived from community forests for relatively middle income and rich category of households (Mitra and Mishra 2011). Thus, in absolute terms, the richer sections derive greater benefits from the community forests. Another study, on the basis of data collected from three villages in West Kameng district, notes that around 24 per cent of the total income of the households is derived from forests (A. Mishra 2005). The extent of forest dependency does not necessarily change as a consequence of increased levels of earnings, but the nature of forest use and the composition of forest products collected changes significantly. While poorer households tend to depend on forests for their survival, the not-so-poor households operate more in the products that are marketed. Mitra and Mishra (2011) find that while the consumption of relatively poor households consisted more of fuel wood and bamboo, leafy vegetables, etc., on the other hand, consumption of timber was much higher among the rich households. In fact, the study shows that as the income of the households increased, the percentage consumption of timber increased but the consumption of minor forest products like bamboo, leafy vegetables, reduced.

Thus, the nature of forest consumption changes from one dependent on household necessities like food, fuel and fodder, to one based on the motive of accumulation, as one moves across the income ladder. Women are more centrally involved in the former case than in the latter. The collection of forest products has been found to be based on product-specific gender-based division of labour. For example, a study in West Kameng, notes that while the contribution of women in the collection of marketed forest products like timber, bamboo and medicinal plants was negligible, women contributed more labour than men in the collection of firewood, grass, leafy vegetables, fruits and roots. In the collection of house-building materials men contribute more than women (A. Mishra, 2005). Commercial extraction of forest products has meant that traditional subsistence activities have been turned into income-generating occupations. Commercialisation has also meant greater interaction with traders and dealers and travel to marketplaces. This has led to a situation where either the entire activity has been turned into predominantly male-dominated, or a division of labour has emerged where women and children join in collecting the forest products and male members take over the responsibility of selling them. In either case, the cash flows get concentrated in male hands. This is exactly what has happened in the Dirang circle of Arunachal Pradesh, where a market for medicinal plants has developed in the past few years. In the neighbouring Nafra circle, with the opening of pine oil processing units, it is the males who have taken over the collection of the oil, while women continue to shoulder the responsibility of collecting household consumption items from forests (Mishra, 2007).

This multiplicity and diversification of livelihood sources have altered the foundation of the traditional labour institutions in the area. In the past, most of the agricultural activities were being carried out by using family and clan labour. Cooperation and labour-sharing were almost indispensable given the low population density and labour-intensive method of cultivation. The institutional arrangements for collective labour mobilization showed considerable tribe-to-tribe variations and it ranged from organized youth labour-groups called *patang* among the Apatanis, to the spontaneous formation of groups under the *Haria* system in Papumare district (Furer-Haimendrof, 1980: 43-44; Roy and Kuri, 2001: 24). In our field surveys we observed two kinds of labour-sharing processes: generalized and specific (Mishra, 2002a; 2006; Harriss-White, Mishra and Upadhyay, 2009). Under *generalized* cooperative labour-sharing, the entire village worked as a single unit. In such cases, reciprocity was generalized and monitoring was a collective responsibility, institutionalized through the traditional village-level decision-making and enforcing structures. Two or more households, independent of other households in the village community, on the other hand, agreed on *specific* labour-sharing arrangements. It was found during the field survey that in recent years, generalized labour-sharing has been limited to work relating to religious festivals and village commons. In other spheres of economic activity, specific reciprocity was found to be the dominant mode of labour-sharing. Under this system, two types of sharing arrangements were noticed. In the first case, two or more families combined their resources—primarily labour, but sometimes other resources like implements, draft-animals as well—to carry out farm and forest-related activities. The second form of specific labour-sharing is in terms of mutually agreed number of labour days to be exchanged between the participating households. Here, the range of cooperation and mutual commitment was found to be narrower than in the first case. Both these forms of specific labour-sharing were noticed in all the villages, but the second case is increasingly becoming the standard practice. Under conditions of increasing environmental degradation, low-productivity and prevalence of a variety of risks, these labour-sharing arrangements can be viewed as a general bilateral contract that involves resource pooling, risk dispersion and mutual insurance.

Although it is difficult to establish the causal mechanisms in such an institutional transition, most of these changes can be linked to the processes of increasing individualization of land holdings, commoditization of the productive resources and increasing state intervention. The opening up of state and market activities has led to large-scale immigration and as noted above, the rural labour market has been substantially changed by this development. This has not only meant an increase in demographic pressure on forest resources, but has also changed the nature of resource-consumption by households.

The response of the village communities to these new challenges emerging from demographic and economic changes ranges from passive acceptance to innovative, nuanced and sophisticated institutional responses. In some of the villages, for example, a differentiated structure of rights over forest resources has been developed, which clearly distinguishes between the claims of the original inhabitants and those of the new settlers. When village communities, particularly those in close proximity to urban centres, find it difficult to effectively monitor resource extraction by non-members, they have tried to develop a graduated system of entry fee, which can be both lump sum or *ad valorem*. With rising economic inequality, however, the allocation rules have been diluted to accommodate the interests of the rich.

The traditional rule that does not specify any quota on forest resources for self-consumption (mainly firewood, timber and bamboo for house construction), fails to monitor the resource-extraction because of relocation of households, in-migration of tenants, government officials and businessmen to the rural areas. But substantial damage to the institutional structures at the local level has been done by the timber-trade, which has been restricted following an order by the Supreme Court. Timber extraction activities paved the way for emergence of a neo-rich contractor class who monopolized the supply contracts and hence the pattern of resource-use was transformed from a need-based one to a profit-oriented one. Apart from the environmental impact of deforestation, the institutional impact was that the traditional rules of resource-use, which had been designed in a resource-abundant context and hence involved almost zero costs of monitoring, became redundant so rapidly that communities did not have the social capital to address the problem. The emergence of the labour market itself transformed the labour-sharing practices, and since most of the traditional institutional mechanisms were based on the implicit assumption of labour-shortage, their distributive egalitarianism lost the capacity for conflict-minimization.

The migration of the relatively richer and younger sections of the population to urban areas has led to the breakdown of collective monitoring and management practices. The attempt to impose a cash fine for absence has hardly altered the scenario. Along with the emergence of private property over agricultural land, the use of common property like forests for individual benefits has led to the creation of alternative institutional mechanisms mediated by the markets. The new institutional space provided by the panchayati raj institutions and electoral democracy has effectively undermined the legitimacy of the traditional resource management practices. The simultaneous existence of alternative and competing sources of power and authority at the grassroots level in some cases has resulted in 'institutional crowding out'.

The Political Economy of Ethnicity and Development

The politics of identity and difference in Northeast India has a long and complex history. The colonial project of building the Empire and post-colonial politics of nation-building have created the broader context in which the ethnic landscape of Northeast India has taken shape. The extraordinary ethnic diversity in the region makes its politics more complex and fragmented, but the roots of the fragmented nature of the polity do not emanate from the co-existence of diverse the ethnic groups alone, it also has resulted from the multiple ways external forces such as the state and capital have interacted with this diversity. One of the ways the state and the markets have interacted with, and have, changed the ethnic landscape of the region, at least since the encounters with colonialism, is the way property rights over crucial livelihood resources have been altered or created. The micro-ethnic communities had their respective institutions of governance at the community level and these institutional arrangements not only regulated the religious and social life of the members, but also governed access to a range of tangible and non-tangible resources that were crucial for the survival of the people.

Depending on the resource endowment position of the community, its settings and type of economy, these rules were different, well-defined or ambiguous, strictly or loosely applied. But the state-induced move towards modernisation and integration of the local economies with the broader regional and national economies led to significant alterations in the way property rights were created, destroyed or rearranged to suit the demands of the changing economic and political contexts. Often, there is a tendency to view these changes through the binary prisms of 'destruction of the old and creation of the new' institutional forms. A detailed study of the changes in various dimensions of property rights and institutional mechanisms however, shows that the transition was often complex (Harriss-White, Mishra and Upadhyay, 2009). It involved destruction, survival, adaptation and modifications of the pre-capitalist institutional structures, along with the creation of newer institutional forms. The institutional diversity and complexity that underlies such transitions is to be seen not simply as a leftover of the past, but as the defining characteristic of the nature of capitalist transition in the region. What adds to the specificity of the situation is, of course, the continuing significance of the traditional institutions governing access to natural resources. The state and market forces are constantly interacting with and by implication changing various dimensions of the resource-management practices in Arunachal; but as of now, the institutional milieu is defined more by heterogeneity and hybridism rather than by institutional convergence. In a recent field survey in 11 villages in five districts of Arunachal Pradesh, Harriss-White, Mishra and Upadhyay (2009) have found that 'institutional adaptation, continuity and hybridism are as integral to the emergence of the market economy as are the processes of creation of new institutions and demise of others. There is no necessary correspondence between the emerging commercialization of the different productive dimensions of the agrarian economy. These uneven processes are deeply influenced by existing and emerging power relations and by the state'.

As the discussions in the earlier sections show, in Arunachal Pradesh, where nearly 63 per cent of forests categorised as 'unclassified state forest' are in fact in the hands of village communities and clans, the effective control of these forests varies a lot among the communities. Unconstrained individual property rights over land co-exist with collective rights in forests. However, irrespective of the precise nature of the property rights regime operating at the ground, there is an unmistakable tendency towards *de facto* privatisation of the ownership or at least use-rights over forests. The individual ownership rights, particularly with regard to alienation rights, are necessarily subject to community control in many areas (D Souza 2001: 46; Mishra 2006; Harriss-White, Mishra and Upadhyay 2009), but exploitation of forest resources, particularly timber, before the imposition of restrictions by the Supreme Court, has no doubt weakened the ethos of collective management. Apart from the environmental impact of deforestation, induced by the wanton exploitation of the 'common' forest for private gains, the institutional impact was that the traditional rules of resource-use, which had been designed in a resource-abundant context and hence involved almost zero costs of monitoring became redundant so rapidly that communities did not have the social capital to address the problem.

The emergence of the labour market itself transformed the labour-sharing practices and since most of the traditional institutional mechanisms were based on the implicit assumption of labour-shortage, their distributive egalitarianism lost the capacity for conflict-minimisation (Mishra, 2002a; Mishra 2004).

Needless to add, the transformation of property relations has hastened the processes of peasant differentiation and landlessness has been increasing (Fernandes and Pereira 2005; Mishra, 2002a). It is important to note that this process of shift from communal economy to increasing economic and gender differentiation was not primarily because of factors like internal population growth (although migration from outside has played a significant catalytic role), but because of state interventions in terms of discouragement of shifting cultivation, provisions of incentive to 'progressive' farmers for growing commercial crops, etc. The institutional strategies of agricultural extension services in these areas are based on the usual assumptions of an individual male, autonomous farmer as the decision-maker in agriculture, which in turn has facilitated the processes of recognition of private property rights over land (Mishra, 2006). In Arunachal Pradesh, studies show that although the state has not formally recognised private property rights in land, it has been a passive observer of the systematic informal transition to private property rights. In this informal transition, women, and other marginalised sections, tend to lose out (Mishra, 2003; 2007). Thus, in such contexts, the state, on the one hand, has facilitated the emergence of private property rights through a series of direct and indirect measures[3], while on the other, by not taking cognisance of the move towards privatisation, it has virtually left the process in the hands of 'traditional' community institutions. These institutions, notwithstanding their other strengths as institutions of decentralised, local-level governance, are hardly 'participatory' when it comes to women (Krishna, 2004; Goswami, 2002; Mishra and Upadhyay, 2007).

An important dimension of the development process in Arunachal Pradesh is the reworking of the 'traditional' community identities under the influence of the state-led modernisation drive. It is widely recognised that 'ethnicity is not a primordially given essence, but the outcome of complex socio-cultural and political processes of labelling and identifying people' (Peters, 1998: 400; Collier, 1998). Contrary to neo-classical theorisation of the market economy as one where impersonal exchanges predominate and identities of agents are of lesser significance, recent theoretical and empirical research, in a number of different settings, has brought home the significance of identity for economic transactions and economic development in general (Kaul, 2008; Meagher, 2010). The politics of identity and difference in Arunachal Pradesh, like elsewhere, involves considerable rediscovery and invention of the past in the light of the present and it has not only been influenced by the introduction of electoral democracy, but also by the unequal distribution of the fruits and burdens of economic prosperity. The ethnic politics in Northeast India has been an important aspect of the transition in the region, particularly in the context of the heavy military presence of the state and its relative inability to protect the life, livelihoods and dignity of its citizens (Baruah, 2004). The relative weakness of the state in safeguarding property rights and enforcing contracts typically creates a scope for the emergence of ethnic groups to provide private means of securing property rights (Bates, 1998). Unlike in many of the Northeastern states, where this has resulted in the proliferation of numerous insurgent groups defending the interest of specific ethnic communities, in the case of Arunachal Pradesh, it has led to competition and bargaining among different tribal groups to acquire a larger share of the government's resources—a form of 'quiet pressure' exercised from within the system (Mishra and Upadhyay, 2007). Nevertheless, the overall framework of ethnic politics has weakened the 'universal' principles of civic rule to a considerable extent and has provided substantial scope for community leaders and elites to exercise considerable control over the everyday politics of survival and accumulation. This nature of politics has been possible within a specific kind of transition in the economic sphere, which has been shaped by as well as shapes the nature of ethnic politics in the state.

The other significant dimension of this transition, noted in Harriss-White, Mishra and Upadhyay (2009) is that it is basically the non-agricultural surplus that has been the moving force behind this transition. Secondly, access to political power and resources of the state acted as key factors in the creation and sustenance of this surplus flow. Another source of surplus for the local elites, until recently, was the huge 'profits' from timber trade. Although timber trade was by and large controlled by large-scale business from outside the state, the local business class, as junior partners and facilitators, managed to corner a substantial share for themselves. Some of them invested the surplus in establishing sawmills, plywood factories and transportation businesses. 'Although in the first instance the timber trade appears to be independent of the state, the manner in which the state allowed the plundering of the commonly owned forests for private profit makes it clear that state support and protection was essential for the timber trade. While the forest department retained control over the supply of permits to cut trees, these permits were issued with such frequency and under such a framework of political patronage, that community control over forests remained at best a minor irritant both for the traders, belonging to indigenous tribal groups as well as people from outside the state (Harriss-White, Mishra and Upadhyay, 2009).

Since state support was crucial for the surplus extraction activities of the elites and access to the resources of the state was being governed within the framework of ethnic politics, it was quite natural for the elites to protect the institutional diversities that provided a scope for them to exercise control and power at the local level. To put it rather bluntly, the ability of the local elites to draw a share from the state's resources or to extract rent from the state or the outsiders, depended upon their ability to perpetuate the politics of ethnicity and difference on the one hand, and also on their capacity to represent their 'community' in the competition over tangible and non-tangible resources. Thus, while the state has been influential in initiating the capitalist transition and also in changing the community institution in diverse ways, the overall framework of ethnic politics, in turn, has created the context in which the politics of democracy and state intervention is being played out today. These mutually reinforcing roles of state, market and community institutions have shaped and have, in turn, been shaped by the trajectories of development in the state.

Concluding Remarks

This article attempts to look at the changes in local-level institutional arrangements for natural resource management along with the changes in agrarian relations in rural Arunachal Pradesh. Along with individualization oi property rights and peasant differentiation, and the consequent changes in labour-use patterns, the 'traditional' institutional mechanisms for natural resource managements face new crises. These institutional arrangements do not necessarily have the social capital to devise new monitoring and allocation mechanisms in the face of rising inequality, heterogeneity of interests and loss of autonomous space for decision-making. Thus, the dynamics of community-level institutional arrangements can probably be better understood by endogenising the emerging power relations in the context of differential access to productive resources rather than an essentialized and homogenized notion of 'community'.

The simultaneous existence of several institutional modes in the rural economy of Arunachal Pradesh, notwithstanding its peculiarities, raises specific doubts about the notion of 'dissolution of the old and emergence of the new' institutional forms that have informed the studies on agrarian change for decades. Institutional diversity appears not to be an impediment to the development of capitalist relations, but, under the specific conditions mentioned here, it is this diversity and complexity of institutional mechanisms that has helped the tribal elites to accumulate and invest the surplus generated within and outside agriculture. The state, while undermining the authority of the traditional community institutions through its developmental initiatives, has nevertheless created new spaces for assertion of identities. By invoking the notion of community rights selectively, the tribal elites have not only been able to acquire large portions of land, but have also been able to 'capture' the local state for their own benefits. In such a context, there is a need to move beyond the analytical prism of the state-versus-community or the state-versus-market framework and to take note of the existing and emerging differentiations within and across the communities.

Notes

1. This article builds on my earlier works on economic transformation in Arunachal Pradesh (Mishra, 2004; Mishra, 2006; Harriss-White, Mishra and Upadhyay, 2009). A slightly different version of the article was presented at a seminar at Lucknow University (Mishra, 2010). The empirical results presented here draws on several rounds of field survey in Arunachal Pradesh, supported by funding from UGC-NER, ICSSR, UNDP, Planning Commission and Government of Arunachal Pradesh. Support, encouragement and insightful criticisms from colleagues at the Department of Economics, Rajiv Gandhi University and at Government College, Bomdila helped a lot in developing these arguments. The usual disclaimers apply.
2. The results of this survey indicate that the livelihood combination having the highest frequency is agriculture, combined with forest-based activities, animal husbandry and wage labour. The simpler combination of agriculture, forest and animal husbandry has also a significant

presence. So, has the livelihood combination with agriculture, forest, animal husbandry and government service. Together, these three combinations explain the diversification strategy of around 60 per cent of all the households (Mishra, 2003).

3. For example, when rubber plantation was introduced in the Garo area of Meghalaya, the Rubber Board and the financial bodies encouraged privatisation of land rights by insisting on individual *pattas* as preconditions for loans and subsidies (Fernandes, nondated; Fernandes and Pereira, 2005). This enforced individual ownership strengthened the demand of middle class men for male ownership, which has been in existence for many decades on a low scale (Kar, 1982; Marak, 2002).

References

Baland, Jean-Marie and Jean-Philippe Platteau (1996). *Halting Degradation of Natural Resources: Is there a Role for Rural Communities?*, Rome: FAO.

Baruah, Sanjib (2004). 'Historicizing Ethnic Politics in North East India', Keynote Address, Seminar on '*Inter-ethnic Conflict and Ethnic Crisis in North East India'*, Department of Political Science, Dibrugarh University, 16-17 February.

Bates, Robert H. (1998). Comment on "Structure and Strategy in Ethnic Conflict" by Donald L. Horowitz in Boris Bleskovic and Joseph E. stiglitz (eds) *Annual World Bank Conference on Development Economics,* Washington: World Bank, pp. 371-376.

Bordoloi, B.N. (1998). 'Tribal land Tenure System and Land Alienation in Northeast India'. In *Antiquity to Modernity in Tribal India*, Vol. III, (ed.) S.N. Mishra, New Delhi: Inter-India.

Byres, T.J. (1996). *Capitalism from Above and Capitalism from Below: An Essay in Comparative Political Economy.* London: Macmillan Press.

Collier, Paul (1998). 'The Political Economy of Ethnicity', in Boris Bleskovic and Joseph E. Stiglitz (ed) *Annual World Bank Conference on Development Economics,* World Bank: Washington, pp. 387-399.

D Souza, Alphonsus (2001). *Traditional systems of forest conservation in North-East India: The Angami tribe of Nagaland.* Guwahati: North-Eastern Social Research Centre.

Das, G. (1995). *Tribes of Arunachal Pradesh in Transition*, New Delhi: Vikas.

Demsetz, H. (1967). 'Toward a Theory of Property Rights', *American Economic Review* 57 (May): 347-359.

Deori, R.K. (1982). *The Sulungs.* Shillong: Department of Research, Government of Arunachal Pradesh.

Dutta, P.C. (2003). *Tribal Chieftanship*, Itanagar and New Delhi: Himalayan Publishers.

Fernandes, Walter (nondated). Tribal Customary and Formal Law Interface in North-Eastern India: Implications for Land Relations, available at siteresources.worldbank.org/INTINDIA/Resources/walter_fernandes_paper.doc retrieved on 5th Sept 2007.

Fernandes, Walter and Pereira, M. (2005). *Changing Land Relations and Ethnic Conflicts: The Case of North-Eastern India*, Guwahati: North-Eastern Social Research Centre.

Gibbs, C.J.N. and D.W. Bromely (1991). 'Institutional arrangements for Management of Rural Resources: Common-Property Regimes' in Berkes, F. (ed.). *Common property Resources: Ecology and Community-based Sustainable Development*, Dehradun: International Book Distributor.

Goswami, A. (2002). Introduction. In: A. Goswami (ed.) *Traditional self-governing institutions among the hill tribes of north-east India*. New Delhi: Akansha.

Government of Arunachal Pradesh (2006). *Arunachal Pradesh Human Development Report 2005*. Itanagar: Government of Arunachal Pradesh.

Hanna, Susan, Carl Folke and Karl-Goran Maler (1995)'Property Rights and Environmental Resources' in Susan Hanna and Mohan Munasinghe (ed.) *Property Rights and the Environment: Social and Ecological Issues,* Washington: The Beijer International Institute of Ecological Economics and the World Bank.

Harriss, John (2002). *Depoliticizing Development: The World Bank and Social Capital*, Leftword Books, New Delhi.

Harriss-White, Barbara (2003). 'On Understanding Markets as Social and Political Institutions in Developing Economies', in Ha-Joon Chang (ed) *Rethinking Development Economics*, London: Anthem Press, pp. 481-497.

Harriss-White, Barbara (2005). *India's Market Society: Three Essays in Political Economy*, Three Essays Collective,

Harriss-White, Barbara, Deepak K Mishra and Vandana Upadhyay (2009). 'Institutional Diversity and Capitalist Transition: The Political Economy of Agrarian Change in Rural Arunachal Pradesh', *Journal of Agrarian Change*, 9 (4): 512-547.

Hart, Gillian A. Turton and B. White, (eds.) (1989). *Agrarian Transformations: Local Processes and the State in Southeast Asia.* Berkeley: University of California Press.

Hart, Gillian, 1989. 'Agrarian Change in the Context of State Patronage'. In *Agrarian Transformations: Local Processes and the State in Southeast*

Asia, Eds. Gillian Hart, A. Turton and B. White, 31-49. Berkeley: University of California Press.

Jodha, N.S. (2001). *Life on the Edge: Sustaining Agriculture and Community Resources in Fragile Environments.* New Delhi: Oxford University Press.

Kar P.C. (1982). *The Garos in Transition.* New Delhi: Cosmo Publication.

Kaul. Nisha (2008). *Imagining Economics Otherwise: Encounters with Identity/Difference*, Routledge, Abingdon.

Krishna, S. (2004). Gender, Tribe and Political Participation: Control of Natural Resources in North-Eastern India. In: Sumi Krishna (ed.) *Livelihood and gender: Equity in community resource management.* New Delhi: Sage.

Leach, Melissa, Robin Mearns and Ian Scoones (1999). 'Environmental Entitlements: Dynamics and Institutions in Community-based Natural Resource Management', *World Development*, Vol. 27, No. 2: 225-247.

Marak, Caroline (2002). Matriliny and Education among the Garo. In: Walter Fernandes and Sanjay Barbora (eds.) *Changing women's status in India: Focus on the North-East,* Guwahati: North-Eastern Social Research Centre., pp. 159-165.

Meagher, K. (2010). *Identity Economics: Social Networks and The Informal Economy in Nigeria*, James Curry, Suffolk.

Mishra, A. (2005). A Study of Economic Transformation, Environmental Degradation and Female Work Participation in Arunachal Pradesh, Ph D Thesis submitted to Rajiv Gandhi University, Itanagar.

Mishra, A. (2006). Occupational Structure and Gender-based segregation in North-East India: The Case of Arunachal Pradesh. *Social Change and Development*. 4(1), pp. 125-145.

Mishra, Deepak K. (2010). 'Interrogating community management: state, market and community in Arunachal's agrarian transition' in M Rajput (ed.) *Understanding North East India: Cultural Diversities, Insurgency and Identities*, Manak, New Delhi.

Mishra, Deepak K. (2003). Environmental Degradation and Changing Livelihood Strategies in Rural Arunachal Pradesh. Paper presented at the 45th Annual Conference of the Indian Society of Labour Economics, Kolkata, 15-17 Dec.

Mishra, Deepak K. (2004). Institutional Sustainability in Natural Resource Management: A Study on Arunachal Pradesh (India). *Asian Profile*, 32 (6).

Mishra, Deepak K. (2006). 'Institutional Specificities and Agrarian Transformation in Arunachal Pradesh: Changing Realities and Emerging Challenges'. *Indian Journal of Agricultural Economics,* 61 (3): 314-27.

Mishra, Deepak K. and V Upadhyay (2007). 'In the Name of the Community: Gender, Development and Governance in Arunachal Pradesh', in Sumi Krishna (ed), *Women's Livelihoods Rights: Recasting Citizenship for Development*, Sage Publications India, New Delhi, (2007), pp. 167-208.

Mishra, Deepak K. and V Upadhyay (2008). *Background paper on Agriculture and Allied Sectors*, Arunachal Pradesh State Development Report, draft.

Mishra, Deepak K., (2007). 'Gender, Forests and Livelihoods: A Note on the Political Economy of Transition in North-East India', *Social Change,* 37 (4): 65-90.

Mishra, Deepak K., 2001. 'Political Economy of Agrarian Change in Arunachal'. *Man and Development*, 23 (3): 40-50.

Mishra, Deepak K. (2002a). 'Agrarian Structure and Labour-Use Patterns in Rural Arunachal Pradesh: A Case Study'. *Arunachal University Research Journal*, 5 (2): 31-56.

Mishra, Deepak K. (2002b). 'Institutional Arrangements and Agrarian Structure during periods of Transition: Evidence from Rural Arunachal Pradesh'. In *Sustainable Agriculture, Poverty and Food Security. Agenda for Asian Economies*, Vol. 2, (eds.) S.S. Acharya, Surjit Singh and V. Sagar, 891-902. Jaipur: Rawat Publications.

Mishra, S.N. (1983). 'Arunachal's Tribal Economic Formation and Their Dissolution'. *Economic and Political Weekly*, 18 (43): 1837-46.

Misra, B.P., (1979). 'Kirata Karyokinesis: Mode of production in Tribal Communities of North East India'. In *Agrarian Relations in India*, eds. A.N. Das and V. Nilkanth, Delhi: Manohar.

Mitra, Amitava and Deepak K. Mishra (2011). Environmental Resource Consumption Pattern in Rural Arunachal Pradesh, *Forest Policy and Economics*, 13 (3)

North, D.C. (1990). *Institutions, Institutional Change and Economic Performance,* Cambridge: Cambridge University Press.

Ostrom, E. (1990). *Governing the Commons: The Evolution of Institutions for Collective Action*, Cambridge: Cambridge University Press.

Ostrom, E. (2000). 'Collective Action and the Evolution of Social Norms', *Journal of Economic Perspectives*, 14(3): 137-158.

Ostrom, V., D. Freny and H. Picht (eds) (1993). *Rethinking Institutional Analysis and Development*, San Fransisco: ICS Press.

Pandey, B.B., D.K. Duarah and N. Sarkar (eds) (1999) *Tribal Village Councils of Arunachal Pradesh*, Itanagar: Directorate of Research, Government of Arunachal Pradesh.

Peters, Pauline E. (1998), 'Comment on "The Political Economy of Ethnicity" by Paul Collier', in Boris Bleskovic and Joseph E. Stiglitz (ed) *Annual*

World Bank Conference on Development Economics, World Bank: Washington

Prakash, Assem and Anil K. Gupta (1997). 'Ecologically Sustainable Institutions' in Smith, Frasser (ed) *Environmental Sustainability: Practical Global Implications*, St. Lucie Press, Boca Raton, Florida.

Roy, N.C. and P.K. Kuri (1995). 'Traditional Institution of Land Ownership and Risk-Coping Mechanism in Rural Arunachal Pradesh', *Resarun*, 21(1-2).

Roy, N.C. and P.K. Kuri (2001). *Land Reforms in Arunachal Pradesh*, Classical Publishing House, New Delhi.

Toye, J. (1995). 'The New Institutional Economics and Its Implication for Development Theory' in J. Harriss, J. Hunter and Colin M Lewis (eds.) *The New Institutional Economics and Third World Development*, London and New York: Routledge.

13

Problems of Technological Modernization and Industrialization in Arunachal Pradesh

N.C. Roy

The trajectories of both technological progress and economic development appear to move together. In spite of their synchronized movement spanning all stages of development and showing a relation which is more deterministic than random, the inordinate delay in comprehending the potentialities of technology seems rather bizarre. Even classical economists of the stature of Ricardo and Mill who lived and worked in England at a time—in the first half of nineteenth century when the Industrial Revolution was in full bloom—could not fathom fully the power of technology, the power which would in one form enhance the productivity of agriculture and in another, reduce human fertility. The development of chemical technology whose output is fertilizers, and much later the emergence of biotechnology leading to the invention of high-yielding varieties of crops neutralized the effects of the operation of diminishing returns in agriculture. The coming into being of the technology of effective contraceptives was instrumental in reducing the fertility rate and much later replacing the nightmare of overpopulation by the nightmare, in some countries, of depopulation.

It is not only the classical economists but also others who did not place adequate importance on technology. Karl Marx, for example, emphasized capital, Stalinists stressed on industrialization and neoclassical economists on the market as the engine of development (Lewis, 1984). The relative neglect of technology might be due to the low frequency of inventions and their applications. That is, a low visibility of high-impact innovations might be the reason why technology was not assigned the central position in the socio-economic dynamics. However, the innovative activities do not take place in isolation societal support in the form of conducive institutional configuration and political patronage are a *sine qua non* for their flourishing (Lazonick, 2001).

The focus of this article is to identify the factors which have conditioned the growth of technology and industrialization in Arunachal Pradesh, a state whose journey to modernization began only after independence. Prior to independence no development took place in the state. It had at the time of independence only three primary schools. So the literacy rate was extremely low; moreover there was no modern industry in the area now forming Arunachal Pradesh. The post-independence days witnessed the launch of development programmes by the Government of India which aimed first to construct the various infrastructural facilities, roads, communication systems, educational institutions, hospitals, etc. The programme later made a switchover to industrialization, but the outcome could not keep pace with the resources invested in the process. This article tries to identify the institutional weaknesses responsible for the unexpectedly poor outcomes of the industrialization efforts. For convenience, the rest of the article is divided into three sections. Section-I is a description of the broad technological structure of production in Arunachal Pradesh. The relationship between technological progress, industrialization and development is highlighted in Section-II. The problems of industrialization and an outline of their solution appear in Section-III. Concluding remarks are also made in this section.

I

The capital intensity of production in Arunachal Pradesh is in general low. Since most of technology is embodied in machinery, a low intensity of capital is indicative of a low level of technology. However, there is a substantial inter-sectoral variation. At one end, there are modern industries—their number as well as scale is low—where the level of technology is high and production is capital-intensive; at the other end, there is traditional agriculture with an extremely low level of technology. The traditional agriculture practiced by the majority of the farmers is based even today on jhuming, the slash-and-burn method. Most of the manufacturing activities in the state are of cottage industry-scale, carried out by the members of the household. The overall value-added by industrial activities is extremely low. In 2007-08 the contribution of manufacturing amounted to only 2.28 per cent of the state's Gross Domestic Product (GDP). During the triennium ending 2007-08, the average value-added by manufacturing amounted to 2.31 per cent of the GDP. This is indeed small compared with even other states in the Northeast, the region least industrialized in the country. In absolute terms, the value-added at current prices by manufacturing activities in 2007-08 was Rs. 83.97 crore, an amount which appears rather dwarfed compared with the revenue earned by a small-scale firm in the rest of the country.

In rural Arunachal most of the households' manufacturing activities have a low technological level which results in productivity being low. Technology is related to capital intensity in production and a simple measure of capital intensity is the capital-labour ratio. So the capital-labour ratio is used here as the indicator of the level of technology. In general, the traditional economic activities in the state are characterized by low capital intensity. Jhuming, the traditional agricultural practice is highly land extensive and not labour-intensive but traditional manufacturing is highly labour-intensive. In *jhum* cultivation land is not tilled and so no plough or harrow is used. Most often, even clod-crushers are not required. The tools used are hoe, digging stick, rake, dao (a kind of machete), axe, scythe and spade. In jhuming, neither a chemical fertilizer nor pesticide is applied. The seeds used are traditional. The cottage industries of Arunachal Pradesh produce most of the goods required in a traditional household. These activities use a minimum of capital and utilize the household's labour very intensively.

When we move from the traditional production activities to those introduced after independence we see a steep rise in the capital intensity. In most of the plains of the state the permanent cultivation which is also known locally as wet-rice cultivation, was introduced in the 1950s and 1960s. The bullock-driven plough became the common symbol of permanent cultivation. Gradually power tillers and even tractors were introduced, but their use till date remains very limited. In manufacturing, if one moves from traditional to modern industry, one finds a steep rise in capital intensity.

Estimation of Capital-Labour Ratio

A simple method is used to calculate the value of the capital-labour ratio for the year 2009-10. In the estimation, fixed capital in all activities is assumed to have a life-term of 10 years with a linear depreciation. A 10 per cent rate of interest is taken to estimate the amount of interest cost. Capital is represented by the sum of interest and depreciation costs per annum. Labour is measured by the yearly wage rate which is taken to be Rs. 36,000 for both the *jhum* and permanent cultivation. This is the average wage rate for the agricultural sector in the state. The transport operator's yearly salary on average turns out to be Rs. 72,000. This is the average salary of the conductor and driver found in Itanagar- Naharlagun area of the state. For modern industry, a raw mill is taken. The capital-labour ratio for these activities is shown in Table 13.1.

Table 13.1: Capital Intensity of Production During 2009-10

Activity	*Capital-labour Ratio*	*Index of capital-labour Ratio*
Jhum cultivation	0.0045	100
Permanent cultivation		
(a) by plough	0.0600	1327
(b) by power tiller	1.6670	36881
Bus service	1.3889	30728
Modern industry	4.1667	92184

Source: Data collected from Papumpare District, Arunachal Pradesh.

The information in Table 13.1 gives a bird's eye view of the technological contrast that exists in the Arunachal economy. The capital intensity in jhuming is so low that the production can be called least-capitalised, that is, the production is carried out with the lowest possible intensity of capital—no further reduction is possible. The capital intensity rises abruptly in permanent cultivation. The cultivation by bullock-driven plough has a capital intensity which is 13 times higher than that in jhuming. The power tiller-based cultivation has a capital intensity which soars to 369 times that of jhuming. Modern industry's capital intensity, as expected, is highest—it is 922 times the capital intensity of jhuming.

The analysis done here is based on a sample which covers small segments of the economy. It does not cover the cottage industry, but it can safely be surmised that the intensity of capital in cottage industry production would not differ significantly from that of jhuming. Again, in some modern or rather urban industrial activities, capital intensity is low. For example, a cobbler's activity in a street corner belongs to the modern industrial category in Arunachal Pradesh because of its introduction in the post-independence days, but the capital intensity in shoe-making/repairing is extremely small. So the information in Table 13.1 suffers from the small sample bias, but it gives an idea of the technological dichotomy that exists in the state between the traditional and modern technologies.

II

In terms of a simplistic input-out framework, industrialization can be seen as the sustained accumulation of both physical and human capital, and expansion of output of a large variety of goods and services. The newly-accumulated capital often embodies a new technology and additional human capital is usually an acquisition of new industrial skill and know-how through what is known as learning by doing. But industrialization along with its propulsive force, the new technology, is more a process than a mere expansion of industrial output. Had it been a mere mechanical relation between input and output determined by technology, then perhaps industrialization would have been an easy task achievable by making a good amount of physical investment. But a high failure rate of the efforts of industrialization is indicative of failure of the instrumentalist approach, and especially of 'physicalism'.

Industrialization is a complex process resolvable into two sub-processes: one is translational and the other transformational. The translational process entails a shifting of industrial focus from scatteredness to concentrations, from dispersed manufacturing activities carried on at households to new centres located mostly in urban and semi-urban areas. The shift of industrial location and 'deindustrialisation' cause flows of migration of workers from rural to urban areas. The process of translation or shifting in space is inseparably related to a transformative process, the change of operational scale of manufacturing. Household manufacturing is enlarged into factory scale manufacturing. The other change is social—the members of different primary groups are transformed into a secondary group whose members operate the factory. So, successful industrialization means a successful social transformation, first in the factory, then in the society at large. However, the argument can be made from the opposite direction: in a transformable society, the one which is waiting for mobility to be set in operation, industrialization is likely to enjoy easy success.

In household-level manufacturing, there is no dearth of incentives—one is working for the immediate family members. But in a factory with workers from different social groups there may be problems of incentives. Workers from different social denominations may not find it easy to perform as a team. However, modern manufacturing, which has the flexibility to adopt more productive technology, whenever it is available, can provide sufficient incentives to its workers. The technology-induced high productivity and high profitability creating a situation of the positive-sum game succeeding n effecting a 'social transformation' at the factory level. The traditional or a low level of technology with its low productivity cannot effect such a transformation because it creates a situation of the zero-sum game in a team of people drawn from different caste or ethnic groups.

In order to show the centrality of technology in the process of industrialization and development, we use the data on patents and economic structure of five countries: China, India, Japan, Korea and the US. Table 13.2 shows the level of income, sectoral composition of the Gross Domestic Product (GDP) and the patents granted, which is a proxy for inventions and innovations. In the group, China is the most industrialized, with 48 per cent of its GDP being generated by industry; the US is most post-industrial, 76 per cent of its income comes from tertiary activities—and India is most agricultural with 18 per cent of its GDP being contributed by agriculture. At the other sectoral extreme, the US is least agricultural and also least industrial, and China is least post-industrial. Japan which is free from any sectoral extreme in the group, granted the highest number of patents, 1.64 lakh, which is 22 times the number granted by India in 2009. The second position is occupied by the US with 1.57 lakh patents, 4.65 per cent less than Japan's. South Korea's position is third with 1.24 lakh patents.

It will be more informative if the number of patents per million population of a country is found out. This is done in Table 13.3. However, patents are granted not only to the residents but also to the non-residents. In 2009, for example, the numbers of patents filed in India were as high as 28,940 of which only 18 per cent were from residents. In China, the resident patent fields were 62 per cent of the total (Prasanth 2010). The resident-non-resident classification carries hardly any substance while considering the technological change in a country. It is the growth of technology which carries more economic meaning and weight than the identity of its creators.

Tables 13.2 and 13.3 provide some evidence to arrive at a tentative conclusion on the relation between economic structure and technological change. The rank correlation between the total number of patents granted and the percentage of GDP from services is positive (0.80) and significant but the rank correlation between patents and

Table 13.2: Income, Economic Structure and Patents Granted in Selected Countries

Country	*Income per head*	*Value added as % of GDP*			*Patents granted in 2009*
		Agriculture	*Industry*	*Services*	
China	5370	12	48	40	67948
India	2740	18	29	53	7539
Japan	34600	2	30	68	1,64,948
Korea	24750	3	39	58	1,23,705
US	45850	1	23	76	1,57,283

NB: Income per head is in purchasing power parity (PPP) US dollar.

Source: Data on income and composition of GDP which relate to year 2007 is from World Bank (2009). The data on patents is from Prasanth (2010).

Table 13.3: Patents Granted Per Million Populations

Country	*Population (million) in 2007*	*Patents per million population in 2009*
China	1320	51
India	1123	7
Japan	128	1289
Korea	49	2525
US	302	521

Source: Population data is from World Bank (2009).

industrial share in GDP is insignificant with a value of -0.20. A very small sample size does not allow us to press this relation hard, but one can safely conclude that the technological progress which nourishes industrialization and in turn is nourished by it, propels an industrialized economy towards its post-industrial stage where a significant part of the population becomes engaged in the creation of new technology. This point can be exemplified. In 2009, IBM got 4914 patents in the US (*The Hindu Business Line*, 2010). Two other corporations in order of patents granted in the US were Samsung Electronics (3611 patents) and Microsoft Corporation (2906 patents). It is remarkable that IBM's patents rose by as high as 50 per cent in the course of just five years from 2004 to 2009. The total number of patents granted to these three corporations was 11431 which is 51.62 per cent higher than the number granted in India. So post-industrialization is a transition from goods-making to technology-making.

III

Given the primacy of industrialization in development, it is relevant to shed some light on why Arunachal Pradesh suffered a setback in the process. The developmental optimism that prevailed throughout the developing world in the decades following the Second World War swept the state partly in the 1950s and mainly in the 1960s after the Chinese invasion. The rich natural resources in the state were thought to be able to support a number of industries. With all sincerity, industrialization began in the 1970s and a number of industries under the ownership of the Government were set up in the 1980s. However, the operational efficiency of most of these industries was so low that they could not generate any profit. Rather, they were incurring losses year after year. In order to escape from the mounting losses, most of these industrial concerns were gradually closed down.

Arunachal Pradesh is not alone in suffering a setback in its maiden effort of industrialization. There are many areas inside and outside our country which have suffered the same fate, and this is the flip side of the instrumentalist approach which assumes that society is like a lump of soft earth capable of being moulded by the Government through the agency of material objects. In the context of Arunachal Pradesh, the project of industrialization did not take into consideration the tastes and preferences of the local people, their strengths and their weaknesses. Rather, industries were imposed, assuming that they would bring linkages through which new technology would propagate. The approach was from industry to people, not from people to industry, an approach that could not work.

From the start, modern industrialization in the state did not pay attention to the productive use of the transformational power of technology and human capital. The industries established in the state were neither technology-incentive nor human capital-intensive; they failed to promote learning. Many industrial skills are acquired only through engaging in actual work. Learning by doing tends to raise the productivity of the workers, which enables the management to pay higher salaries, the incentives which tend to develop the team spirit in the factory. It is the team spirit that is an important factor of high productivity and a type of social transformation is affected by an industrial concern. Such an industrial concern is always after high technology.

In a multinational company, people from different nationalities work together and a strong team spirit is created. It seems like magic. The secret of this magic is partly managerial proficiency and technological efficiency, both being the product of a healthy combination of rich human capital and productive technology. In Arunachal Pradesh the industrialization process suffered from the deficiency of both human capital and technology. The government-run management lacked sufficient human capital; it also could not promote it through the induction of productive technology.

Notes

1. *The Hindu Business Line* (2010): *'IBM tops in US Patents' Report 2009*, 14 January, Delhi.
2. Arthur W. Lewis (1984): *"The State of Development Theory", American Economic Review*, Vol. 74 No. 1, pp. 1-10.
3. W. Lazonick (2001): "*Social Organization and Technological Leadership*", in F.J. Lechner and J. Boli (ed.), *The Globalization Reader*, Oxford, Blackwell, pp. 164-193.
4. G.N. Prasanth (2010), "India Lagging in Research Output", *The Times of India,* 11 February, 2010.
5. The World Bank (2009), *World Development*, Washington DC.

14

Patterns of Employment in Arunachal Pradesh

Implications for Inclusive Development

Vandana Upadhyay

Inclusive Development

Access to employment is one of the fundamental ways to gain access to earnings and by implication, a range of goods, services and institutions, which enhances human well-being. Providing productive employment opportunities to the increasing labour force has been a cornerstone of policymaking in many developing economies, more so in the case of densely populated countries like India in order to make development more inclusive. There has been a concern with the slower growth of employment opportunities with the onset of economic reforms in India. With increasing skill-intensity in many of the newly emerging and rapidly expanding sectors, such as the Information and Communication Technology (ICT), and declining employment elasticity in organized manufacturing, the prediction of 'jobless growth' is increasingly being voiced in many quarters. With the slowing down of agricultural growth in the nineties as well as signs of relative stagnation in the rural non-farm sector employment, the prospects for the rural workers seem less than promising (Chadha and Sahu, 2002; Chadha, 2002). Increasingly, more and more emphasis is being given to inclusive growth and development. Inclusive growth focuses on economic growth, which is in fact a necessary and crucial condition for poverty reduction. It is a broad-based, long-term perspective focusing on sustainable growth. It is inclusive in nature and focuses on both the pace and pattern of growth and productive employment rather than income distribution as a means of increasing incomes for excluded groups. In fact, inclusiveness is a concept that encompasses equity, equality of opportunity, and protection in market and employment transitions and is an essential ingredient of any successful growth strategy (Commission on Growth and Development, 2008). Thus the definition of inclusive growth implies a direct link between the macro and micro determinants of growth and captures the importance of structural transformation for economic diversification and competition. Inclusive development therefore is a process of ensuring that all marginalized and excluded groups are included in the development process.

Issues of Development in Arunachal Pradesh

In Arunachal Pradesh as well as in many neighbouring northeastern states the question of employment and unemployment has additional significance and implications. The spiral of high unemployment, political instability and slow economic growth has been part of the recent history of many states of the region. Due to a number of problems, both at the regional as well as the state levels, the growth of private sector investment in these states has been rather tardy. While the problems of insurgency and violence have diverse roots, portraying them as the results of economic backwardness alone would be highly reductionist; many observers would agree that unemployment in general and unemployment of the youth in particular, acts as a supporting factor in creating political instability (Sarma, 2005; Upadhaya, 2005). The continuing political violence, on the other hand, acts as a cause of slow economic growth, which in turn, serves as reason for increasing unemployment. In Arunachal Pradesh, which, barring a few districts in recent past, has witnessed a lesser degree of insurgency and other forms of political violence, the right kind of employment policy, apart from its intrinsic value, has additional relevance and urgency as part of the strategy towards providing greater social stability and human security. One of the fundamental problems in designing such a strategy, however, is the thin database on various aspects of the employment and unemployment scenario in the state. Based on the available secondary information and the insights from a few micro-studies, the article provides a broad overview of the employment scenario in the state.

The data from the NSS' 50th round (July 1993-June 1994), 55th round (July 1999-June 2000) and 61st round (July 2004-June 2005) has been used to analyze various aspects of the employment scenario in Arunachal Pradesh. While the choice of periods has been dictated by the availability of data, the limited insights that one can get from this exercise, will have to be judged from the specific constraints and challenges faced by Arunachal Pradesh. This period, 1993-94 to 2004-2005, is generally taken to be the post-reform period in the discussions on poverty and unemployment in India. While, given the overall significance of the state as the dominant economic actor in the state's economy, the economy of Arunachal Pradesh was not entirely immune from the processes of liberalization which were initiated at the Centre; nevertheless, there was a noticeably limited impact of the liberalization of the economy so far as the policies of the state government were concerned. Apart from the difficulties associated with a relative reduction in the flow of funds from the central government, two other developments contributed to the state of the economy significantly. The nineties was also the decade in which various 'financial packages' were announced for the Northeast by successive central governments, apart from the creation of a special ministry, at the Centre, for the development of the northeastern region (Ramesh, 2005). Thus, there were many new projects, particularly aiming at infrastructural development, which complemented the usual central government initiatives. Secondly, the restrictions imposed on the commercial use of timber, had a drastic effect not only on the forestry and logging sector, but also on other sectors of the economy, most ostensibly on non-household manufacturing. The changes between 1993-94 and 2004-2005, on which most of the subsequent discussions concentrate, thus, cannot be assumed simply to be the changes in the post-reform period, so far as the Arunachal economy is concerned.

Patterns of Employment in Arunachal Pradesh

The changing composition of employment in Arunachal Pradesh, for various categories of workers, has been presented in Tables 14.1, 14.2 and 14.3 for the three NSS rounds. In order to get an insight into the employment patterns of different social groups within the state, disaggregated figures for males and females in rural and urban areas, belonging to the Scheduled Tribes (ST) and other social groups has been presented. In 2004-2005, it is found that out of the total workers in Arunachal Pradesh, 79.7 per cent were self-employed, while nearly 6.1 per cent worked as casual labourers and the rest worked as regular salaried workers. The proportion of self-employed workers was remarkably higher in the rural areas than in the urban areas. In fact, it is regular salaried employment that has the largest category of employment in urban Arunachal Pradesh. The share of the self-employed was around 93 per cent among rural women, while it was 40.5 per cent among urban women. In terms of social groups, the share of regular salaried employment was remarkably low in the case of ST workers (9 per cent) than non-ST workers (27 per cent). The casual labour category also had a lower share among the ST workers than the non-ST workers. In rural areas, as high as 90 per cent of the total workers and 95 per cent of women workers in the ST category, were self-employed.

The important changes that took place during 1993-94 and 2004-05 are as follows: Firstly, between 1993-94 and 1999-2000, there was a decrease in the share of self-employed workers, a marginal decline in the share of salaried employment and a rise in the share of casual workers. During the period 1993-94 and 2004-05, while in the urban areas the share of self-employed and that of salaried employment had declined, as far as the share of casual workers is concerned, which was around 15 per cent in the earlier two rounds, it had gone down to 8.4 per cent in 2004-05. Between 1999-00 and 2004-05, however, there had been an increase in the share of the self-employed people and a decline in the share of casual labourers. Thus, between 1993-94 and 2004-05, there had only been a marginal change in the composition of employment in Arunachal Pradesh. In the rural areas, there had been a growth of casual wage labour along with a decline in the share of salaried employment, while the share of self-employment had remained almost stagnant. Given the substantial role of the government sector in providing regular salaried jobs in the state, the impact of a job squeeze in the government sector on the overall employment structure comes out very clearly from the data presented here. Secondly, it is important to note that there had been a decline in the relative importance of self-employment among the ST workers, which has been accompanied by a rise in the share of both regular salaried employment as well as casual labour. Thirdly, among the male workers in rural areas belonging to the ST category, there had been a fall in the share of self-employment, along with a corresponding rise in the share of casual labour and regular employment. The only group of workers which had not witnessed any significant change in the structure of employment, is rural women belonging to the ST category. In fact, their share in regular salaried employment had increased marginally, while the shift away from self-employment, which has been a consistent feature in the case of most categories, has not been seen in the case of women workers of this category. Although, given the small size of the sample in some of the disaggregated categories, some of these trends might not be reflecting the ground realities. But by and large, the restructuring of employment as shown in these Tables brings out the broad contours of change in the employment scenario of the state.

Distribution of Workers Across Industries

Tables 14.4 through 14.6 present the distribution of workers at the broad industry level in Arunachal Pradesh. The share of agriculture in 2004-2005, among all workers, was 76 per cent, implying the continuing significance of agriculture in the state's economy. It is important to note that the next important industry was public administration followed by education and community services, which clearly underlines the significance of the government sector in generating employment outside agriculture. Manufacturing has a low share of 0.6 per cent, while construction has a share of nearly 4 per cent. Among other activities, trade, hotel and industries, account for 4 per cent of the workers employed. The industrial diversification of workers is even less pronounced in the case of rural workers in general and rural women workers in particular. The share of rural men and women in public administration and other areas is significantly less than that of their urban counterparts. In urban areas, the share of women workers was higher than that of male workers in construction. Among urban males, around 51 per cent were in public administration, while 27 per cent were in trade, hotels and restaurants. The share of ST workers in agriculture, particularly in rural areas and among females, was considerably high.

So far as changes between 1993-94 and 2004-05 are concerned, in overall terms, there had been a marginal decline in the share of workers employed in agriculture, while a marginal increase was noticed in the share of those employed in public administration, etc. The increase in the share of workers employed in public administration was more pronounced in the case of urban workers in general and urban male workers in particular. Among the ST workers, there was a decrease in the share of those employed in agriculture, while there was an increase in the share of those engaged in public administration.

In the urban areas, ST women have increased their visibility in two industries, namely, construction and trade, hotels and restaurants. As a consequence, the share of those employed in public administration has declined. Thus, the unevenness in the process of occupational diversification is clear from the disparities in the access to non-agricultural occupations by various categories of workers. Rural workers in general and rural women workers have continued to be tied to agriculture. While at one level it signifies the unequal opportunities available to women as compared to men, micro-studies suggest that the shift of the rural male workers to activities other than agriculture has led to a process of 'feminization' of agriculture in the sense that women are substituting men in farm work (Mishra, 2003).

Growth of Women's Employment: 1993-94 to 2004-2005

As far as the growth of employment between 1993-94 and 1999-2000 is concerned, for the state as a whole, in overall terms, while employment growth was negative for all workers, it was more significant for the women workers. Location-wise, deceleration in employment growth was sharper for urban men, urban women and rural women. There was a contrasting pattern of employment growth for non-ST and ST workers—while for non-ST workers in general and non-ST women workers in particular, the employment scenario worsened, for the ST workers employment gains were substantial. Thus, the overall negative growth in employment was because of a strong decline in employment of the non-ST workers (Table 14.7).

Between 1999-2000 and 2004-05, employment growth was 5.8 per cent for all workers. It was remarkably higher in the urban areas than in the rural areas. Unlike the earlier period, employment growth was positive for all categories of workers. While there was substantial gain in employment for both men and women workers of ST category, for non-ST workers, employment growth was negative, primarily because of shrinking employment opportunities for rural non-ST workers (Table 14.8).

The limited coverage of the data makes it difficult to draw a conclusion regarding the growth of employment at the industry level. However, from 1993-94 to 1999-2000 there was negative growth in sectors like agriculture, electricity, gas and water supply, transport, finance and business services, public administration, education and community services, while employment increased in manufacturing, construction, trade, hotel and restaurants. In fact, in the latter period, rural employment growth was robust. Between 1999-00 and 2004-05, the significant changes were the decline in employment in manufacturing and substantial growth in electricity, gas and water supply, trade, hotels, restaurants, transport, finance and business services and public administration. Also remarkable was the fact that rural women gained in sectors like construction, trade, hotels and restaurants, apart from public administration. Another noticeable pattern was that there was significant employment growth for ST workers in agriculture and public administration, education and community services, while in these industries, non-ST workers experienced a negative employment growth.

Youth and Unemployment Among the Educated

Youth and unemployment among the educated is normally found to be higher than the general unemployment rate. At the all-India level, for all groups except urban women, it has increased significantly over the 1990s (Planning Commission, 2002). In the case of Arunachal Pradesh, the problem of unemployment is generally considered to be a problem of the educated and the young population. The data from the employment exchange shows that the number of unemployed persons in the live register has crossed twenty-six thousand. The NSS data also shows a relatively higher level of unemployment among the relatively better educated. The rate of unemployment among those having a secondary or higher level of education was higher than that among the general population. Between 1993-94 and 2004-05, the level of unemployment among the relatively better educated has declined. However, an important change between these two years is that, while in 1993-94 unemployment among the educated in the ST group was virtually non-existent it started showing some presence since 1999-2000.[1] Although, given the thin spread of the sample across all these categories, conclusions should be drawn rather cautiously. The available data suggests that, between 1993-94 and 2004-05, the decline in the unemployment rates among the relatively better educated groups, was accompanied by a rise in unemployment among the relatively better educated ST youths in the rural areas (Tables 14.9-14.11).

Among the different age groups, the unemployment rate was highest in the age group of 20-24 years followed by the category 25-29 years in 2004-05. The unemployment rate was particularly high among the urban youth in the state. Urban women belonging to the age group of 15-24 years have a high level of unemployment in the state (Tables 14.12-14.14). Another important aspect of the unemployment scenario in the state is that the extent of youth unemployment among the population is higher among the ST population than the general levels of youth unemployment in the state. Between 1993-94 and 2004-05, there has been an increase in the extent of youth unemployment among the ST population.

The problem of unemployment among the youth and the educated in Arunachal Pradesh, though considerably lower than many other parts of the country, basically exemplifies the mismatch between the available jobs and the skills, expectations and aspirations of young job seekers. Given the negligible presence of organized manufacturing in the state, and the dominance of public administration as a source of employment, so far, the major source of employment has been the Government sector. There are, however, obvious limits to the possibility of expanding employment opportunities in the Government sector, particularly in the context of increasing emphasis on fiscal responsibilities of the Government at various levels. The analysis of sectoral issues in employment generation brings out these problems and inadequacies in a clearer manner.

Growth Rate of Labour Force and Unemployment

Between 1999-2000 and 2004-05, the labour force in Arunachal Pradesh increased at the rate of 5.9 per cent, while unemployment increased at the rate of 13.1 per cent for all categories of workers. Unemployment has decreased in urban areas but it has increased in the rural areas of the state. For the ST workers, overall unemployment has increased, mainly due to the increase in rural unemployment (Table 14.15).

Drop-Out Rates: A Cause of Concern

Access to education plays a significant role in expanding opportunities for individuals, households and communities. Given the positive externalities of education in general, it is hardly surprising that expansion of educational opportunities has been regarded as one of the fundamental means for social transformation, thereby making development more inclusive.

Improvements in enrolment, however, do not guarantee access to adequate levels of education. The drop-out rates in relatively underdeveloped regions are very high. In Arunachal Pradesh drop-out rates in classes I-V for children have come down substantially from 73.9 per cent in 1981-82 to 46.85 per cent in 2004-05 (Table 14.16). It is still higher than the national average, but there seems to be very little improvement in reducing the drop-out rate at this stage in the past few years. The drop-out rate at this stage in 1998-99 was already 46.89 per cent. The drop-out rate in classes I-VIII for children, similarly, reduced from 84.20 per cent in 1981-82 to 63.23 per cent in 2004-05. Similarly, the drop-out rate for children in classes I-X has reduced from 90.70 per cent in 1981-82 to 70.79 per cent in 2004-05. In this case, in classes I-X, girls in the state have a higher drop-out rate than boys. The drop-out rates for scheduled tribe students are higher than that of all categories of students.

In Arunachal Pradesh access to formal education has been one of the most important means for achieving a better quality of life and the rapid transformation and modernization of the economy, society and polity. The gender disparity index[2] in Arunachal Pradesh is higher at all levels of schooling than that of most of the other northeastern states. This disparity is even more pronounced in higher education. At this stage, with the sole exception of Tripura, Arunachal Pradesh has a higher gender disparity index than all other states of the region. Thus, as pointed out earlier, greater emphasis has to be given to expand access for girls to higher education in order to make it more inclusive.

Towards a Policy Framework for Inclusive Development

Arunachal Pradesh is a predominantly tribal state and a substantial proportion of its area is mountainous. Often it is argued that conventional employment generation strategies conceived at the level of the central government and other agencies are inadequate and inappropriate for the state. Thus, there is an urgent need for a serious re-evaluation of the employment generation strategy in the state, keeping in mind the local specificities. For a number of reasons, the standard model of employment generation is less likely to be effective in Arunachal Pradesh.[3] Given the fact that most of the poor in the state are self-employed in agriculture, it is quite natural that the standard programmes that attempt to tackle poverty by providing more employment opportunity through labour-intensive casual work would not be successful in Arunachal Pradesh.[4] In fact, given the labour market characteristics of the state, such programmes have helped the people who are well above the poverty line (viz., contractors) more than the poor.

There is a need to integrate the problems of unemployment and poverty. As in the case of many other underdeveloped regions of India, poverty doesn't necessarily reflect itself through unemployment, as the poor are too poor to be unemployed. So far as the problems of the self-employed poor who are mainly cultivators in rural areas, are concerned, there are only two viable policy options: a) to increase productivity and profitability of agriculture; and b) to provide alternative sources of earnings and employment in non-agricultural occupations. No doubt, there is scope for increasing earnings within agriculture through crop diversification, technological change, value addition at local levels, etc., but given the ecological constraints and weak market linkages, there are limits to which agricultural growth could be projected as the sole hope for rural development. The alternative is to provide education and gradually shift labour from low to high productive occupations. But this strategy has its own problems as well. In Arunachal Pradesh, manufacturing in general, and private industries in particular, have a marginal presence. Provision of non-agricultural jobs has been mainly through expansion of employment in the government sector; so much so that, the basic purpose of public investment is thought to be 'job creation' rather than development per se. This strategy is wasteful, unproductive and unsustainable in the long-run, but more importantly, it would almost certainly bypass the poor.

In this context, the increasing participation of women in a number of micro-enterprises provides an alternative strategy to address the problems of the poor. Many of these women are found in retail trade and seasonal enterprises, but some of them are also involved in the traditional manufacturing. Given the ecological preconditions and the spatial dispersion of settlements in the state, these enterprises cater to a locally differentiated market. There is a strong linkage with the household economy as well, with many of them selling output produced or collected by themselves and other family members. Most importantly, these activities are not directly dependent on state support or subsidies. These are micro-level responses of women, who might be less educated and less skilled, but who have a keen understanding of their household level strengths and constraints (Upadhyay, 2005).

Several policy implications could be noted on the basis of the existing employment situation in Arunachal Pradesh. The real problem confronting the economy of Arunachal Pradesh, apart from the slowing down of the growth of per capita NSDP in the 1990s, is the lop-sided nature of the growth itself. This is also reflected in the employment structure of the economy. Till now the major chunk of employment generated outside the agriculture sector has been either in public administration or sectors like construction, which have strong linkages with Government spending. The inadequate expansion of employment opportunities in the manufacturing sector has to be addressed in a forward-looking perspective, giving due emphasis to the relative advantages and disadvantages of the state in specific sectors. The crux of the problem is however, to create enough employment opportunities outside the Government sector. Given the low level of development of the state as well as the strong presence of the state in various sectors of the economy, it may be possible to expand employment in the Government sector at least for a few more years. But there are obvious limits to this and any forward-looking strategy has to take cognizance of this limitation.

The problem of youth and unemployment among the educated, which exists along with shortages of skilled manpower in specific sectors and occupations, needs urgent attention, particularly because of its potential role as a source of social destabilization. The policy options here range from harmonization of skill requirements and skill creation to create additional avenues of earnings for the youth, particularly for those living in the rural areas. Strengthening the system of vocational education will go a long way in addressing the skill deficit in the state. Lack of entrepreneurial ability has acted as a major constraint in making self-employment an attractive option for the youth and the unemployed.

There is a tremendous scope for the expansion of the rural non-farm occupations in the state. At present, the growth of the non-farm economy seems to be restricted to a few well-communicated rural localities of the state. There has been a great deal of spatial concentration in rural non-farm sector employment in the state. There is a clear need for a more *dispersed* rural non-farm sector growth. There is a sharp difference in access to non-farm occupations, along both ethnic and class lines. While in overall terms, the non-ST households have a higher presence in the non-farm occupations, even in the rural areas, most of the ST households which are in the non-farm sectors are in the relatively high-earning jobs within the sector (Mishra, 2007). The growing inequality of opportunities in Arunachal Pradesh, particularly among the indigenous communities of the state, is, at least partially, responsible for this kind of a hiatus in the rural labour market. There is also an urgent need to identify and prioritize the rapidly growing rural non-farm occupations to dove-tail their sector-specific needs to a comprehensive strategy of employment generation in rural Arunachal Pradesh.

Some sectors like rural manufacturing and petty trading need additional attention. Over the past decades, partly as a result of the growing demonstration effect of urban consumption patterns in the rural areas, there has been a phenomenal growth of these sectors in the rural areas. Women, particularly those belonging to the tribal communities have already taken a lead in establishing small self-financed micro-enterprises in petty trading (Upadhyay, 2005; 2007). In the urban areas of the state there has been a modest growth of traditional handicraft manufacturing as well. All these activities should be made part of the strategy to generate more employment, particularly more self-employment in the rural areas. Among the basic needs of these enterprises is credit and marketing support. There is a scope for better horizontal as well as vertical coordination among various agencies working in these areas.

Finally, given the overwhelming significance of education as a determinant for entry into more remunerative occupations, education has to be made more accessible to all sections of the population. There is a significant rural-urban as well as a gender divide in terms of access to education in the state. Apart from addressing these glaring inequalities, there is a clear case for special educational drives for specific marginalized groups such as villagers in inaccessible and border areas, traditionally marginalized ethnic groups, migrant casual labourers, tenants, as well as those living in labour camps, in order to make it more inclusive.

Acknowledgements

This article is part of a larger study undertaken for the preparation of the State Development Report of Arunachal Pradesh. The author is grateful to Prof. Atul Sarma and Dr. Deepak Mishra for their comments on earlier drafts and to Rajiv Kumar for his research support. The usual disclaimers apply.

Appendices

Table 14.1: Composition of Employment in Arunachal Pradesh: 1993-94 (UPSS basis)

Location	*Employment Category*	*Male*	*Female*	*Persons*
		All Social Groups		
Rural	Self-Employed	76.19	93.57	83.61
	Regular Employed	17.39	5.07	12.13
	Casual Labour	6.42	1.36	4.26
Urban	Self-Employed	18.93	31.18	20.66
	Regular Employed	67.01	52.55	64.97
	Casual Labour	14.06	16.27	14.37
All	Self-Employed	68.99	91.65	78.09
	Regular Employed	23.63	6.53	16.76
	Casual Labour	7.38	1.82	5.15
		ST Social Group		
Rural	Self-Employed	90.57	96.68	93.24
	Regular Employed	7.79	2.26	5.38
	Casual Labour	1.64	1.05	1.38
Urban	Self-Employed	0.00	25.94	3.95
	Regular Employed	36.44	74.06	42.16
	Casual Labour	63.56	0.00	53.89
All	Self-Employed	88.28	96.26	91.73
	Regular Employed	8.52	2.69	6.00
	Casual Labour	3.20	1.05	2.27
		Non-ST Social Group		
Rural	Self-Employed	73.29	92.91	81.62
	Regular Employed	19.33	5.67	13.52
	Casual Labour	7.39	1.42	4.85
Urban	Self-Employed	19.53	31.36	21.19
	Regular Employed	67.96	51.81	65.69
	Casual Labour	12.51	16.82	13.12
All	Self-Employed	65.56	90.70	75.52
	Regular Employed	26.32	7.32	18.79
	Casual Labour	8.12	1.98	5.69

Source: NSS 50th Round

Table 14.2: Composition of Employment in Arunachal Pradesh: 1999-2000 (UPSS basis)

Location	*Employment Category*	*Male*	*Female*	*Persons*
			All Social Groups	
Rural	Self-Employed	70.17	92.98	79.31
	Regular Employed	20.14	1.38	12.63
	Casual Labour	9.69	5.64	8.07
Urban	Self-Employed	21.57	35.54	23.89
	Regular Employed	59.31	58.10	59.11
	Casual Labour	19.13	6.36	17.00
All	Self-Employed	66.24	91.51	76.01
	Regular Employed	23.31	2.83	15.39
	Casual Labour	10.45	5.66	8.60
			ST Social Group	
Rural	Self-Employed	80.48	97.01	88.10
	Regular Employed	12.51	1.14	7.27
	Casual Labour	7.02	1.84	4.63
Urban	Self-Employed	19.90	60.71	30.12
	Regular Employed	72.25	39.29	64.00
	Casual Labour	7.85	0.00	5.88
All	Self-Employed	77.43	96.28	85.98
	Regular Employed	15.51	1.91	9.34
	Casual Labour	7.06	1.81	4.68
			Non-ST Social Group	
Rural	Self-Employed	60.81	86.69	69.42
	Regular Employed	27.07	1.75	18.65
	Casual Labour	12.12	11.56	11.93
Urban	Self-Employed	22.23	12.40	20.99
	Regular Employed	54.13	75.39	56.83
	Casual Labour	23.64	12.21	22.19
All	Self-Employed	56.68	84.18	65.35
	Regular Employed	29.97	4.24	21.86
	Casual Labour	13.35	11.58	12.79

Source: NSS 55th Round.

Table 14.3: Composition of Employment in Arunachal Pradesh: 2004-05 (UPSS basis)

Location	*Employment Category*	*Male*	*Female*	*Persons*
		All Social Groups		
Rural	Self-Employed	76.4	92.6	83.3
	Regular Employed	16.5	2.9	10.8
	Casual Labour	7.0	4.4	5.9
Urban	Self-Employed	41.3	47.9	42.7
	Regular Employed	51.1	40.5	48.9
	Casual Labour	7.5	11.6	8.4
All	Self-Employed	72.3	90.6	79.7
	Regular Employed	20.6	4.7	14.2
	Casual Labour	7.1	4.7	6.1
		ST Social Group		
Rural	Self-Employed	84.7	94.9	89.3
	Regular Employed	11.5	3.0	7.6
	Casual Labour	3.8	2.1	3.1
Urban	Self-Employed	40.8	50.0	44.1
	Regular Employed	55.9	41.8	50.7
	Casual Labour	3.3	8.2	5.1
All	Self-Employed	82.5	93.4	87.4
	Regular Employed	13.7	4.3	9.4
	Casual Labour	3.8	2.4	3.2
		Non-ST Social Group		
Rural	Self-Employed	55.2	82.3	63.8
	Regular Employed	29.5	2.9	21.0
	Casual Labour	15.3	14.8	15.1
Urban	Self-Employed	41.6	44.7	42.0
	Regular Employed	49.3	38.4	47.9
	Casual Labour	9.1	16.9	10.1
All	Self-Employed	51.7	78.7	59.2
	Regular Employed	34.6	6.3	26.7
	Casual Labour	13.7	15.0	14.1

Source: NSS 61st Round.

Table 14.4: Industry-Group wise Distribution of Workers in Arunachal Pradesh: 1993-94

Industry Group	*Category of Workers*								
	R_M	*R_F*	*R_P*	*U_M*	*U_F*	*U_P*	*T_M*	*T_F*	*T_P*
					All Social Groups				
Agriculture	79.07	96.16	86.39	7.09	19.27	8.65	70.15	94.09	79.79
Mining & Quarrying	0.06	0.04	0.05	0.00	0.00	0.00	0.05	0.04	0.05
Manufacturing	0.42	1.32	0.80	12.36	9.84	12.04	1.90	1.55	1.76
Manufacturing	0.00	0.00	0.00	2.19	0.00	1.91	0.27	0.00	0.16
Electricity, Gas & Water Supply	1.38	0.11	0.84	4.01	1.73	3.72	1.70	0.15	1.08
Construction	3.90	1.00	2.66	9.56	7.72	9.32	4.60	1.18	3.22
Trade, Hotels & Restaurants	0.32	0.00	0.18	17.14	5.24	15.62	2.41	0.14	1.49
Transport	2.56	0.37	1.62	6.37	0.00	5.56	3.03	0.36	1.96
Finance & Business Services	0.66	0.00	0.37	3.20	1.90	3.03	0.97	0.05	0.60
Public Admn, Education & Community Services	11.64	0.99	7.08	38.08	54.30	40.16	14.91	2.43	9.89
All	100.00	100.00	100.00	100.00	100.00	100.00	100.00	100.00	100.00
					ST Social Group				
Agriculture	90.10	96.82	93.06	0.00	0.00	0.00	87.78	96.38	91.52
Mining & Quarrying	0.00	0.00	0.00	0.00	0.00	0.00	0.00	0.00	0.00
Manufacturing	0.00	0.19	0.08	13.36	0.00	11.79	0.34	0.19	0.28
Manufacturing	0.00	0.00	0.00	0.00	0.00	0.00	0.00	0.00	0.00
Electricity, Gas & Water Supply	0.00	0.00	0.00	8.64	0.00	7.62	0.22	0.00	0.13
Construction	1.86	1.06	1.51	0.00	0.00	0.00	1.81	1.06	1.48
Trade, Hotels & Restaurants	0.00	0.00	0.00	0.00	0.00	0.00	0.00	0.00	0.00
Transport	0.56	0.00	0.31	0.00	0.00	0.00	0.54	0.00	0.31
Finance & Business Services	0.56	0.00	0.31	0.00	0.00	0.00	0.54	0.00	0.31
Public Admn, Education & Community Services	6.93	1.93	4.73	78.00	100.00	80.58	8.76	2.37	5.98
All	100.00	100.00	100.00	100.00	100.00	100.00	100.00	100.00	100.00

(*Contd.*)

Industry Group	Category of Workers								
	R_M	R_F	R_P	U_M	U_F	U_P	T_M	T_F	T_P
				Non-ST Social Group					
Agriculture	76.87	96.03	85.02	7.32	19.83	8.92	67.06	93.62	77.59
Mining & Quarrying	0.07	0.05	0.06	0.00	0.00	0.00	0.06	0.05	0.06
Manufacturing	0.50	1.56	0.95	12.33	10.13	12.05	2.17	1.83	2.04
Manufacturing	0.00	0.00	0.00	2.26	0.00	1.97	0.32	0.00	0.19
Electricity, Gas & Water Supply	1.65	0.13	1.01	3.86	1.78	3.60	1.96	0.19	1.26
Construction	4.30	0.99	2.89	9.86	7.95	9.62	5.09	1.21	3.55
Trade, Hotels & Restaurants	0.39	0.00	0.22	17.69	5.39	16.11	2.83	0.17	1.77
Transport	2.96	0.45	1.89	6.58	0.00	5.73	3.47	0.44	2.27
Finance & Business Services	0.68	0.00	0.39	3.30	1.95	3.13	1.05	0.06	0.66
Public Admn, Education & Community Services	12.57	0.80	7.56	36.80	52.98	38.87	15.99	2.44	10.62
All	100.00	100.00	100.00	100.00	100.00	100.00	100.00	100.00	100.00

Notes: R_M= Rural Males, R_F = Rural Females, R_P= Rural Persons, U_M= Urban Males, U_F = Urban Females, U_P = Urban Persons, T_M= Total Males, T_F= Total Females, T_P = Total Persons

Source: NSS 50th Round.

Table 14.5: Industry-Group wise Distribution of Workers in Arunachal Pradesh: 1999-2000

Industry Group	*Category of Workers*								
	R_M	*R_F*	*R_P*	*U_M*	*U_F*	*U_P*	*T_M*	*T_F*	*T_P*
					All Social Groups				
Agriculture	75.62	95.11	83.42	6.45	19.95	8.69	70.02	93.19	78.98
Mining & Quarrying	0.00	0.00	0.00	0.00	0.00	0.00	0.00	0.00	0.00
Manufacturing	2.80	2.68	2.75	0.50	0.00	0.42	2.62	2.61	2.62
Electricity, Gas & Water Supply	0.53	0.00	0.32	2.19	0.00	1.83	0.66	0.00	0.41
Construction	6.66	1.12	4.44	12.93	2.56	11.20	7.17	1.16	4.84
Trade, Hotels & Restaurants	1.00	0.09	0.63	33.32	34.21	33.47	3.61	0.96	2.59
Transport	0.19	0.00	0.12	1.20	0.00	1.00	0.28	0.00	0.17
Finance & Business Services	0.27	0.21	0.24	1.00	0.52	0.92	0.33	0.21	0.28
Public Admn, Education & Community Services	12.93	0.79	8.07	42.41	42.76	42.46	15.32	1.87	10.12
All	100.00	100.00	100.00	100.00	100.00	100.00	100.00	100.00	100.00
					ST Social Group				
Agriculture	86.25	98.51	91.90	14.32	41.64	21.16	82.64	97.36	89.31
Mining & Quarrying	0.00	0.00	0.00	0.00	0.00	0.00	0.00	0.00	0.00
Manufacturing	0.00	0.00	0.00	0.00	0.00	0.00	0.00	0.00	0.00
Electricity, Gas & Water Supply	0.72	0.00	0.39	1.13	0.00	0.85	0.74	0.00	0.40
Construction	7.35	0.85	4.35	17.54	0.00	13.15	7.86	0.84	4.68
Trade, Hotels & Restaurants	0.50	0.07	0.30	16.73	30.85	20.27	1.32	0.69	1.03
Transport	0.00	0.00	0.00	0.00	0.00	0.00	0.00	0.00	0.00
Finance & Business Services	0.09	0.00	0.05	0.00	0.00	0.00	0.08	0.00	0.05
Public Admn, Education & Community Services	5.09	0.57	3.01	50.27	27.51	44.57	7.36	1.11	4.53
All	100.00	100.00	100.00	100.00	100.00	100.00	100.00	100.00	100.00

(Contd.)

Industry Group	Category of Workers								
	R_M	R_F	R_P	U_M	U_F	U_P	T_M	T_F	T_P
					Non-ST Social Group				
Agriculture	65.97	89.80	73.89	3.30	0.00	2.88	59.26	0.00	67.93
Mining & Quarrying	0.00	0.00	0.00	0.00	0.00	0.00	0.00	0.00	0.00
Manufacturing	5.35	6.86	5.85	0.70	0.00	0.61	4.85	6.63	5.41
Electricity, Gas & Water Supply	0.36	0.00	0.24	2.62	0.00	2.29	0.60	0.00	0.41
Construction	6.04	1.54	4.54	11.08	4.91	10.30	6.58	1.65	5.02
Trade, Hotels & Restaurants	1.44	0.13	1.01	39.96	37.31	39.62	5.57	1.39	4.25
Transport	0.37	0.00	0.25	1.67	0.00	1.46	0.51	0.00	0.35
Finance & Business Services	0.43	0.53	0.46	1.40	1.00	1.35	0.53	0.54	0.54
Public Admn, Education & Community Services	20.05	1.14	13.76	39.26	56.78	41.48	22.10	3.02	16.09
All	100.00	100.00	100.00	100.00	100.00	100.00	100.00	100.00	100.00

Notes R_M= Rural Males, R_F = Rural Females, R_P= Rural Persons, U_M= Urban Males, U_F = Urban Females, U_P = Urban Persons, T_M= Total Males, T_F= Total Females, T_P = Total Persons.

Sourc : NSS 55th Round.

Table 14.6: Industry-Group wise Distribution of Workers in Arunachal Pradesh: 2004-05

Industry Group	*Category of Workers*								
	R_M	*R_F*	*R_P*	*U_M*	*U_F*	*U_P*	*T_M*	*T_F*	*T_P*
	All Social Groups								
Agriculture	74.0	92.7	81.9	4.7	35.3	11.1	65.8	90.1	75.6
Mining & Quarrying	0.0	0.0	0.0	0.0	0.0	0.0	0.0	0.0	0.0
Manufacturing	0.4	0.3	0.4	4.5	0.0	3.6	0.9	0.3	0.6
Electricity, Gas & Water Supply	1.5	0.0	0.9	0.3	0.0	0.2	1.4	0.0	0.8
Construction	5.0	2.8	4.0	9.0	4.7	8.1	5.4	2.9	4.4
Trade, Hotels & Restaurants	3.6	0.4	2.3	25.6	14.1	23.2	6.2	1.0	4.1
Transport	1.1	0.0	0.6	3.0	0.0	2.3	1.3	0.0	0.8
Finance & Business Services	1.0	0.2	0.6	1.6	0.0	1.2	1.1	0.1	0.7
Public Admn, Education & Community Services	13.4	3.6	9.3	51.4	45.9	50.2	17.9	5.6	12.9
All	100.0	100.0	100.0	100.0	100.0	100.0	100.0	100.0	100.0
	ST Social Group								
Agriculture	83.3	94.9	88.6	13.0	37.9	22.1	79.8	92.9	85.8
Mining & Quarrying	0.0	0.0	0.0	0.0	0.0	0.0	0.0	0.0	0.0
Manufacturing	0.1	0.2	0.1	1.6	0.0	1.0	0.2	0.2	0.2
Electricity, Gas & Water Supply	0.7	0.0	0.4	0.0	0.0	0.0	0.6	0.0	0.3
Construction	2.5	1.3	1.9	11.2	3.8	8.5	2.9	1.4	2.2
Trade, Hotels & Restaurants	1.3	0.2	0.8	12.9	14.7	13.6	1.9	0.7	1.4
Transport	0.5	0.0	0.3	1.7	0.0	1.1	0.6	0.0	0.3
Finance & Business Services	1.1	0.2	0.7	0.0	0.0	0.0	1.1	0.1	0.6
Public Admn, Education & Community Services	10.6	3.2	7.2	59.6	43.6	53.7	13.0	4.6	9.2
All	100.0	100.0	100.0	100.0	100.0	100.0	100.0	100.0	100.0

(*Contd.*)

Industry Group	Category of Workers								
	R_M	R_F	R_P	U_M	U_F	U_P	T_M	T_F	T_P
	Non-ST Social Group								
Agriculture	50.3	82.6	60.6	1.5	31.4	5.3	37.8	77.7	48.9
Mining & Quarrying	0.0	0.0	0.0	0.0	0.0	0.0	0.0	0.0	0.0
Manufacturing	1.2	0.8	1.1	5.7	0.0	4.9	2.3	0.7	1.9
Electricity, Gas & Water Supply	3.8	0.0	2.6	0.4	0.0	0.4	2.9	0.0	2.1
Construction	11.3	9.6	10.8	8.1	6.0	7.8	10.5	9.2	10.2
Trade, Hotels & Restaurants	9.4	1.1	6.7	30.5	13.3	28.3	14.8	2.3	11.3
Transport	2.7	0.0	1.8	3.4	0.0	3.0	2.9	0.0	2.1
Finance & Business Services	0.7	0.2	0.5	2.2	0.0	1.9	1.1	0.1	0.8
Public Admn, Education & Community Services	20.7	5.8	15.9	48.2	49.3	48.4	27.7	10.0	22.7
All	100.0	100.0	100.0	100.0	100.0	100.0	100.0	100.0	100.0

Notes: R_M= Rural Males, R_F = Rural Females, R_P= Rural Persons, U_M= Urban Males, U_F = Urban Females, U_P = Urban Persons, T_M= Total Males, T_F= Total Females, T_P = Total Persons

Source: NSS 61st Round.

Table 14.7: Industry–Group wise Growth of Employment in Arunachal Pradesh: 1993–94 to 1999–2000

Industry Group	*Growth of Employment (%)*								
	R_M	*R_F*	*R_P*	*U_M*	*U_F*	*U_P*	*T_M*	*T_F*	*T_P*
					All Social Groups				
Agriculture	–0.76	–2.07	–1.37	–9.05	–2.20	–6.83	–0.84	–2.07	–1.42
Mining & Quarrying	–100.00	–100.00	–100.00				–100.00	–100.00	–100.00
Manufacturing	37.12	10.45	21.78	–47.29	–100.00	–48.12	2.31	7.04	3.97
Electricity, Gas & Water Supply	–14.78	–100.00	–15.60	–16.45	–100.00	–17.30	–15.25	–100.00	–16.08
Construction	9.32	0.02	8.07	–2.84	–19.12	–4.02	6.80	–2.22	5.70
Trade, Hotels & Restaurants	20.62		21.81	3.22	32.95	5.70	6.14	35.10	8.22
Transport	–34.91	–100.00	–36.02	–30.09		–30.09	–33.48	–100.00	–34.33
Finance & Business Services	–13.92		–7.76	–23.83	–21.62	–23.65	–17.27	24.47	–12.89
Public Admn, Education & Community Services	1.75	–5.52	1.38	–5.94	–6.56	–6.04	–0.37	–6.14	–0.87
All	–0.02	–1.89	–0.80	–7.61	–2.76	–6.91	–0.81	–1.91	–1.25
					ST Social Group				
Agriculture	18.30	21.18	19.66				18.47	21.36	19.84
Mining & Quarrying									
Manufacturing		–100.00	–100.00	–100.00		–100.00	–100.00	–100.00	–100.00
Electricity, Gas & Water Supply				–4.69		–4.69	46.13		46.13
Construction	49.84	16.57	43.10				52.83	16.57	45.72
Trade, Hotels & Restaurants									
Transport	–100.00		–100.00				–100.00		–100.00
Finance & Business Services	–12.52		–12.52				–12.52		–12.52
Public Admn, Education & Community Services	13.20	–1.44	11.20	24.29	25.74	24.50	16.24	6.84	14.88
All	19.16	20.83	19.91	33.73	55.92	37.42	19.67	21.15	20.32

(Contd.)

Industry Group	Growth of Employment (%)								
	R_M	R_F	R_P	U_M	U_F	U_P	T_M	T_F	T_P
				Non–ST Social Group					
Agriculture	–9.79	–14.35	–11.84	–23.09	–100.00	–27.27	–9.94	–14.44	–11.95
Mining & Quarrying	–100.00	–100.00	–100.00				–100.00	–100.00	–100.00
Manufacturing	37.12	10.93	22.14	–47.04	–100.00	–47.89	2.72	7.42	4.37
Electricity, Gas & Water Supply	–28.32	–100.00	–29.02	–17.70	–100.00	–18.59	–24.57	–100.00	–25.32
Construction	–2.09	–6.73	–2.70	–10.47	–19.12	–11.21	–4.04	–8.69	–4.61
Trade, Hotels & Restaurants	15.21		16.04	0.59	20.99	2.00	2.93	22.90	4.13
Transport	–34.51	–100.00	–35.66	–30.09		–30.09	–33.18	–100.00	–34.06
Finance & Business Services	–14.16		–7.08	–23.83	–21.62	–23.65	–17.78	24.47	–12.92
Public Admn, Education & Community Services	0.01	–8.01	–0.28	–11.23	–11.34	–11.25	–2.97	–10.22	–3.52
All	–7.47	–13.39	–9.75	–12.19	–12.36	–12.21	–8.06	–13.35	–9.98

Notes: (i) R_M= Rural Males, R_F = Rural Females, R_P= Rural Persons, U_M= Urban Males, U_F = Urban Females, U_P = Urban Persons, T_M= Total Males, T_F= Total Females, T_P = Total Persons

(ii) Blanks occur in the cells where employment was zero in the 50th Round; –100% occur in the cells where employment was zero in the 55th Round

Source: NSS 50th and 55th Round.

Table 14.8: Industry–Group wise Growth of Employment in Arunachal Pradesh: 1999–2000 to 2004–05

Industry Group	*Growth of Employment (%)*								
	R_M	*R_F*	*R_P*	*U_M*	*U_F*	*U_P*	*T_M*	*T_F*	*T_P*
					All Social Groups				
Agriculture	3.8	5.8	4.8	6.4	34.7	20.4	3.9	6.1	4.9
Mining & Quarrying									
Manufacturing	–29.4	–31.0	–30.0	75.9		75.9	–15.4	–31.0	–20.1
Electricity, Gas & Water Supply	29.3		29.3	–23.6		–23.6	22.1		22.1
Construction	–1.7	27.7	3.2	5.3	35.6	7.3	–0.6	28.2	3.8
Trade, Hotels & Restaurants	35.0	43.1	35.6	7.5	0.7	6.5	17.2	8.3	16.1
Transport	47.4		47.4	35.9		35.9	43.8		43.8
Finance & Business Services	35.7	0.3	27.6	23.9	–100.0	21.5	33.2	–1.0	26.5
Public Admn, Education & Community Services	5.0	44.3	8.1	17.8	21.8	18.5	8.4	33.0	11.1
All	4.3	6.4	5.1	13.3	20.1	14.6	5.2	6.8	5.8
					ST *Social* Group				
Agriculture	12.5	12.1	12.3	10.7	23.5	17.7	12.5	12.2	12.3
Mining & Quarrying									
Manufacturing									
Electricity, Gas & Water Supply	11.6		11.6	–100.0		–100.0	9.8		9.8
Construction	–9.0	23.1	–3.8	3.2		7.0	–7.3	25.6	–2.4
Trade, Hotels & Restaurants	36.9	46.6	38.0	7.2	8.5	7.7	21.5	14.9	19.6
Transport									
Finance & Business Services	88.4		92.5				88.4		92.5
Public Admn, Education & Community Services	31.1	59.3	34.6	16.8	38.0	21.1	26.8	50.2	30.4
All	13.3	12.9	13.1	12.9	25.9	16.7	13.2	13.2	13.2

(*Contd.*)

Industry Group	*Growth of Employment (%)*								
	R_M	*R_F*	*R_P*	*U_M*	*U_F*	*U_P*	*T_M*	*T_F*	*T_P*
					Non–ST Social Group				
Agriculture	–12.8	–10.6	–11.9	–3.5		28.2	–12.7	–9.8	–11.5
Mining & Quarrying									
Manufacturing	–31.7	–41.5	–34.9	72.3		72.3	–17.5	–41.5	–23.6
Electricity, Gas & Water Supply	47.8		47.8	–21.1		–21.1	31.2		31.2
Construction	4.4	31.2	9.0	6.6	18.4	7.5	4.8	30.1	8.7
Trade, Hotels & Restaurants	33.8	40.0	34.1	7.6	–7.5	6.2	16.0	1.9	14.8
Transport	36.4		36.4	31.1		31.1	34.6		34.6
Finance & Business Services	1.8	–27.9	–5.5	23.9	–100.0	21.5	10.0	–28.9	2.9
Public Admn, Education & Community Services	–7.4	25.7	–5.6	18.3	10.5	17.1	–0.2	17.0	1.2
All	–7.9	–9.1	–8.3	13.5	13.7	13.5	–4.5	–7.8	–5.5

Notes: (i) R_M= Rural Males, R_F = Rural Females, R_P= Rural Persons, U_M= Urban Males, U_F = Urban Females, U_P = Urban Persons, T_M= Total Males, T_F= Total Females, T_P = Total Persons

(ii) Blank means there was no employment in relevant cell in 1999–2000. –100% means that whatever employment was there in 1999–2000 was no more in 2004–2005 for relevant cells.

Source: NSS 55th and 61st Round.

Table 14.9: Unemployment Rate by Educational Standards in Arunachal Pradesh (as a Proportion of Labour Force): 1993–94

Education Level	*Proportion of Labour Force*								
	R_M	R_F	R_P	U_M	U_F	U_P	T_M	T_F	T_P
					All Social Groups				
Illiterate	14.25	0.64	7.60	0.00	0.00	0.00	13.56	0.63	7.35
Below Primary	0.00	0.00	0.00	76.74	285.70	93.91	16.38	23.68	17.75
Primary	5.82	0.00	5.00	0.00	0.00	0.00	4.94	0.00	4.29
Middle	16.49	0.00	13.90	30.47	0.00	26.96	20.45	0.00	17.47
Secondary	76.26	38.66	73.57	0.00	295.97	27.25	49.39	146.21	57.01
Higher Secondary	5.00	246.57	26.16	29.19	167.65	64.92	12.75	196.79	40.38
Graduate & Above	107.10	106.44	106.93	0.00	0.00	0.00	47.38	80.15	52.88
All	16.37	2.26	10.40	17.73	73.91	26.07	16.54	4.63	11.79
					ST Social Group				
Illiterate	26.54	4.07	15.34	0.00	0.00	0.00	25.97	4.06	15.15
Below Primary	0.00	0.00	0.00	0.00		0.00	0.00	0.00	0.00
Primary	17.87	0.00	14.34				17.87	0.00	14.34
Middle	0.00	0.00	0.00	0.00	0.00	0.00	0.00	0.00	0.00
Secondary	0.00	0.00	0.00	0.00		0.00	0.00	0.00	0.00
Higher Secondary	0.00		0.00	0.00	0.00	0.00	0.00	0.00	0.00
Graduate & Above	0.00	0.00	0.00	0.00		0.00	0.00	0.00	0.00
All	19.51	3.38	12.53	0.00	0.00	0.00	19.03	3.36	12.32

(Contd.)

Education Level	Proportion of Labour Force								
	R_M	R_F	R_P	U_M	U_F	U_P	T_M	T_F	T_P
					Non–ST Social Group				
Illiterate	12.06	0.00	6.20	0.00	0.00	0.00	11.43	0.00	5.97
Below Primary	0.00	0.00	0.00	79.04	285.70	96.49	19.96	44.19	23.13
Primary	0.00	0.00	0.00	0.00	0.00	0.00	0.00	0.00	0.00
Middle	21.47	0.00	17.73	30.96	0.00	27.75	24.66	0.00	20.92
Secondary	82.57	54.72	81.02	0.00	295.97	27.48	52.13	176.35	60.78
Higher Secondary	5.37	246.57	27.90	30.96	176.37	68.71	13.63	203.13	42.95
Graduate & Above	128.43	353.80	153.27	0.00	0.00	0.00	51.37	169.28	62.43
All	15.74	2.02	9.96	18.27	76.25	26.87	16.10	4.90	11.69

Notes: R_M= Rural Males, R_F = Rural Females, R_P= Rural Persons, U_M= Urban Males, U_F = Urban Females, U_P = Urban Persons, T_M= Total Males, T_F= Total Females, T_P = Total Persons

Source: NSS 50th Round.

Table 14.10: Unemployment Rate by Educational Standards in Arunachal Pradesh (as a Proportion of Labour Force): 1999–2000

Education Level	*Proportion of Labour Force*								
	R_M	R_F	R_P	U_M	U_F	U_P	T_M	T_F	T_P
					All Social Groups				
Illiterate	0.00	0.00	0.00	0.00	0.00	0.00	0.00	0.00	0.00
Below Primary	5.85	0.00	4.00	0.00	0.00	0.00	5.31	0.00	3.71
Primary	37.26	0.00	25.05	38.46	0.00	32.48	37.32	0.00	25.37
Middle	17.35	0.00	13.44	0.00	0.00	0.00	15.67	0.00	12.34
Secondary	2.53	42.82	6.92	16.67	149.81	43.99	5.33	79.50	14.98
Higher Secondary	2.16	0.00	2.07	0.00	220.31	36.31	1.72	118.89	9.80
Graduate & Above	7.36	661.06	30.84	0.00	31.97	4.90	4.42	180.75	19.67
All	7.72	1.41	5.20	6.50	89.97	21.30	7.62	3.85	6.16
					ST Social Group				
Illiterate	0.00	0.00	0.00	0.00	0.00	0.00	0.00	0.00	0.00
Below Primary	16.02	0.00	10.45	0.00	0.00	0.00	14.02	0.00	9.40
Primary	91.05	0.00	54.98	0.00	0.00	0.00	87.52	0.00	53.13
Middle	37.13	0.00	26.39	0.00	0.00	0.00	34.82	0.00	24.93
Secondary	2.08	46.57	9.02	47.94	0.00	42.70	7.76	42.58	13.00
Higher Secondary	0.00	0.00	0.00	0.00	540.26	141.05	0.00	203.19	45.61
Graduate & Above	8.02	800.61	38.67	0.00	0.00	0.00	5.56	233.06	25.45
All	13.71	1.75	8.23	11.21	102.28	35.56	13.59	3.98	9.26

(Contd.)

Education Level	Proportion of Labour Force								
	R_M	R_F	R_P	U_M	U_F	U_P	T_M	T_F	T_P
					Non–ST Social Group				
Illiterate	0.00	0.00	0.00	0.00	0.00	0.00	0.00	0.00	0.00
Below Primary	0.00	0.00	0.00	0.00	0.00	0.00	0.00	0.00	0.00
Primary	9.20	0.00	6.57	50.86	0.00	46.10	11.74	0.00	8.50
Middle	0.00	0.00	0.00	0.00		0.00	0.00	0.00	0.00
Secondary	3.23	0.00	3.15	0.00	179.48	44.56	2.29	151.48	17.60
Higher Secondary	2.48	0.00	2.45	0.00	0.00	0.00	2.02	0.00	1.95
Graduate & Above	6.80	524.05	24.16	0.00	51.05	7.17	3.67	145.52	15.85
All	2.20	0.89	1.76	4.57	78.11	14.42	2.45	3.64	2.82

Notes: R_M= Rural Males, R_F = Rural Females, R_P= Rural Persons, U_M= Urban Males, U_F = Urban Females, U_P = Urban Persons, T_M= Total Males, T_F= Total Females, T_P = Total Persons

Source: NSS 55th Round.

Table 14.11: Unemployment Rate by Educational Standards in Arunachal Pradesh (as a Proportion of Labour Force): 2004–05

Education Level	*Proportion of Labour Force*								
	R_M	*R_F*	*R_P*	*U_M*	*U_F*	*U_P*	*T_M*	*T_F*	*T_P*
					All Social Groups				
Illiterate	0.0	0.0	0.0	27.8	0.0	20.3	0.8	0.0	0.4
Below Primary	8.6	10.1	9.1	38.3	6.1	23.3	10.7	9.7	10.4
Primary	17.7	15.8	17.0	0.0	14.8	1.9	15.2	15.7	15.4
Middle	14.1	20.6	16.3	0.0	35.9	7.8	12.1	21.9	15.2
Secondary	8.5	7.7	8.3	0.0	0.0	0.0	7.1	6.2	6.9
Higher Secondary	33.2	46.8	35.8	6.0	47.9	11.3	23.1	47.0	27.2
Graduate & Above	61.4	70.6	62.1	18.0	135.5	29.4	48.5	93.7	52.2
All	11.1	5.8	8.9	10.6	24.3	13.5	11.1	6.6	9.3
					ST Social Group				
Illiterate	0.0	0.0	0.0	165.9	0.0	74.2	1.0	0.0	0.5
Below Primary	3.4	12.9	6.9	0.0	0.0	0.0	3.3	12.0	6.5
Primary	22.2	19.7	21.3	0.0	26.3	10.7	21.6	19.9	21.0
Middle	21.8	23.5	22.5	0.0	39.7	19.5	20.4	24.9	22.3
Secondary	14.4	8.8	12.6	0.0	0.0	0.0	13.4	7.3	11.3
Higher Secondary	44.3	51.2	46.1	0.0	72.7	13.6	31.7	55.7	37.5
Graduate & Above	68.4	52.7	67.0	32.1	286.9	57.7	60.2	111.2	64.9
All	11.3	6.7	9.2	15.9	32.7	22.1	11.5	7.6	9.7

(Contd.)

Education Level	Proportion of Labour Force								
	R_M	R_F	R_P	U_M	U_F	U_P	T_M	T_F	T_P
				Non–ST Social Group					
Illiterate	0.0	0.0	0.0	0.0	0.0	0.0	0.0	0.0	0.0
Below Primary	21.2	0.0	15.4	59.0	11.1	38.7	26.8	2.8	19.5
Primary	5.3	0.0	3.8	0.0	0.0	0.0	3.4	0.0	2.7
Middle	0.0	0.0	0.0	0.0	0.0	0.0	0.0	0.0	0.0
Secondary	0.0	0.0	0.0	0.0	0.0	0.0	0.0	0.0	0.0
Higher Secondary	15.1	0.0	14.3	10.3	0.0	9.5	12.8	0.0	12.0
Graduate & Above	54.7	95.2	57.3	11.0	54.5	15.1	39.2	76.5	42.0
All	10.8	1.4	7.9	8.6	11.1	8.9	10.3	2.4	8.1

Notes: R_M= Rural Males, R_F = Rural Females, R_P= Rural Persons, U_M= Urban Males, U_F = Urban Females, U_P = Urban Persons, T_M= Total Males, T_F= Total Females, T_P = Total Persons

Source: NSS 61st Round.

Table 14.12: Unemployment Rate by Age Group in Arunachal Pradesh (as a Proportion of Labour Force): 1993–94 (*per thousand population*)

Age Group	*Proportion of Labour Force*								
	R_M	R_F	R_P	U_M	U_F	U_P	T_M	T_F	T_P
					All Social Groups				
10–14	209.28	0.00	142.73		1000.00	1000.00	209.28	84.36	167.13
15–19	44.33	1.61	25.27	110.86	254.56	177.72	46.40	10.11	30.19
20–24	71.38	18.13	41.92	74.51	207.82	108.67	71.76	25.15	47.04
25–29	27.79	0.00	13.51	0.00	0.00	0.00	23.67	0.00	12.23
30–34	8.52	0.00	5.43	0.00	0.00	0.00	7.58	0.00	4.92
35–39	0.00	0.00	0.00	0.00	0.00	0.00	0.00	0.00	0.00
40–44	0.00	0.00	0.00	0.00	0.00	0.00	0.00	0.00	0.00
45–49	0.00	0.00	0.00	0.00	0.00	0.00	0.00	0.00	0.00
50–54	0.00	0.00	0.00	0.00		0.00	0.00	0.00	0.00
55–59	0.00	0.00	0.00	0.00		0.00	0.00	0.00	0.00
60 & Above	0.00	0.00	0.00	0.00		0.00	0.00	0.00	0.00
All Age Groups	16	2	10	18	74	26	17	5	12
					ST Social Group				
10–14	0.00		0.00				0.00		0.00
15–19	140.63	0.00	72.35				140.63	0.00	72.35
20–24	23.86	52.01	32.72	0.00	0.00	0.00	23.35	47.63	31.34
25–29	38.73	0.00	19.31	0.00		0.00	37.72	0.00	19.06
30–34	25.01	0.00	8.89				25.01	0.00	8.89
35–39	0.00	0.00	0.00	0.00		0.00	0.00	0.00	0.00
40–44	0.00	0.00	0.00	0.00		0.00	0.00	0.00	0.00
45–49	0.00	0.00	0.00	0.00		0.00	0.00	0.00	0.00
50–54	0.00	0.00	0.00				0.00	0.00	0.00
55–59	0.00	0.00	0.00				0.00	0.00	0.00
60 & Above	0.00	0.00	0.00				0.00	0.00	0.00
All Age Groups	19.51	3.38	12.53	0.00	0.00	0.00	19.03	3.36	12.32

(*Contd.*)

Age Group	Proportion of Labour Force								
	R_M	R_F	R_P	U_M	U_F	U_P	T_M	T_F	T_P
					Non–ST Social Group				
10–14	214.92	0.00	145.33		1000.00	1000.00	214.92	84.36	170.09
15–19	28.47	1.93	16.82	110.86	254.56	177.72	31.45	12.04	22.91
20–24	88.66	14.42	43.86	77.80	272.19	119.68	87.00	22.55	50.20
25–29	25.82	0.00	12.49	0.00	0.00	0.00	21.50	0.00	11.15
30–34	7.50	0.00	5.02	0.00	0.00	0.00	6.62	0.00	4.50
35–39	0.00	0.00	0.00	0.00	0.00	0.00	0.00	0.00	0.00
40–44	0.00	0.00	0.00	0.00	0.00	0.00	0.00	0.00	0.00
45–49	0.00	0.00	0.00	0.00	0.00	0.00	0.00	0.00	0.00
50–54	0.00	0.00	0.00	0.00		0.00	0.00	0.00	0.00
55–59	0.00	0.00	0.00	0.00		0.00	0.00	0.00	0.00
60 & Above	0.00	0.00	0.00	0.00		0.00	0.00	0.00	0.00
All Age Groups	15.74	2.02	9.96	18.27	76.25	26.87	16.10	4.90	11.69

Notes: R_M= Rural Males, R_F = Rural Females, R_P= Rural Persons, U_M= Urban Males, U_F = Urban Females, U_P = Urban Persons, T_M= Total Males, T_F= Total Females, T_P = Total Persons

Source: NSS 50th Round.

Table 14.13: Unemployment Rate by Age Group in Arunachal Pradesh (as Proportion of Labour Force): 1999–2000 (*per thousand population*)

Age Group	*Proportion of Labour Force*								
	R_M	R_F	R_P	U_M	U_F	U_P	T_M	T_F	T_P
					All Social Groups				
10–14	0.00	0.00	0.00				0.00	0.00	0.00
15–19	37.04	0.00	17.11	0.00	533.09	123.10	35.86	4.49	19.16
20–24	41.05	9.96	25.55	141.16	317.38	216.11	45.11	19.33	32.32
25–29	7.56	0.00	4.54	87.84	24.45	70.89	11.92	0.74	7.52
30–34	1.18	0.00	0.84	0.00	0.00	0.00	1.10	0.00	0.79
35–39	0.00	0.00	0.00	0.00	71.21	10.47	0.00	4.55	1.43
40–44	0.00	0.00	0.00	0.00	0.00	0.00	0.00	0.00	0.00
45–49	0.00	0.00	0.00	0.00	0.00	0.00	0.00	0.00	0.00
50–54	0.00	0.00	0.00	0.00	0.00	0.00	0.00	0.00	0.00
55–59	0.00	0.00	0.00	0.00	0.00	0.00	0.00	0.00	0.00
60 & Above	0.00	0.00	0.00				0.00	0.00	0.00
All Age Groups	7.71	1.41	5.20	16.40	88.38	29.13	8.42	3.84	6.65
					ST Social Group				
10–14	0.00	0.00	0.00				0.00	0.00	23.71
15–19	61.22	0.00	24.07	0.00	0.00	0.00	59.59	0.00	64.16
20–24	102.41	14.53	53.07	215.24	338.28	298.81	106.18	32.04	11.46
25–29	15.55	0.00	8.37	150.96	0.00	98.43	21.14	0.00	0.74
30–34	1.18	0.00	0.77	0.00	0.00	0.00	1.12	0.00	0.00
35–39	0.00	0.00	0.00	0.00	0.00	0.00	0.00	0.00	0.00
40–44	0.00	0.00	0.00	0.00	0.00	0.00	0.00	0.00	0.00
45–49	0.00	0.00	0.00	0.00	0.00	0.00	0.00	0.00	0.00
50–54	0.00	0.00	0.00	0.00	0.00	0.00	0.00	0.00	0.00
55–59	0.00	0.00	0.00	0.00	0.00	0.00	0.00	0.00	0.00
60 & Above	0.00	0.00	0.00				0.00	0.00	9.73
All Age Groups	13.71	1.75	8.23	28.34	101.41	47.72	14.46	3.98	23.71

(*Contd.*)

Age Group	Proportion of Labour Force								
	R_M	R_F	R_P	U_M	U_F	U_P	T_M	T_F	T_P
					Non–ST Social Group				
10–14	0.00	0.00	0.00				0.00	0.00	0.00
15–19	21.00	0.00	10.97	0.00	1000.00	193.49	20.26	9.50	15.19
20–24	0.00	5.08	2.26	105.02	0.00	98.33	4.75	5.06	4.88
25–29	2.50	0.00	1.62	61.94	42.56	57.52	6.20	1.48	4.57
30–34	1.18	0.00	0.93	0.00	0.00	0.00	1.08	0.00	0.85
35–39	0.00	0.00	0.00	0.00	117.33	14.99	0.00	13.16	2.78
40–44	0.00	0.00	0.00	0.00	0.00	0.00	0.00	0.00	0.00
45–49	0.00	0.00	0.00	0.00	0.00	0.00	0.00	0.00	0.00
50–54	0.00	0.00	0.00	0.00	0.00	0.00	0.00	0.00	0.00
55–59	0.00	0.00	0.00				0.00	0.00	0.00
60 & Above	0.00	0.00	0.00				0.00	0.00	0.00
All Age Groups	2.19	0.89	1.76	11.53	76.06	20.22	3.20	3.63	3.34

Notes : R_M= Rural Males, R_F = Rural Females, R_P= Rural Persons, U_M= Urban Males, U_F = Urban Females, U_P = Urban Persons, T_M= Total Males, T_F= Total Females, T_P = Total Persons

Source: NSS 55th Round.

Table 14.14: Unemployment Rate by Age Group in Arunachal Pradesh (as Proportion of Labour Force): 2004–05 (*per thousand population*)

Age Group	*Proportion of Labour Force*								
	R_M	R_F	R_P	U_M	U_F	U_P	T_M	T_F	T_P
					All Social Groups				
10–14	0.0	0.0	0.0	0.0	0.0	0.0	0.0	0.0	0.0
15–19	20.8	7.9	14.4	92.3	66.0	77.8	24.0	11.1	17.6
20–24	35.6	13.0	25.1	107.6	110.2	108.5	40.3	17.0	29.6
25–29	31.1	25.6	28.7	23.0	36.4	26.7	30.1	26.2	28.5
30–34	10.9	0.0	6.1	0.0	0.0	0.0	9.6	0.0	5.6
35–39	3.9	0.0	2.1	0.0	0.0	0.0	3.2	0.0	1.9
40–44	0.0	0.0	0.0	0.0	0.0	0.0	0.0	0.0	0.0
45–49	0.0	0.0	0.0	0.0	0.0	0.0	0.0	0.0	0.0
50–54	0.0	0.0	0.0	0.0	0.0	0.0	0.0	0.0	0.0
55–59	0.0	0.0	0.0	0.0	0.0	0.0	0.0	0.0	0.0
60 & Above	0.0	0.0	0.0	0.0		0.0	0.0	0.0	0.0
All Age Groups	11.1	5.7	8.9	10.6	24.3	13.5	11.1	6.6	9.3
					ST Social Group				
10–14	0.0	0.0	0.0	0.0	0.0	0.0	0.0	0.0	0.0
15–19	5.1	11.4	8.4	0.0	80.1	69.0	5.0	15.8	10.9
20–24	44.9	16.6	31.2	240.8	142.5	186.0	48.7	19.8	34.7
25–29	26.0	30.1	27.8	34.5	44.0	38.7	26.6	31.1	28.6
30–34	15.2	0.0	8.0	0.0	0.0	0.0	14.6	0.0	7.7
35–39	6.2	0.0	3.0	0.0	0.0	0.0	5.9	0.0	2.8
40–44	0.0	0.0	0.0	0.0	0.0	0.0	0.0	0.0	0.0
45–49	0.0	0.0	0.0	0.0	0.0	0.0	0.0	0.0	0.0
50–54	0.0	0.0	0.0	0.0	0.0	0.0	0.0	0.0	0.0
55–59	0.0	0.0	0.0	0.0		0.0	0.0	0.0	0.0
60 & Above	0.0	0.0	0.0	0.0		0.0	0.0	0.0	0.0
All Age Groups	11.3	6.7	9.2	15.9	32.7	22.1	11.5	7.6	9.7

(*Contd.*)

Age Group	Proportion of Labour Force								
	R_M	R_F	R_P	U_M	U_F	U_P	T_M	T_F	T_P
					Non–ST Social Group				
10–14	0.0	0.0	0.0	0.0		0.0	0.0	0.0	0.0
15–19	44.4	0.0	25.3	110.3	0.0	87.7	50.3	0.0	29.4
20–24	10.7	0.0	6.4	73.9	80.7	75.7	21.6	7.6	16.2
25–29	46.5	8.5	31.6	15.5	0.0	13.9	38.8	8.0	28.4
30–34	0.0	0.0	0.0	0.0	0.0	0.0	0.0	0.0	0.0
35–39	0.0	0.0	0.0	0.0	0.0	0.0	0.0	0.0	0.0
40–44	0.0	0.0	0.0	0.0	0.0	0.0	0.0	0.0	0.0
45–49	0.0	0.0	0.0	0.0	0.0	0.0	0.0	0.0	0.0
50–54	0.0	0.0	0.0	0.0		0.0	0.0	0.0	0.0
55–59	0.0	0.0	0.0	0.0	0.0	0.0	0.0	0.0	0.0
60 & Above	0.0	0.0	0.0	0.0		0.0	0.0	0.0	0.0
All Age Groups	10.8	1.4	7.8	8.6	11.1	8.9	10.2	2.4	8.1

Notes: R_M= Rural Males, R_F = Rural Females, R_P= Rural Persons, U_M= Urban Males, U_F = Urban Females, U_P = Urban Persons, T_M= Total Males, T_F= Total Females, T_P = Total Persons

Source: NSS 61st Round.

Table 14.15: Growth Rates of Labour Force and Unemployment: 1993–94 to 1999–2000 and 1993–94 to 2004–05

Category	*UPSS Growth Rates (%) – 1993–94 to 1999–2000*					
	Labour Force			Unemployment		
	Rural	*Urban*	*Total*	*Rural*	*Urban*	*Total*
ST	19.56	37.61	19.99	11.47		15.37
Non–ST	–9.92	–12.90	–10.20	–32.51	–16.94	–27.14
All	–0.96	–7.49	–1.46	–11.78	–5.77	–10.43
	UPSS Growth Rates (%) – 1993–94 to 2004–05					
ST	13.1	16.1	13.2	15.6	–0.5	13.2
Non–ST	–8.2	13.3	–5.4	23.7	–3.8	12.8
All	5.2	14.2	5.9	17.0	–2.0	13.1

Table 14.16: Drop-out Rates in Arunachal Pradesh and India: 2004–05

State	*Category*	*Class I–V*			*Class I–VIII*			*Class I–X*		
		Boys	*Girls*	*Total*	*Boys*	*Girls*	*Total*	*Boys*	*Girls*	*Total*
Arunachal Pradesh	All	45.86	48.01	46.85	63.23	61.90	62.63	69.59	72.30	70.79
	ST	47.91	47.74	47.83	68.03	66.58	67.37	73.38	74.89	74.05
India	All	31.81	25.42	29.00	50.49	51.28	50.84	60.41	63.88	61.92
	ST	42.55	42.04	42.32	64.97	67.09	65.87	77.75	80.66	78.89

Source: Selected Educational Statistics 2004–05, Ministry of Human Resource Development, Government of India.

Notes

1. In 2004-05, for example, unemployment among the ST population with an education level of higher secondary but less than graduation, was nearly 3.75 per cent of the labour force, while that among those having graduation or higher level of education in the ST group was 6.49 per cent.
2. Gender Parity Index (GPI) is girls' GER divided by boys' GER at a given level of education. GPI=1 indicates that there is no gender disparity at that level.
3. In 1993-94, among the very poor category, more than 45 per cent were landless in states like Bihar, Assam, Andhra Pradesh and many others, but in the case of Arunachal Pradesh, only 6.7 per cent of the very poor were landless. Among the poor only 7.4 per cent were landless. However, 54 per cent among the very poor and 41 per cent among the poor were sub-marginal farmers. Around 90.2 per cent of the very poor were *self-employed* and only 3.7 per cent were wage earners in the state. In no other state of India were such a high proportion of very poor people self-employed (Chaudhri, 2002).
4. Between 1987-88 and 1993-94, as per estimates based on NSS data, the percentage of poor in Arunachal Pradesh has increased from 29.76 per cent to 47.70 per cent (Dubey and Srivastava, 2003; 2004). In fact, among the northeastern states, it is only in Arunachal Pradesh where such a rise in the incidence of poverty has been noticed. Moreover, in terms of human development parameters, the progress of the state has been less than satisfactory (Upadhyay and Mishra, 2004).

References

Chadha, G.K. and P.P. Sahu (2002). "Post-reform Setbacks in Rural Employment: Issues that Need Further Scrutiny", *Economic and Political Weekly*, Vol. 37, No. 21, pp. 1998-2026.

Chadha, G.K. (2002). "Rural Non-farm Employment in India: What does Recent Experience Teach us?", *The Indian Journal of Labour Economics,* Vol. 45, No. 4, pp. 665-694.

Chaudhuri, D.P. (2002). "Poverty and Equity Issues in Indian agriculture" In S.S. Acharya, S. Singh and V. Sagar (eds) *Sustainable Agriculture, Poverty and Food Security*, Rawat Publications, Delhi.

Commission on Growth and Development (2008). *Growth Report: Strategies for Sustained Growth and Inclusive Development*, the World Bank.

Mishra, Deepak K. (2003). "Gender and Agrarian Relations in Arunachal

Pradesh: A Study on West Kameng District", *Assam Economic Journal*, Vol. 16, pp. 71-81.

Mishra, Deepak K. (2007). Rural Non-farm Employment in Arunachal Pradesh: Growth, Composition and Determinants, NLI Research Studies Series, No. 075/2007, Noida: V V Giri National Labour Institute.

Planning Commission (2002). *Special Group on Targeting Ten Million Employment Opportunity per Year: Employment Generating Growth*, available on-line.

Ramesh, Jairam (2005). "North East India in a New Asia", *Seminar: 550*, June.

Sarma, Atul (2005). "Why the North-eastern States Continue to Decelerate", *Man and Society*, Vol. 1, No. 2, pp. 1-20.

Srivastav, Nirankar and Dubey, A. (2003). "Unemployment in North East India: Some Issues" in A.C. Mohapatra and C.R. Pathak (eds.) *Economic Liberalisation and Regional Disparities in India: Special Focus on North Eastern Region*, Star Publishing House, Shillong, pp. 208-220.

Srivastav, Nirankar and Dubey, A. (2004). "How and why the Access to Public Distribution System does not enhance the Food security among the people of North-East India", In M.C. Behera (ed), *Globalisation and Development Dilemma: Reflection from North East India.* Mittal Publications, New Delhi, pp. 295-308.

Sundaram, K. (2001). "Employment-Unemployment Situation in the Nineties: Some Results from NSS 55th Round Employment-Unemployment Survey, 1999-2000", *Economic and Political Weekly*, Vol. 39, No. 11, pp. 931-940.

Sundaram, K. (2001). "Employment and Poverty in 1990s: Further Results from NSS 55th Round Employment-Unemployment Survey, 1999-2000", *Economic and Political Weekly*, Vol. 39, No. 32, pp. 3039-3049.

Upadhyay, V. (2005). "Women as Micro-Entrepreneurs: Towards an Alternative Strategy of Poverty Reduction in Arunachal Pradesh", *Rajiv Gandhi University Research Journal*, Vol. 8, No. 2, pp. 41-54.

Upadhyay, V. (2007). "Employment and Earnings in Urban Informal Sector: A Study on Arunachal Pradesh", NLI Research Studies Series No.: 076/2007, V.V. Giri National Labour Institute, Noida.

Upadhyay, V. and Mishra, D.K. (2004). "Micro Enterprises in Hill Economies: A Study on Arunachal Pradesh", *The Indian Journal of Labour Economics*. Vol. 47, No. 4, pp. 1027-1038.

Vaidyanathan, A. (1994), "Labour-Use in Rural India: A Study of Spatial and Temporal Variations", in Visaria, P. and R. Basant (eds.) *Non-agricultural Employment in India: Trends and Prospects,* Sage, New Delhi.

15

Tourism Development in Northeast India

A Study in Arunachal Pradesh

Maila Lama and *Amitava Mitra*

Arunachal Pradesh, one of the eight states of Northeast India, is located in the easternmost part of India and is blessed with abundant natural resources. The presence of numerous peaks, passes, valleys, lakes and rivers has enriched the state with enchanting natural and scenic beauty. At the same time, the state is highly rich in biodiversity and forest resources. As per the estimate of the Forest Survey of India, based on satellite imagery, the forest area in this state constitutes around 81.9 per cent of the total area, which is one of the highest among the states of the Northeast. An analysis reveals that in around 2.5 per cent of India's landmass, the state of Arunachal Pradesh contains nearly 16 per cent of the total timber growing stock of the country and more than 20 per cent of the fauna of the country. Moreover, Arunachal Pradesh with its unique geographical position and climate offers excellent growing conditions for orchids. The state is an abode of more than 545 species of orchids which is perhaps the highest number of species of orchids known from any single state of India. This fact clearly shows the potentiality of developing tourism in Arunachal Pradesh.

However, despite being rich in natural resources, the state is one of the most backward. This is mainly because of the limited scope for industrial activities and underdeveloped agriculture. In this background, the promotion of tourism appears to be one of the best ways of generating internal revenue, employment, income and accelerating the pace of development in the state. In addition, the promotion of nature-based and eco-tourism can play an important role in the state's strategy to conserve the rich forest resources as well as cultural heritage.

But statistical data shows that the inflow of tourists in the state is very limited. The share of Arunachal Pradesh in total tourist arrivals in Northeast India is one of the lowest. For example, in 2009 the state accounted for only 3.42 per cent of the total domestic tourist inflow in the region which is the third lowest. However, in recent years, the state has been witnessing inflow of increasing number of tourists (both domestic and foreign). Arunachal Pradesh recorded 47.84 per cent annual average growth rate of domestic tourist arrivals during 2006-09 against the regional average of 14.7 per cent (Table 15.3). In fact, the annual average growth rate of domestic tourist arrivals during 2006-09 was the highest in Arunachal Pradesh among the Northeastern states.

Potentiality of Tourism

Arunachal Pradesh is a tourist paradise. It has abundant resources for attracting tourists from various states of India as well as from other countries. The state is gaining popularity due to its cultural heterogeneity, monasteries, mountains, snow-clad peaks, crystal clear lakes and rich biodiversity. There are eleven identified tourist spots in the state, the details of which are given in Table 15.1.

These tourist spots can be grouped into different categories as follows:

Heritage Tourism

Tawang, Bhismarknagar and Itanagar are historical and heritage tourist spots. Tawang has a 350 year-old Buddhist monastery which is the second oldest monastery in Asia and the largest in the Himalayan region. The monastery is named "Galden Namgyal Latse" and is popularly known as the Tawang Monastery. There is also a Stupa called 'Gorsam Chorten' at Gorsam village of the Zemithang Circle which is one of the largest stupas in Asia. So, Tawang can be developed as a Buddhist tourist centre which can attract Buddhist tourists from Thailand, Japan, Korea, Sri Lanka, Nepal, Bhutan, etc. The Itafort of Itanagar which was built in the 14th century A.D. and is a historical site as also Bhismarknagar in Dibang Valley district can be developed as heritage tourist spots.

Pilgrimage Tourism

Malinithan and Parasuram Kund are pilgrim centres of Arunachal

Table 15.1: Identified Tourist Spots in Arunachal Pradesh

Name of the Tourist Spot	*District*	*Distance from the State Capital (in km)*
Itanagar	Papum Pare	0
Tawang	Tawang	540
Bomdila	West Kameng	360
Dirang	West Kameng	403
Tipi	West Kameng	210
Ziro	Lower Subansiri	168
Malinithan	West Siang	162
Along	West Siang	335
Pasighat	East Siang	280
Parasuram Kund	Lohit	795
Namdapha National Park	Changlang	640

Source: North East India Data Bank-Tourism, 2003, 5-6.

Pradesh. Malinithan, situated at Likabali in the West Siang district is a unique site developed between the 10th and 12th centuries A.D. It has an ancient temple housing sculptures of Gods and Goddesses. Parasuram Kund in the Lohit district is one of the important pilgrim sites in Northeast India. It is a place where Lord Parasuram is believed to have washed away his sin of matricide. During Makar Sankranti (around 14 or 15 January) thousands of pilgrims from all over the country come here for a holy dip.

Cultural Tourism

Arunachal Pradesh is rich in cultural resources. In fact, the state is home for twenty-six major and one hundred and ten minor tribes with rich cultural traditions. The added attractions are the colourful festivals of different tribes which form essential aspects of the socio-cultural life of the people of the state. Arunachal Pradesh is a sought after destination for the cultural tourists who are interested in understanding tribal life and culture.

Nature-Based Tourism and Eco-Tourism

Arunachal Pradesh is rich in forest resources and biodiversity. The state provides an opportunity to develop nature-based tourism and eco-tourism. The tourist spots like Bomdila, Bhalukpong and Dirang in the West Kameng district, Tawang in Tawang district, Ziro in the Lower Subansiri district and Along in the West Siang district can be developed as major destinations for eco-tourism. Tawang and Bomdila can be developed as mountain resorts.

Adventure Tourism

The state has a huge potential to develop adventure tourism. It has numerous voluminous rivers such as Kameng, Siang, Lohit, and Subansiri which are suitable for river rafting and boating. It also has a number of mountain peaks such as the Kangte peak (7,090 mtrs.) in West Kameng district and the Gorichen peak (6,488 mtrs.) in Tawang district, which attract climbers. There are numerous passes in the state such as the Bomdila Pass, the Sela Pass, the Bumla Pass, the Lumla Pass, which can be used for trekking. The lakes of the state such as the Sela Lake, the Bangachanga Lake and the Sangester Lake in Tawang district and the Ganga Lake in Itanagar, are suitable for boating. Tourists activities like mountaineering, trekking, boating, and river rafting and angling can be popularized and developed in most of the tourist spots of the state.

Wildlife Tourism

Wildlife tourism is also a type of eco-tourism which promotes sustainable tourism and significantly contributes to sustainable development. In Arunachal Pradesh, there are two national parks, viz., the Namdapha National Park in Changlang district and the Mouling National Park in Upper Siang district, eight wildlife sanctuaries, one Biosphere Reserve which houses diverse species of animals, and one orchid sanctuary at Tippi in West Kameng district. Viewing wild animals can be a satisfying experience for the tourists in the state.

Challenges for Tourism Development

Though the state has an enormous potential for the development of tourism, the tourist inflow in the state is very limited. The share of Arunachal Pradesh in total tourist arrivals in Northeast India is one of the lowest. For example, in 2009 the state accounted for only 3.42 per cent of the total domestic tourist inflow in the region which is the third lowest. Hence, it is time to identify the factors which have acted as barriers for growth of the tourism sector in the state and formulate appropriate policy measures. The study has identified the following challenges for the development of tourism in the state:

Infrastructural Constraints

The state is one of the most backward in India in terms of infrastructural facilities. The remoteness and inaccessibility of most of the tourist spots, due to a lack of proper infrastructural facilities, has hindered the development of tourism in the state. Even after more than sixty years of the country's independence, the state does not have a functional airport. The status of railways in the state is also dismal. Even the capital is not connected by rail, not to mention the other parts of the state. The state possesses a metre gauge railway line of just 1.2 kms. Thus, the principle mode of transport and communication in the state is by road. However, the density of roads in the state is one of the lowest in the country. In 2004, the state had a road density of 18 km per 100 sq. km against the national average of 75 km per 100 sq. km and the Northeastern average of 52 km per 100 sq. km.

Inadequate Accommodation Facilities

Availability of proper accommodation facilities near the tourist spots is also an important determinant of tourism development. Eco-tourists are nature lovers and they basically want to stay close to Nature. They prefer accommodation facilities located near the tourist spots. However, in Arunachal Pradesh, it has been found that accommodation facilities in the identified tourist spots are not well developed except in some tourist spots like Bomdila, Tawang, Itanagar and Ziro. The service facilities in the tourist lodges are also found to be below par.

Institutional Constraints

Certain institutional constraints also hinder the development of tourism in Arunachal Pradesh. The main among them are the provision of Inner Line Permits (ILP) and Restricted Area Permits (RAP). All domestic tourists are required to obtain ILP for visiting Arunachal Pradesh which can be obtained from just a few places like Delhi, Kolkata, Shillong, Guwahati, and Dibrugarh. All the foreign tourists intending to visit Arunachal Pradesh are required to obtain RAP from the Ministry of Home Affairs, Government of India. Of late though, the central government has recently delegated power to the state government to issue Restricted Area Permits (RAP) to foreign tourists visiting in a group of three or more persons for a maximum period of thirty days. It has been observed that the procedure for obtaining ILP and RAP is very complex and time-consuming. This acts as a disincentive for the potential tourists intending to visit the state.

Marketing Constraints

The lack of a proper marketing strategy for tourism products is also a major constraint (Mitra, 1998). The Arunachal tourism industry is poorly developed because of lack of coordination between the Government agencies and the virtual absence of information and marketing of the state's attractions. The success of Singapore and China in the tourism industry would suggest that the marketing of tourism products is just as important as its nature and quality, for promoting the tourism industry.

Other Constraints

Other major constraints for the successful promotion of tourism in Arunachal Pradesh include growing insurgent activities and agitations in the neighbouring states. These have disrupted the development of tourism in the entire Northeast in general and Arunachal Pradesh in particular. Tourism as an industry is highly sensitive to potential disturbances. There may be some grievances of the local people but it has acted as a psychological barrier for the potential tourists.

Trend and Growth of Tourist Inflow

The state has no doubt an enormous potential to attract tourists from various parts of the country as well as, but the number of tourist arrivals is limited as compared to the other states of the country as well as other states of the region. However, in recent years it has been observed that the total tourist arrivals in the state have been increasing at a faster rate (Tables 15.2 and 15.3).

Arunachal Pradesh has witnessed a rapid increase in tourist inflow since 2004. The total tourist inflow in Arunachal Pradesh has increased from 40,088 in 2004 to 93,312 in 2007 and further to 1,99,092 in 2009 (Table 15.2). During the period 2006 and 2009, the average annual growth rate of tourist arrivals was the highest in Arunachal Pradesh (47.84 per cent) among the Northeastern states (Table 15.3).

At the same time, there has also been a slight change in the composition of tourists visiting the state. In 2004, foreign tourists constituted just 0.80 per cent of the total visiting the state. However, the share of foreign tourists increased to 2.37 per cent in 2007. In 2009, the foreign tourists constituted 1.98 per cent of the total visiting the state. Though the share of foreign tourists is increasing, the domestic tourists constitute the major proportion (Table 15.2).

Since the foreign tourists have a relatively higher propensity to spend during their visit, it is important for the state to increase their

Table 15.2: Trend in Domestic and Foreign Tourist Inflow in Arunachal Pradesh

Year	Domestic	Foreign	Total
2004	39767 (99.20)	321 (0.80)	40088
2005	50560 (99.38)	313 (0.62)	50873
2006	80137 (99.13)	706 (0.87)	80843
2007	91100 (97.63)	2212 (2.37)	93312
2008	149292 (98.02)	3020 (1.98)	152312
2009	195147 (98.02)	3945 (1.98)	199092

Source: Directorate of Tourism Government of Arunachal Pradesh.
Note: Figures in the bracket indicate percentage of the total.

Table 15.3: Domestic Tourist Inflow in Northeast India 2006-09

Sl. No	States	2006	2007	2008	2009	Annual Average Growth of Tourist Arrival during 2006-2009
1.	Arunachal Pradesh	80137 (2.02)	91100 (1.93)	149292 (2.90)	195147 (3.42)	47.84
2.	Assam	2768824 (69.96)	3436833 (72.72)	3617306 (70.31)	3850521 (67.50)	13.02
3.	Manipur	116984 (2.96)	101484 (2.15)	112151 (2.18)	124229 (2.18)	2.06
4.	Meghalaya	401529 (10.15)	457685 (9.68)	549936 (10.69)	591398 (10.37)	15.76
5.	Mizoram	50987 (1.29)	43161 (0.91)	55924 (1.09)	56651 (0.99)	3.70
6.	Nagaland	15850 (0.40)	22085 (0.47)	46513 (0.90)	20953 (0.37)	10.73
7.	Sikkim	292486 (7.39)	329075 (6.96)	368451 (7.16)	547810 (9.60)	29.10
8	Tripura	230645 (5.83)	244795 (5.18)	245438 (4.77)	317541 (5.57)	12.56
NER Total		3957442 (100)	4726218 (100)	5145011 (100)	5704250 (100)	14.71

Source: Ministry of DoNER, Government of India.
Note: Figures in the bracket show percentage of total.

share. At the same time, there is a need to attract more and more domestic tourists to the state. This can be accomplished by developing the required infrastructure.

Socio-Economic Characteristics and Expenditure Pattern of Tourists

The survey of tourists to ascertain their socio-economic characteristics and expenditure pattern in Arunachal Pradesh revealed that around 88.49 per cent of the tourists visiting the state were between the ages 20 to 50 years. The average age of the domestic tourist was calculated as 35 years and that of the foreign tourist was 36 years. This fact emphasizes the need to organize more and more challenging adventure activities for the energetic and youthful tourist population. This would mean greater investment in activities like mountaineering, trekking, hiking, river rafting and allied sports along with fascinating cultural activities (Mitra, 2008).

Furthermore, it was revealed that viewing Nature was a satisfying experience and most of the respondents (98.11 per cent) wanted to return to Arunachal Pradesh provided transportation facilities and institutional facilities were improved. At the same time, a high proportion of the respondents (98.75 per cent) pointed out that they would talk to their friends and relatives about their experience in Arunachal Pradesh and presumably advice them to visit these places. This was also supported by the fact that the recommendations of friends and relatives have induced 79.4 per cent of the tourists to visit the state as against other factors such as publicity in newspapers, television or the Internet.

These factors demonstrate the existence of a large market, particularly for eco-tourism in the state and also strengthen the case for further expansion and development of tourism sector. However, on the supply side, we found that the tourism infrastructure is underdeveloped in the state. The roads are not properly developed. The conditions of roads leading to many tourist spots are bad. In fact, a very high proportion of the surveyed tourists also called for improving conditions of roads. The accommodation facilities were insufficient at tourist destinations. But in the recent years, there has been substantial improvement in accommodation facilities in the state barring a few destinations. However, the quality of food, basic facilities and services in the hotels/lodges need further improvement.

An attempt was also made to study the tourists' expenditure pattern in the selected tourist spots of Arunachal Pradesh. The analysis of the study revealed that the surveyed tourists spent 39.92 per cent of their total expenditure on accommodation, followed by food and beverages (30.06 per cent), shopping (15.84 per cent) and local transport (12.90 per cent). The relatively less percentage of the total expenditure spent on local transport reflects that tourists hired transport from outside the state. This reveals that the local transport system is underdeveloped and relatively costly. This is supported by the fact that around 77.87 per cent of the surveyed tourists were of the opinion that there is a need to improve the mode of transportation for developing tourism in Arunachal Pradesh (Mitra, 2008).

Policy Suggestions

The study suggests following for promoting sustainable tourism in the state:

1. A tourism masterplan may be prepared and more circuits identified. The circuits should be developed in terms of two primary categories. The first category should cover some of the locally important attractions. The second category should cover those attractions which have more local importance and which can be linked to tourist centres of the Northeastern region. Detailed circuit routes and location-specific recommendations should be drawn up with a phased approach. Commercial viability and competitive advantage of each route should be worked out.
2. Public-private partnership should be treated as an essential ingredient of the policy for the development of tourism in the State. The Government can build the infrastructural facilities for tourism like Helipads, short landing run-ups for small aircraft, tourist lodges and huts, etc. The private sector is best suited for the management and delivering of services. The tourist lodges are few in number and also scattered in different parts of the state. Hence, it is proposed to construct tourist lodges in the remaining Eleventh Five Year Plan in selected places like Itanagar, Ziro, Malinithan, Sela Pass, Tipi, Yingkiong, Pasighat, Tuting, Anini, Daporijo, Hayuliang, etc.
3. The Government should also encourage adventure tourism by building necessary infrastructure for angling, river rafting, winter sports, etc. Angling and river rafting can be developed in West Kameng, Lower Subansiri, West Siang and East Siang

districts. Winter sports can be developed in Tawang, West Kameng and Upper Siang districts.

4. The participation of local people should be encouraged. The local management and skills must be developed so that the local people can preserve and propogate their culture and also improve sites. For example, the tourist destination will be developed in consonance with the local communities. It may be possible to provide a unique experience to tourists by building low-cost infrastructure in the villages adjoining district headquarters by using local materials and local design inputs. This will create local employment opportunities.
5. The simplification of entry formalities can lead to more tourist inflow throughout the year. This is expected to generate sufficient economic benefits to the local people and much needed revenue for the state exchequer.

Conclusion

The study reveals that Arunachal Pradesh, blessed with abundant resources, has an enormous potential for development of tourism. But the inflow of tourists in the state is found to be very less compared to other states of the country. This is mainly because of various challenges and constraints which hinder the growth of its tourism sector. However, there is good prospect for the development of tourism in the state if the infrastructural facilities and institutional mechanisms are improved. In recent years, the state has been witnessing a high level of growth of tourist inflow among the Northeastern states. The study shows that sustainable policies and guidelines for tourism could make Arunachal Pradesh one of the most frequently visited tourist states in the entire Northeastern region. This could provide very significant and much needed revenue to the state government and employment opportunities and income to the local populace. Tourism development also assumes significance in the state because of underdeveloped agriculture, where productivity is low and the non-existence of industries except a few forest-based ones. Hence, in the present situation, promotion of tourism can help the state to accelerate the development process as well as to maintain its rich biodiversity. However, tourism development must be integrated within the Northeastern region as a whole, in order to reap maximum benefits.

Notes

Data Bank (2003), Ministry of DoNER, Government of India, New Delhi.

Data Bank (2010), Ministry of DoNER, Government of India, New Delhi.

A.I. Fazili and S. Hussain Ashraf (2006), *Tourism in India, Planning and Development,* Sarup & Sons, New Delhi.

Indian Tourism Statistics (2007), *Ministry of Tourism, Government of India,* New Delhi.

K.K. Kamra (1997), *Tourism Theory, Planning and Practice,* Indus Publishing Company, New Delhi.

K.K. Kamra and M. Chand (2004), *Basics of Tourism, Theory, Operation and Practice*, Kanishka Publishers and Distributors, New Delhi.

A. Mitra (1998), "Tourism Development in Hilly Regions of North-East India: A study in Arunachal Pradesh", in Roy, K.C. and C.A. Tisdell (eds.); *Tourism in India*, Nova Science Publishers, New York, pp. 175-186.

A. Mitra, *et al.* (2003), *Environment and Nature-based Tourism: An Endeavour at Sustainability*, Kanishka Publishers, New Delhi.

A. Mitra (2008), "Tourism Development", in *State Development Report of Arunachal Pradesh,* Planning Commission, Government of India, New Delhi.

A. Mitra and M. Lama (2010), "The Potentiality and Challenges of Developing Eco-tourism in Arunachal Pradesh: An Empirical Study", in M.C. Behera and J. Basar (eds.), *Globalisation and the Marginalized: Issues and Concerns for Development.*, Commonwealth Publishers Pvt. Ltd., New Delhi, pp. 142-152.

K.K. Sharma (2004), *Tourism and Socio-Cultural Development,* Sarup & Sons, New Delhi.

C.A. Tisdell (ed.) (2001), *Tourism Economics: the Environment and Development, Analysis and Policy*, Edward Elgar, Cheltenham, UK.

Contributors

Amitava Mitra, Professor, Department of Economics, Rajiv Gandhi University, Itanagar.

Annada C. Bhagabati, Former Vice-Chancellor, Rajiv Gandhi University, Itanagar.

Deepak K. Mishra, Associate Professor, Centre for the Study of Regional Development, Jawaharlal Nehru University, New Delhi.

Jagdish Lal Dawar, Professor, Department of History and Ethnography, Mizoram University, Aizawl.

Jayanti Alam, Project Fellow, Maulana Abul Kalam Azad Institute of Asian Studies, Kolkata.

Krishnan Srinivasan, former Indian Foreign Secretary and currently Maulana Azad Fellow at the Maulana Abul Kalam Azad Institute of Asian Studies, Kolkata.

Maila Lama, Assistant Professor, Department of Economics, Rajiv Gandhi University, Itanagar.

Moji Riba, Assistant Professor, Department of Mass Communications, Rajiv Gandhi University, Itanagar.

Mrinal Kanti Chakma, Fellow, Maulana Abul Kalam Azad Institute of Asian Studies, Kolkata.

N.C. Roy, Professor, Department of Economics, Rajiv Gandhi University, Itanagar.

Philip Mody, Assistant Professor, Department of Commerce, Rajiv Gandhi University, Itanagar.

Rakhee Bhattacharya, Fellow, Rajiv Gandhi Institute for Contemporary Studies, Rajiv Gandhi Foundation, New Delhi.

Sanjay Pulipaka, Fellow, Maulana Abul Kalam Azad Institute of Asian Studies, Kolkata.

Sarit K. Chaudhuri, Professor, Departmnet of Anthropology, Rajiv Gandhi University, Itanagar.

Sucheta Sen Chaudhuri, Associate Professor, Centre for Indigenous Culture, Central University of Jharkhand.

Tajen Dabi, Assistant Professor, Department of History, Rajiv Gandhi University, Itanagar.

Tamo Mibang, Head, Arunachal Institute of Tribal Studies, Rajiv Gandhi University, Itanagar.

Teshi Sohang, Research Scholar, Department of Commerce, Rajiv Gandhi University, Itanagar.

Vandana Upadhyay, Assistant Professor, Department of Economics, Rajiv Gandhi University, Itanagar.

Index